THE GODDESS FORTUNA
IN
MEDIAEVAL LITERATURE

"Of chaunges newe lady and princesse."

Lydgate, *Fall of Princes*, vi, i, 210.

The Goddess Fortuna
in
Mediaeval Literature

BY

HOWARD R. PATCH

OCTAGON BOOKS

A DIVISION OF FARRAR, STRAUS AND GIROUX

New York   1974

PATRI MATRIQUE

PREFACE

THE present study is based on my dissertation on the same subject, which was presented for the doctorate at Harvard University in 1915. Much of the material is substantially the same as that which appeared in my thesis, although it has seemed unwise to present here all the evidence at my disposal. The wealth of what is available would furnish forth a small encyclopaedia; what I have printed here has seemed sufficient in general to indicate the extent and richness of the cult, and the footnotes, limited as they are, will even now be open to the charge of pedantry. Early in the course of this piece of research it became apparent that there was no special reason for trying to be exhaustive. Indeed, of late my temptation has been to meander through the subject, avoiding the systematic, and taking up each bit of material for what it is worth — and from that point of view it is worth a good deal. "For the essence of humanism," at least according to Pater, "is that belief . . . that nothing which has ever interested living men and women can wholly lose its vitality — no language they have spoken, nor oracle beside which they have hushed their voices, no dream which has once been entertained by actual human minds, nothing about which they have ever been passionate, or expended time and zeal." But the more formal method is probably also the more economical, at least in point of time.

My general subject was originally suggested to me by Professor W. A. Neilson, now President of Smith Col-

viii PREFACE

lege. He guided me through the initial perplexities of
my work, and has read the present manuscript with a
care that has produced many fruitful criticisms. Professor G. L. Kittredge of Harvard University has given me
both the particular and the indefinable aid which one can
hardly describe, but which all his students know. Several of the chapters were originally prepared under his
supervision, and his advice and encouragement helped
me at every point when as a graduate student I was living "in sorwe and care." Valuable assistance has come
to me also from Professor F. N. Robinson; and for
special favors I am under obligation to Professors Grandgent, Rand, Woods, and Lowes, and to the late Professor
Edward S. Sheldon. I am indebted as well to the cura-
tors of the Bodleian Library, the library of the University of Cambridge, the British Museum, and the Bibliothèque Nationale of Paris, for permission to have the
photographs made which appear in the plates of the
present volume. My attention was drawn by Professor
Roger S. Loomis of Columbia University to the inlay
in the door at Siena, represented by plate 11; and Professor E. K. Rand of Harvard gave me the photograph
of the painting shown in plate 12.

It is a pleasure for me to acknowledge these many
kindnesses. More than a word should be added, however,
with regard to the tireless and painstaking efforts of Miss
Addie F. Rowe in checking up the details of this study;
her conscientiousness and her bland indifference to reward should be known by more than those who are likely
to have the advantage of her help.

H. R. P.

CONTENTS

ILLUSTRATIONS

ILLUSTRATIONS

THE GODDESS FORTUNA

IN

MEDIAEVAL LITERATURE

2

Τί γὰρ εὑρετὸν ἢ τί μαθητόν ἐστίν ἀνθρώποις,
εἰ πάντα περαίνεται κατὰ τύχην;
PLUTARCH, *De Fortuna*, 98, A.

Quapropter effigiem dei formamque quaerere
imbecillitatis humanae reor.
PLINY, *Natural History*, ii, 14.

I pray thee fortune, (fortune if thou be)
Come heere aside, for I must braule with thee.
THOMAS BASTARD, *Epigrams*, ii, 35.

INTRODUCTION

ANYONE who has investigated the literature of the Middle Ages or that of the Renaissance will be fully aware that at least one pagan deity seems to have survived the decline and fall of ancient Rome. Allusions to the Goddess Fortuna abound in the literature of those periods, as references to Venus and Jove and other members of the classical pantheon do not. Even now, in our own day, we find some mention of the capricious deity in passages where there is no conscious intention of a classical allusion; and pictures of the goddess, standing on a ball or turning her prepotent wheel, still adorn magazines and gift-cards, and even invade the pages of our dignified journalism. But in earlier times the instances were far more numerous. An author could hardly compose a poem without devoting at least a stanza to the goddess; books introduced some mention of her on nearly every page; the philosopher seriously discussed the meaning of such a figure; clerk and layman alike paid her a really extraordinary amount of attention. The result inevitably is that the wealth of all this material constitutes a special problem in itself, for the history of philosophy and literature, and also for the history of mankind.

One may easily dispose of the question how it is that Fortuna of all the deities was the only one to survive the change in religion with the advent of Christianity. I shall deal with some of the details of that process later,

but now I may briefly indicate the underlying principle
which governs the matter. As investigators have several
times observed, Fortuna is not the goddess of a special
function, like Venus or Diana; she is not even the personification of a special aspect of fate, like Lachesis or Atropos. She represents one view, degraded if you like, of a
universal, omnipotent god; and therefore her only rival
could be such a figure as that of Jove. But in the period
of decadent Rome, and in the early Middle Ages, it was
not the figure of Jove that held sway, but that of the
fickle goddess. And why? Because men at that time so
regarded the universe — not as an ordered and properly
ruled domain, but as the realm of the mutable and haphazard forces which we generalize and characterize as
"chance." With the coming of Christianity the idea of
Jove, in so far as a trace of it survived during the Empire, was supplanted by that of the Christian God; but
there was no new equivalent for the figure of ruling
"chance," and Fortune, accordingly, had that field to
herself.

The problem of the element of "chance" in life was not
considered in that period for the first time. It is one that
almost certainly everybody has to face, and that mankind has had to deal with since first religious processes
came to occupy its attention. Whether we acknowledge
the existence of this element or not, somehow we seem to
be forced to settle the problem, in so far, at least, as it
involves ourselves. If life is in part a process of adjust-
ment to one's environment, it is necessary at the outset
to have some conception about the nature of that environment, especially in the way in which it affects experience and conduct. Thus, by a gradual shaping of

opinion, which includes testing and rejecting, and no doubt much bungling of the matter, we come to hold our own views about the working of the universe, our views of whatever gods there be. In the material which serves to guide us in this development, the seemingly casual is bound to play a large part. Events which seem to happen by chance, or the interrelation of which, at least, seems to be wholly casual, greatly outnumber those which we can definitely ascribe to the visible working of some force. Furthermore, what direction controls the force itself? In order to guide one's own conduct into channels that lead profitably — and with what else is the world eternally occupied? — one has to make up one's mind as to the dependability and profit of things in general.

On such matters surely every human being has come to some conclusion, if only to decide that life is, or is not, worth living, and that on the whole he is willing to "take a chance." In this way the Goddess Fortuna is the reflection, simply, of one kind of human temperament. She is the answer which a certain type of person will give to these questions. The cynic has remarked that mankind creates its god in its own image; but let us observe rather that our apprehension of the Divine is necessarily qualified by the personality through which we have our vision. Human beings who perceive the validity of law and order will cherish faith in an ordered universe. Those, on the other hand, who find that order sometimes imposes restraint, and that restraint is sometimes tyranny, will rejoice in the freedom that beckons from uncharted ways, and for them a universe of chance will mean a universe of opportunity. The point of contrast is probably fundamental, and I suspect that, if we followed this matter through and listened long enough to the wrangling of the contestants, we should find ultimately that it involves that ancient battle of the books, the age-old quarrel about classicism and romanticism. Some suggestion of this, at least, will be forthcoming later when we look into the history of the problem of Fortune.

The study of the goddess, then, is philosophical as well as literary, and on that basis I shall proceed. In the first place, I shall review the general history of the cult of Fortune in the Middle Ages; and afterward the more literary problems will be dealt with, including motifs and formulae (or themes) used in the accounts devoted to her, and various descriptions of her house and her wheel. But even these later chapters have a distinct bearing on the whole question of her philosophy and her meaning in the history of mankind. The trappings, the ritual of her worship, if we may call it so, have their own significance,— in their elaborateness, for one thing, and in the steadiness even unto monotony of their tradition, for another. The very number of these references means something. It would have been justifiable, even if not humanly possible, to include in my footnotes all the references to the goddess in all accessible literature, up to thousands upon thousands of items, no matter how confounding such a mass of footnotes might have been to a certain type of critic and to the "literati." How indispensable the lady was to the mediaeval mind (as well as to that of later times) no one knows who has not tried to accumulate the vast number of passages in which she makes her everlastingly debonair appearance. But, while it is hardly possible to be really "exhaustive," the present material may suggest the extent of her popularity.

Another limitation, however, is that of time: the full account of Fortune's career would reach back into the remote antiquity of ancient Rome and come down to the modern era; but here I have taken for my field only the Middle Ages, with a glance or two at what preceded and what followed. And I have necessarily been forced to exclude the parallel developments of this conception in German and Greek and other literatures, where Fortuna reigned also, but under a different name.

CHAPTER I

THE PHILOSOPHY OF FORTUNE

WHETHER its method is sound or not, or its conclusions fruitful, modern thought is indubitably moving toward the conclusion that man's opinion about God is fully as important for the study of man as it is for theology. It is perfectly obvious that the recorded conceptions of the Divine nature reveal the traces of differing human temperaments. If, as I have urged, the goddess of chance represents at least one of these, then, theoretically one might characterize a man, whether writer, philosopher, or plain layman, according to his confessed belief or disbelief in her. The conclusions one may reach will necessarily show the lack of precision that any attempt to classify human nature always shows; and yet they will have value in so far as they agree with experience, and in that way will gain validity for the reader. This, perhaps pseudo-scientific, task of analyzing human nature is practically what I have attempted in some detailed studies elsewhere [1] concerning the opinions of various important literary men in the Middle Ages. A summary of these opinions, however, may have a special value in itself, to show the general trend of thought on this subject in the period. How did men in general feel about the problem of Fortune? Did opinion vary from one time to another? Was chance regarded as the ruling force of life?

Our estimate of the period is necessarily limited by the

[1] *Smith College Studies in Modern Languages*, vol. III, nos. 3 and 4; vol. IV, no. 4.

fact that we can draw our evidence only from the educated and the philosophical or literary element in the population. The lower classes, among which we should naturally expect to find primitive cults surviving the longest, either as religion or simply as folk-lore, have left us few records of their own ideas and customs. By references in St. Augustine and other early Fathers we know that, for a while at least, Fortuna remained alive among the people; lyrics of a more or less popular kind echo something of their devotion to the figure, whether in jest or in earnest; and the prevalence of the cult among the educated would make it highly probable that it was known to some extent elsewhere — especially if, as seems to be the case, a belief in pure chance is not commonly found in the philosophically-minded. Fortune as nothing more than a literary figure, as a conventional symbol of use to those who had some contact with the classics, would have been worn threadbare long since; but her meaning was really vital to everybody, and so, in spite of the vast number of allusions to her, and the frigid repetition of the formulae associated with her, she persisted.[1] And it requires little time to discover that apparently among all classes of men she is still familiar in our own day. We may therefore, I think, take the reflection in literature and philosophy in the period as fairly typical, and bear in mind that these writers set down their remarks, after all, for an audience.

A special difficulty of another kind, however, must be mentioned at this point. In tracing the history of the

---

[1] The history of personified Nature furnishes an interesting parallel for study. See Dr. Knowlton's investigations, *Journal of English and Germanic Philology*, XXIV, 409 ff., and references; cf. *Palaestra*, CX, Leipzig, 1923.

goddess we cannot always be sure of the precise conception for which she was a symbol. The difficulty is like
that of the exact meaning of any word in any particular
period. Yet a tradition which fixes the denotation of the
name was fairly well established, and in most cases an
author shows by his discussion what figure he had in
mind.

I

In the pre-Christian period the Goddess Fortuna was
not at all times identical with the goddess of chance. The
word *fortuna* itself does not seem to carry any such basic
idea at the outset, or anything indeed beyond the general
conception of Fate. The idea that "Fate" operated in a
casual way was apparently a later addition — after the
lapse of centuries. In other words, from meaning simply
"the one who brings our destiny," the term later came to
signify the one who performs that act in a capricious
way. Although someone may object to this theory of
development on the ground that the word is at start
feminine, we may note that, according to one view, the
original deity was simply known as "Fors," to which
"fortuna" was added as a cognomen, later only to break
off and become independent; [1] but even the latter term
might imply nothing more than the creative power,
whether it served by itself in the first place, or not. In
any case, there is a strong likelihood that at first the word
implied pure Fate, and the development seems to have
been parallel to that of the Greek τύχη. [2] Differing views
of the force that controls external circumstances, or rather
of the nature of the external (and sometimes the internal)

[1] See Carter, *Religion of Numa*, pp. 50 f.
[2] See Wissowa, *Real-Encyclopädie*, XIII, 12.

world, were thus reflected in the history of this expression. A period which saw the universe ruled by order used "Fors Fortuna," or simply "Fortuna," as the equivalent of "Fate"; another, which rejected order and emphasized (at least from the human point of view) caprice, used the term to mean "chance."

For the Middle Ages it is important merely to observe that the second attitude was in vogue at the end of the classical period, when, in fact, the meaning was fixed with that rigor which, more or less invading all classical Latin, meant that it was no longer a living language. From a wealth of possible illustrations two will serve. The first, from Ovid, is one which was well known in mediaeval times:

> Passibus ambiguis Fortuna uolubilis errat
> et manet in nullo certa tenaxque loco:
> sed modo laeta uenit; uultus modo sumit acerbos;
> et tantum constans in leuitate sua est.
> (*Tristia*, V, viii, 15–18.)

The second, taken from the elder Pliny, shows the despair of a thoughtful man at the prevalence of the cult:

> Inuenit tamen inter has utrasque sententias medium sibi ipsa mortalitas numen, quo minus etiam plana de deo coniectatio esset. toto quippe mundo et omnibus locis omnibusque horis omnium uocibus Fortuna sola inuocatur ac nominatur, una accusatur, rea una agitur, una cogitatur, sola laudatur et cum conuiciis colitur, uolubilis . . . que, a plerisque uero et caeca existimata, uaga, inconstans, incerta, uaria, indignorumque fautrix. huic omnia expensa, huic feruntur accepta, et in tota ratione mortalium, sola utramque paginam facit, adeoque obnoxiae sumus sortis, ut prorsus ipsa pro deo sit qua deus probatur incertus.
> (*Natural History*, ii, 22.)

The epithets here applied to the goddess may be found many times elsewhere. Horace speaks of her fickleness:

Transmutat incertos honores,
nunc mihi, nunc alii benigna.
(*Odes*, III, xxix, 51 f.)

She is described in various accounts as *caeca* and *fragilis*; she is a *meretrix*. Plutarch called in the philosophy of Aristotle to give her a reasonable basis of existence,[1] and explained her as the "cause by accident" which is proper only to man, and which is the necessary cause to allow for human free-will. She is not, however, rational enough even to reward virtue and punish vice: "Nihil eripit fortuna, nisi quod dedit: uirtutem autem non dat" (Seneca, *De Constantia Sapientiae*, v, 2).

In the Empire, then, Fortuna flourished with considerable power as the goddess of chance. I am not concerned to prove that she was in every case worshipped as an actual deity, or even so regarded;[2] there is ample evidence to show that, goddess or abstraction, she was enormously popular. There were numerous temples dedicated in her honor; in the differing aspects of her cult her activities became almost universal in scope, until as "Fortuna Panthea" she absorbed the functions of many other gods;[3] and for several emperors she was nothing less than a tutelary. The reason for this remarkable growth is not far to seek. The Empire was an essentially romantic period, when Rome, with a limitless ambition for worldly conquest, ventured forth into the unknown, and in nearly every turn of human life felt the risks which imply chance. It was, moreover, a time of religious skep-

---

[1] *De Fato;* see especially 5–7.

[2] Cf. Fowler's article in Hastings's *Encyclopaedia of Religion and Ethics*, VI, 98 ff.

[3] Roscher's *Lexikon*, 1534 ff., gives a convenient account of this phenomenon.

ticism, with a general dabbling in foreign creeds, and without much spiritual depth. At such a time Fortuna naturally came into her own. To men who felt that life shows no signs of fairness, that whatever lies beyond is at best dubious, that the most you can do is to take what comes your way, Fortuna represented a useful, if at some times flippant, summary of the way things go. "Euentus docuit fortes fortunam iuuare," they said,[1] not, I think, without cynicism. "Trust God and keep your powder dry."

As the Roman, however, came to regard himself as at the mercy of Fortune, so he tried to save himself by limiting her powers. One way to be successful in this was to show courage. Another was to oppose reason to her unreason, to live the life of wisdom; and another, less widely used, perhaps, was to devote one's self to those concerns in which Fortuna had no part — the activities of virtue. It is "prudentia" which Juvenal advocates (*Satires*, x, 363); and Seneca, whom I have already quoted in a similar connection, also writes as follows: "'Vnum Bonum esse, quod Honestum est.' . . . nam, qui alia bona iudicat, in fortunae uenit potestatem, alieni arbitrii fit" (*Epistles*, lxxiv, 1). These methods of dealing with Fortuna move actually in the direction of putting her out of existence. Her power is at least not universal, if one may successfully take a stand against her. If reason maintains a validity above and beyond her caprice, if virtue has a meaning which she is unable to obliterate, she cannot be the only deity that rules the skies. In fact, in proportion as these methods are triumphant, she becomes a subordinate figure. Vigorous as she was, a possibility of a differ-

[1] Livy, *Historia*, viii, 29.

ent conception of things, therefore, was already in the mind of the Romans; and the fact of this possibility shows a need which would call for fulfilment.

II

A new conception was, of course, found in Christianity. Here was the idea of a rational God, who gave validity to reason; and here too virtue had a supreme significance. It can hardly be supposed that such a completely different view of things prevailed everywhere at once, any more than that everybody instantly became a devotee of what was regarded as a foreign and a not too respectable cult. The difficulty of the change, however, may be represented in a more subtle fashion than this. As in ancient Rome not everybody—indeed, probably very few people—had genuinely held the nobler opinions implicit in the opposition to Fortuna which I have described, so there would be a limited number in the early Middle Ages who would be ready for the conception of a rational God, or of a God who gave an essential meaning to virtue. This being the case, there were bound to be many who continued to see things in the old way. It was still possible for the human temperament to persist which believed mainly in chance. Spiritual rebirth could not come automatically to the whole of Europe. How far such a belief in chance was identified with a faith in Fortuna it would be impossible to determine; but the figure of the goddess was at least convenient, and extraordinarily familiar. The great number of allusions to her, the detailed accounts of her activities, the descriptions and portraits in the works of literally hundreds of authors, constitute, it would seem, almost a sufficient argument to prove the survival of her

worship in the Middle Ages. One impression of what happened in this particular is recorded in the statement of
Cumont, that "in Latin Europe in spite of the anathemas
of the church the belief remained confusedly alive all
through the Middle Ages that on this earth everything
happens somewhat 'Per ovra delle rote magne.'" [1]

The Church Fathers refer, with some uneasiness, to the
pagan tradition of the goddess. In Tertullian's day and
in that of St. Augustine, the special fidelity to Fortuna
Muliebris, Fortuna Dux, Fortuna Barbata, and the like,
was still alive. Her chief characteristic as the personification of disorder is presented steadily in the numerous
accounts, which are found in many types of literature,
from Martianus Capella down to the drinking-songs of
the *Carmina Burana* and Nigellus Wircker's *Speculum
Stultorum*, and even afterward. Arturo Graf held that
"the populace, who understand little and care less about
the subtle disputes and more subtle distinctions of the
theologians and the philosophers, never abandoned faith
in one or more powers, occult and irresistible, distinct and
separate from the divine will, and variously designated,
as the case might be, by the name of destiny, fortuna, or
astrological influence." [2]

The Roman goddess, however, could not flourish in her
new background without, at least, readjustment. Belief
in chance was not officially welcome to the new faith
which maintained that even the hairs of the human head
are numbered, and that not a sparrow falls without
God's knowledge. Inasmuch as actual belief in the casual carried with it the assumption that just so much

---

[1] *The Oriental Religions in Roman Paganism*, authorized translation
(Chicago, 1911), pp. 179 ff.
[2] Graf, *Miti, Leggende e Superstizioni*, I, 276.

territory lay outside of the province of the Christian God, the Church waged special war against what was probably at first an unexpected foe in Fortuna. It was no longer sufficient to oppose her with fortitude, with prudence or with philosophy, or even with virtue. It must be made clear that she had no actual existence, that her works were only illusory. Such a definite stand was taken by the Fathers, from Lactantius and St. Augustine to St. Thomas Aquinas. According to such writers as Lactantius and St. Jerome, and others even as late as William of Malmesbury, the goddess is more or less identified with the spirit of evil, as in the case of so much else from pagan sources.

The Aristotelian argument that chance is necessary in order to make room for free-will is adopted in a modified form by St. Augustine and St. Thomas. Both, however, are definite in refusing to accept the figure of the goddess, and they agree in pointing out that in the last analysis what seems to come from chance has really a proper cause of its own. Fortune may be useful as a name for the *causa per accidens* which Aristotle defined, but it will not be ultimately justifiable to delude one's self into thinking that the personified figure has a basis in fact:

> Sed quamuis haec opinio habeat ueram radicem, non tamen bene usi sunt nomine fortunae. Illud enim diuinum ordinans non potest dici uel nominari fortuna; quia secundum quod aliquid participat rationem uel ordinem, recedit a ratione fortunae. Vnde magis debet dici fortuna causa inferior, quae de se non habet ordinem ad euentum fortuitum, quam causa superior, si qua sit ordinans. Praetermittit tamen inquisitionem huius opinionis, tum quia excedit metas scientiae naturalis, tum quia infra manifestat quod fortuna non est causa per se, sed per accidens.[1]

---

[1] St. Thomas Aquinas, *Opera*, ed. Pope Leo XIII, II, 77 (9), *Commentaria Physicorum Aristotelis.*

And further:

Considerandum est autem quod si ea quae fortuito uel casualiter accidunt, idest praeter intentionem causarum inferiorum, reducantur in aliquam causam superiorem ordinantem ipsa; in comparatione ad illam causam non possunt dici fortuita uel casualia: unde illa causa superior non potest dici fortuna.[1]

But it is only naïve opinion which holds that free thought ceases to exist where authority reigns. The Church proclaimed authoritative views on comparatively few points; on the rest men were allowed to differ. St. Thomas's characteristically sound logic, while it was widely representative, was not official. The pagan Fortuna continued on her primrose path, from her appearance in such a work, for example, as the lament of Hildebert of Lavardin, *De Exsilio Suo*,—Hildebert was Bishop of Le Mans and Tours in the early part of the twelfth century,—through the *Anticlaudianus* of Alain de l'Isle, — who was an ecclesiastic of the latter part of the twelfth, — down to the Renaissance. The description in the *Anticlaudianus* is, it is true, so confused, varying between a picture of the goddess and that merely of a personification of the abstract idea (the gifts which Fortune bestows), that one is led to conclude that the author did not take the figure of an actual deity very seriously. But, as far as he has any use for her at all, she reappears in her pagan guise.

A sign that the problem was for many men unsettled appears in the fact that some writers retained both Fortune and the Christian God, without any precise attempt to reconcile the two conceptions. One of the most influential figures in mediaeval thought, the remarkable Boe-

[1] *Ibid.*, p. 86 (13).

thius, of whose words echoes are found in literature for a thousand years, sets forth a clear picture of the pagan goddess and, at the same time, obviously worships the Christian God, without showing us exactly how the two may exist together in one universe. While he gives a character sketch of Fortuna thoroughly in accord with that familiar in classical literature, and almost certainly based in large measure on his reading there,[1] he only suggests a solution of the difficulty, taking his ideas in part from Aristotle. "Chance," we are told, allows for human free-will; fate is a servant of God; and chance, growing out of hidden causes, is also subject to Divine Providence:

> Licet igitur definire casum esse inopinatum ex confluentibus causis in his quae ob aliquid geruntur euentum. concurrere uero atque confluere causas facit ordo ille ineuitabili conexione procedens, qui de prouidentiae fonte descendens cuncta suis locis temporibusque disponit.[2]

An imitation of the *Consolation of Philosophy* by a Christian priest in the twelfth (or early thirteenth) century, Henricus Septimellensis, conveys hardly more than a similar picture of the pagan deity.[3] A compromise of the same kind is found in the long discussion in Albertus Magnus, where, as we should expect, the Aristotelian suggestions are developed more fully.[4]

It remained for Dante to give poetic reality to what is really implicit in the treatment in Boethius. In the familiar account of Fortune which it is Virgil's part to de-

[1] *Cons. Philos.*, II, pr. i, and the sections that follow.
[2] *Ibid.*, V, pr. i, 51 ff.
[3] *De Diversitate Fortunae et Philosophiae Consolatione*, ed. Manni, Florence, 1730; Italian text, Prato, 1841.
[4] See the *Physicorum*, II, tr. ii, cap. x ff. (*Opera*, II, 83 ff.); also the *Ethicorum*, I, tr. vii, cap. vi (*Opera*, I, 67).

PLATE I

BOETHIUS AND FORTUNE

liver in the seventh canto of the *Inferno*,[1] the capricious goddess becomes a ministering angel entirely subservient to the Christian God. She still appears to be arbitrary, she still receives the scorn and reproaches of mankind; but she has her own concealed method in her apparent madness, and to all blame she is serenely indifferent:

> Con l'altre prime creature lieta
> Volve sua spera, e beata si gode.

The pagan and the Christian traditions are thus united in Dante's representation. Boethius at times had made Fortune seem identical with Fate, and Fate itself as changeable as Fortune. Compare in this regard his famous figure of the wheel of which God is the centre and Fate the rim.[2] Fate and chance, too, he maintained, were subordinate to Providence. In Dante's portrait, Fortune is "general ministra e duce," and yet her judgment is concealed from the understanding of man; in a sense, she is a kind of personification of the Aristotelian *causa per accidens*, except that we are told,

> Questa provvede, giudica e persegue
> Suo regno, come il loro gli altri dei.

---

[1] Lines 67–96.

[2] *Cons. Philos.*, IV, pr. vi, ll. 21 ff. The idea of the Christian Fortuna seems implied in certain representations of the wheel in art. A seal of Tyrnau in Hungary of the second half of the xiii century shows Christ in the center of the wheel, with the inscription "Et Deus in Rota." G. Heider, *Das Glücksrad*, p. 119, discusses it as follows: "Die Bedeutung dieser Darstellung liegt klar vor. Der feste Mittelpunkt im Wechsel der irdischen Dinge ist Christ. . . ." He refers to other Christian modifications, with the wheel used for the four Evangelists, etc. (cf. below, p. 58, n. 3). Other instances are mentioned by J. Sauer, *Symbolik*, pp. 272 ff. Also see *Reproductions from Illuminated Manuscript.*, British Museum, Series III, 1908, plate xxiv. Cf. the wheel described in *Les Échecs Amoureux* (referred to below, p. 175, n. 2).

It is this aspect of her greatness, the fact that she is only superficially opposed to reason, that brought one touch of adverse criticism to the poet. Cecco d'Ascoli wrote:

In ciò peccasti florentin poeta,
Ponendo che li ben de la fortuna
Necessitati siano con lor meta.
Non è fortuna che rason non venca.[1]

This is the necessary attitude of the scholastic mind, and yet it appears that Dante answers this objection in his statement that Fortune's orderliness is hidden from the eyes of man.

Italian literature subsequent to Dante is, at least in part, a history of the development of these differing conceptions of Fortuna. She is the pagan deity; or she is allowed to exist along with the Christian God (which of the two was the more vivid probably varied with the attitude of individual men); or she is the angelic intelligence of whom Dante caught a vision. I cannot list here the direct imitations of Dante's account, but what he set forth was not satisfactory to everybody. Petrarch refers to the goddess many times, and in his study *De Remediis Utriusque Fortunae* he counsels mankind to oppose Fortune's wiles with wisdom and with spiritual devotion. In substance the book might have been written by any intellectual person in the classical period. In fact, the model for the work seems to have been Seneca, as Petrarch himself says, although he adds remedies against Good Fortune, whereas most writers in this vein discussed only Bad Fortune (*Fortuna Mala*). But one day

[1] *L'Acerba*, Rosario's ed., Lanciano, 1916, p. 53. My own discussion of the matter may be consulted: *Smith College Studies in Modern Languages*, vol. III, no. 4, pp. 202 ff.

Petrarch was forced to declare himself on the problem of chance even more explicitly, and what happened is a revelation of what was going on in the popular mind at this period.

After King John of France was liberated from his English prison in 1360, Petrarch spoke before the monarch, consoling him for what he had suffered and rejoicing with him at his present relief. Perhaps the analogy to the case of Boethius sprang to his mind. At any rate he attributed all guilt for the King's experiences to Fortuna, and the very mention of her name disturbed his audience. At dinner afterward he was asked to give his opinion about the goddess; escaping from that predicament through an accidental turn of the King's interest, he was visited in his chamber by three *doctori*, who talked with him from *sesta* to *sera*.[1] Five years later Petrarch wrote a letter to a friend on the whole problem.[2] In this he takes the orthodox position of the Church Fathers, denying any existence to the goddess:

> Io miserabile peccatore, inteso peraltro a cure secolaresche, udendolo sulla bocca di tutti, e scritto trovandolo in ogni libro, lo ripetei mille volte nelle mie opericciuole: e tanto fui lungi dal pentirmene che scrissi non ha guari un libro avente per titolo: *I rimedi dell' una e dell' altra fortuna*, ove non già di due Fortune, ma di una sola a due faccie tenni lungo discorso. . . .
> Ed io ti rispondo che la Fortuna veramente ho sempre stimato esser nulla. . . . Credesi generalmente che quando accade alcuna

---

[1] For an account of the affair see Barbeu du Rocher, in *Mémoires de l'Académie des Inscriptions*, etc., 2d series, III, 189 ff. A translation of the letter (to Pietro di Poitiers) is printed in *Lettere Familiari*, ed. Fracassetti, vol. IV, lib. xxii, lett. 13. For the "tragedy" of King John, see the story in Boccaccio's *De Casibus* and subsequent translations.

[2] To Tommaso del Garbo, *Lettere Senili*, ed. Fracassetti, vol. I, lib. viii, lett. 3, pp. 468 ff.

cosa senza cagione apparente (chè senza causa veramente non ac-
cade mai nulla), avvenga per caso, e s'imputa alla Fortuna.[1]

A similar situation is found in the pages of Boccaccio.
In his early works the spirit of what he writes is not unlike that of Ovid, and it is not surprising to find the capricious goddess mentioned on nearly every page, and
several times discussed at length. She was a convenient
figure when he wanted someone on whom to put the
blame for his adversities in love. She fitted neatly into
the classical apparatus when he was composing an epic;
and she furnished a theme for the laments of Arcita and
Troilo when they were speaking the poet's own passion to
the Countess Maria. Jove and even the Christian God
are introduced as well, without apparently much com-
plicated attempt to reconcile them. But this skepticism,
like that which obtained during the Empire in Rome, was
not characteristic of Boccaccio's later life. Here, it is
true, the number of references to Fortune is still great,
but both in the *De Casibus* and in the *De Genealogia
Deorum* the Christian conception seems to be present in
the author's mind. In the latter he wrote as follows:

> Lachesi poi cognominata dal fine: percioche anco Iddio hà dato il
> suo fine alle cose c' hanno a uenire . . . Sono appresso di quelli, che
> uogliono Lachesi esser quella, che noi chiamiamo Fortuna.[2]

That he knew Dante's account is, of course, perfectly
certain; and his own comment on the passage in the *Inferno*, besides showing this, also gives us his real opinion
on the subject; for here he regards Fortuna as a poetic
fiction.[3]

[1] *Lettere Senili*, I, 470–472. He refers to the Christian conception, p. 474.
[2] Betussi's trans., p. 11.
[3] *Commento sopra Dante* (*Opere*, XI, 151 ff.), pp. 155–156.

The pagan Fortune, or a kind of compromise, appears in the works of Fazio degli Uberti, Burchiello, Frezzi, and the novelists Masuccio Salernitano, Sannazaro, and others. Frezzi gives us a long passage describing the realm of Fortune, and seemingly she is regarded as the servant of God, although her function is more diabolic than otherwise.[1] Something like the Christian conception — or is it the scholastic? — is found in a *Ballata della Fortuna:*

> Fortuna nonn' è nulla al mio parere,
> anz' è 'l piacier di Dio in tutte cose.[2]

A tournament dramatized the strife of Reason with Fortune, and the latter won; for the conflict, instead of being settled in the *débat* which preceded, gave rise to the joust itself, where, naturally, Reason was not at a proper advantage.[3] The pagan goddess plays a conspicuous part in the pages of Aeneas Sylvius, as we shall see from his account of her home, and in Boiardo's *Orlando Innamorato*, where the Fata Morgana borrows traits both from her and from Occasio. Alberti, in his treatise *Della Tranquillità dell' Animo*, follows the tradition from Petrarch's *De Remediis*, and opposes wisdom and virtue to the caprices of chance. Giovanni Pontano, in his book *De Fortuna*, presents nothing more than the scholastic doctrine, concluding, "Fortunam non esse Deum." [4]

---

[1] *Quadriregio*, vol. II, cap. xiii, pp. 147 ff.

[2] Ed. A. Medin, in *Il Propugnatore*, 1889, p. 120.

[3] *Ibid.*, App. I, pp. 127 ff.

[4] In a suggestive and interesting article on Fortuna in the Warburg *Vorträge* (II, 1 Teil, 1924), A. Doren objects to my classification of the varying conceptions of Fortune; he finds it "nicht glücklich, weil nicht streng durchzuführen" (p. 139, note). Because he fails to observe that the classifi-

Something like the Christian conception of Dante, with the suggestion that Fortune is both angel and devil, however, is presented in the discussion of the subject by Pico della Mirandola, who quotes from St. Augustine, and brings up the old figure of the man discovering a treasure, which suggests, and rightly, that this author is a late follower of the Aristotelian tradition. On the other hand, the pagan idea continues in the work of Politian, Benivieni, Pulci, Ariosto, and others, until, with the full tide of the Renaissance, with its many features so reminiscent of the Roman golden age, Fortuna comes into her own with as much vitality as ever, defended even on philosophic grounds in a manner unheard of in ancient Rome. To Machiavelli, for instance, she was indispensable, if only to personify the forces from which his conception of the superman is to wrest his triumph. In the past, he maintains, men believed that the world was controlled by the Divine Power and by Fortune, and that therefore everything might as well be left to chance:

Al che pensando io qualche volta, mi sono in qualche parte inchinato nella opinione loro. Nondimanco perchè il nostro libero arbitrio non sia spento, giudico potere esser vero, che la fortuna sia

----

cation is philosophical, — as he shows by misunderstanding why I have listed the poems in the *Carmina Burana* as pagan (and his discussion of my treatment of the love-poetry and of Pontano shows the same mistake), — he does not realize that the method is fundamental and inevitable. On the other hand, his study of Renaissance material is somewhat weakened by the fact that the idea of man as master of his Fortune appears long before the Renaissance — e.g., in the works of John Gower — and is an outgrowth of the classical idea that Fortune aids the brave. A thirteenth-century instance has been recently cited by K. Hampe in the *Archiv für Kulturgeschichte*, XVII (1926), 1 Heft, pp. 20 ff. It is true that the egoistic note found in Machiavelli and others is not heard much before their day.

arbitra della metà delle azioni nostre, ma che ancora ella ne lasci governare l' altra metà o poco meno a noi.[1]

This curious echo of the Aristotelian discussion, if it is an echo, only makes the rest of what Machiavelli has to say stand out as a more striking counterpart to the classical method and the classical conception. With many scattered testimonials to Fortune, the great utilitarian describes the goddess at length, with an account of her dwelling-place and a triumphant paean to her majestic sway. Everyone, including Jove, is afraid of her power, and to only a few does she give real happiness.[2]

"Chi considera bene non può negare che nelle cose umane la fortuna ha grandissima potestà," observes another writer of the same general period and of much the same temper, Francesco Guicciardini.[3] In a significant manner he sets the typically Italian Renaissance conception of *Virtù* against Fortune, as practically one's only resource in dealing with the goddess; that is to say, Fortune yields, not to goodness, nor yet to wisdom, but to power. As Machiavelli remarked in so many words, the goddess is a lady and must be taken by storm. And thus the Renaissance welcomes the pagan figure, and gives her an appropriate place in its elaborate theology. Like the time of Augustus in Rome, it is a restless period, with much traffic and discovery, much hazarding of all that one had, much toying with strange gods for the very delight of their strangeness, much questioning (with little passion for an answer). The goddess of chance admira-

---

[1] *Il Principe*, cap. xxv. Chapter xv speaks of using one's strength to resist Fortune.

[2] *Capitolo di Fortuna* (*Opere*, VII, 366 ff.).

[3] *Ricordi Politici e Civili*, xxx, xxxi (*Opere Ined.*, I, 97 ff.).

bly represented both its weakness and its strength. She is just the deity for the romantically-minded, for those who find life only in flux and change. She represents that conveniently adjustable religion for which certain temperaments long.

III

The survey of the material in the Italian field gives us a sufficiently complete picture of what happened to Fortune in the Middle Ages. Philosophy tried to annihilate her, but poetry was able to keep her, whether in a form agreeable to the Christian Church or not. In the Renaissance she comes into full vigor as an appropriate embodiment of the paganism and superstition of the time. The same process takes place in other countries where she is known, and to present a detailed study of conditions elsewhere would in general involve mere repetition. Yet by this statement I do not mean to imply that the growth in other soil was modelled, consciously or not, on the Italian plan. In each country differing conditions produced an independent life for the goddess; and the similarities which do occur are therefore all the more interesting, and the undeniably similar trend of the general development gains thereby a really profound significance.

It is unnecessary, however, to repeat here the detail that I have printed elsewhere, to which I have already made allusion. Here I shall limit myself to pointing out some special phases of the development in the French and English fields, phases that seem to me to have some meaning in relation to the whole point of this chapter. Apart from that, let it suffice to say that in Old French and Middle English the pagan Fortuna survives;

that wherever we turn in these fields we find the same *motifs*, the same "remedies" for her onslaught; and that occasionally the Christian denied her existence, or retained her by means of a figure not unlike that which is found in Dante's *Inferno*. The allusions and discussions in these literatures are not perfunctory, but show freshness and individuality. Furthermore, when the old conceptions are reproduced, they appear, not as borrowings, but as an independent flowering, with a life of their own.

It is true, of course, that there is an interrelation between England, France, and Italy. Many of the Latin writers of the early part of the period were living in France and studying there — Alanus de Insulis, for one example, and Albertus Magnus, for another. Petrarch, as I have said, was challenged by King John of France on the subject of Fortune. Little argument is necessary, however, to point out that the closer the contact between the two countries the more striking the differences in the accounts of the fickle goddess, and the more important.

If one grants, as I think one is really bound to, that Dante's figure of the Christian Fortuna is a remarkable conception, at once appealing to the imagination and satisfying to the intellect, then the reappearance of this figure, quite independently, in France and England is still more remarkable. In France there is something like a suggestion, in the works of Chrestien de Troyes and in the *Roman du Renart*, that God and Fortune do not work in opposition, or without some measure of concord. In the *Roman*, God apparently punishes some sinners on the wheel of Fortune:

Or prions le Roy Jhesu-Crist
Qui pour nous char humaine prist,
Que de tel roe nous destourgne.[1]

Material from Boethius, in the writings of Simund de Freine, and extensively in the *Roman de la Rose*, may have helped the development. But next we see in the *Manekine* of Philippe de Beaumanoir, and in a dialogue between Fortune and Pierre de la Broche, and in the work of Watriquet de Couvin, the idea of the goddess as definitely in the service of the Christian God.

In the *Manekine* we read that God consents to Fortune's rule of the world.[2] The dialogue with Pierre de la Broche, however, with strong reminiscence of Boethius, shows the goddess as doing God's will and punishing the wicked.[3] Here Reason calls on Fortune to defend herself against the charges raised by Pierre, but her replies simply rebuke Pierre for failure to keep true to God, and in general reveal something of the calm of the blessed figure in Dante. Watriquet, on the other hand, describing not Fortune but Aventure (who really represents the same idea), gives a very clear account of the relation between God and this capricious deity:

> Frère, on m'apele Aventure,
> En terre m'a Diex establie;
> Au main lever pas ne m'oublie,
> Tantost sui où je veil aler;
> Je fas le trop haut devaler,
> Nus n'a en moi juste fiance.
> Bien en vois la senefiance
> A mon cors de double figure,

---

[1] *Renart le Nouvel* (*Roman*, ed. Méon, IV, 461), ll. 77–79.
[2] Philippe de Beaumanoir, *Œuvres*, ed. Suchier, I, 36, ll. 1084 ff.
[3] Monmerqué and Michel, *Théâtre Français*, pp. 208 ff.

Qu'en moi n'a point d'uevre seüre.
Nus n'i do it estr asseürez,
Tant soit riches ne eürez
Ne par fortune aventureus.[1]

It will be seen on detailed investigation that the discussions in the works of these writers do not show the slightest trace of influence from Dante. Indeed, the growth shows every indication of being spontaneous and natural. A little later, in the satiric *Roman de Fauvel*, the Christian Fortune appears again, responsible, we are told, for the present unhappy condition of the Church; and here she is a daughter

Du roy qui sans commencement
Regne et vit pardurablement.[2]

Other examples are found in the works of Jean de Condé, in an independent fourteenth-century manuscript (described by Gorra), and in Martin le Franc,— in addition to the passages already discussed. On the other hand, Fortune as a goddess of love, with nothing more than the pagan conception, flourishes in French literature: in the *Panthère d'Amours* of Nicole de Margival, in *Les Échecs Amoureux*, in the works of Guillaume de Machaut, Froissart, Deschamps, Charles d'Orléans, and elsewhere.

In England the situation is in many respects similar. From its Germanic heritage Old English received the figure of a goddess of ruthless and inscrutable destiny in

[1] *Li Mireoirs as Dames*, ll. 158–169 (*Dits*, ed. Scheler, p. 6).
[2] Ed. Längfors (Société des Anciens Textes Français), ll. 1850 ff. F. von Bezold (*Das Fortleben der antiken Götter im mittelalterlichen Humanismus*, p. 81) finds Fortune as a daughter of the "gottlichen Geistes" in Heinrich of Mailand's *Controversia Hominis et Fortunae* (1254), a book that I have not seen.

Wyrd, who, we remember, "gǣð ā . . . swā hīo scel."[1] There seems to be little doubt that this figure corresponded to the Latin idea of Fate, even as the Germanic Norns are a convenient equation for the three Fates. Fortune became known in England at least as early as the West Saxon translation of Boethius, in which Aelfred quite properly rendered Fortune the goddess by "woruldsǣld" and fortune the abstraction by "wyrd."[2] Considerable mention of the figure does not appear, of course, until much later, when at length the opportunity to distinguish between an ordered fate and a capricious fortune was made possible by the actual borrowing of the words themselves. Many of the English passages regarding Fortune, like the remarkable one in the alliterative *Morte Arthure*, ll. 3250 ff., are suspect, as being at least adaptations from the French.[3] John Gower, as we should properly suppose, annihilates the goddess, unless he takes her as a symbol for astrological influence; *Piers Plowman* presents her simply as the personified abstraction, riches; many writers in English and Scottish keep her in the pagan figure. In the *Book of the Duchesse*, possibly in order to follow the conventions of Court of Love poetry in this point as in all others, Chaucer uses the pagan idea to good effect, the inference being that the death of Blanche could be due only to the caprice of a heartless and irrational deity. After his intensive study of Boe-

[1] *Beowulf*, l. 455. For the situation in Old English, see Jente's *Mythologischen Ausdrücke im altenglischen Wortschatz*, Heidelberg, 1921 (*Angl. Forsch.*, vol. LVI), 196 ff.

[2] Fortune was, of course, known previously in Roman England. Altars dedicated to her may be seen in the library of Durham Cathedral.

[3] Cf. Bruce, *Mort Artu*, Halle, 1910, p. 291, with regard to some similar passages.

thius, however, it is especially significant to notice that he introduced the Christian figure in the *Balade of Fortune*, without the slightest hint of influence from Dante:

> Lo, th'execucion of the magestee
> That al purveyeth of his rightwisnesse,
> That same thing 'Fortune' clepen ye,
> Ye blinde bestes, ful of lewednesse! [1]

Although "Destinee" is described in the *Knight's Tale* (ll. 1663 ff.) with obvious indebtedness to the passage on Fortune in the *Inferno*, Chaucer returns to the Christian conception of Fortune herself, with echoes of both Boethius and Dante, in *Troilus and Criseyde*, showing, I think, that it was Boethius who furnished him with the basis for his idea, even while he was impressed with Dante's account.

Structurally the idea of Fortune as the servant of the Christian God has a profound effect on the plot of the *Troilus*. With its many allusions to the operation of fate, the story nevertheless does not proceed as a sentimental tragedy, in which the characters fall victim to some pitiless force external to themselves; but Troilus, unlike his prototype in the *Filostrato*, eventually discovers that his sufferings are pretty much the result of his own folly. Passages regarding the Christian conception are deliberately introduced by the poet [2] to show that Fortune is the shepherdess of us poor beasts only under the direction of "heighe Jove" (the language distinctly recalling that in the *Balade*), and that therefore the plot does not move by chance, but in accordance with an actual if concealed plan that does not exclude human free-will. These pas-

---

[1] Lines 65–68. See *Essays in Memory of Barrett Wendell*, Cambridge, 1926, pp. 95 ff. I hope to publish a more detailed study of this field later.
[2] *Troilus*, iii, stanza 89; v, ll. 1541 ff.

sages occur at the two main crises of the story. Describing the effect in this isolated fashion may serve to make the purpose of the poem seem too sombre, and even heavy: Troilus, we remember, laughed at the woe of those who wept for his death. The actual result of relieving the poem of a sentimental type of fatalism is to take away the hopelessness of a setting where the pagan Fortune rules, and to show that Troilus is a healthier being when he can ridicule his own weakness than when he utters that interminable discourse on cruel fate in Book IV.[1]

Something like the Christian figure appears in the works of the faithful and industrious Monk of Bury, John Lydgate, when he makes Fortune subject to the goddess Juno:

> For Juno is the tresourere,
> And fortune hir awmonere.[2]

Although this is translated from Les Échecs Amoureux,[3] and may mean much or little in itself, it is in harmony with other references to a similar figure in the poet's writings.[4] The pagan figure endures, on the other hand, in the lines of Hoccleve and in those of numerous other writers, both English and Scottish. At the time of the Renaissance in England Fortune is still with us, abundantly dealt with in the works of Sir Thomas More,[5] and elsewhere.

---

[1] I have discussed this monologue in detail in an article in the *Journal of English and Germanic Philology*, XVII, 399 ff., "Troilus on Predestination."

[2] See the whole passage, *Reson and Sensuallyte*, ll. 1350 ff.

[3] See Sieper's edition, p. 17. For a discussion of the French, cf. *Smith College Studies in Modern Languages*, vol. IV, no. 4, pp. 19 ff. A synopsis of the poem has been printed by Galpin, *Romanic Review*, XI, 283 ff.

[4] Cf. the *Troy Book*, ii, 3036 ff. His ideas may have been derived partly from Laurent de Premierfait's translation of Boccaccio's *De Casibus*.

[5] His *Book of Fortune* is printed in *Anglia*, XXVI, 139 ff.

PLATE 2

THE CONTROVERSY BETWEEN FORTUNE AND VIRTUE

IV

For the mediaeval period, then, Fortune was a lively and ubiquitous figure, a shape-shifter who could not be put down. With the masses the pagan idea survived, apparently, without much change. The philosophically-minded acknowledged the phenomena that gave rise to her creation, but, committed as they were to a belief in a rational and orderly universe, they attributed these phenomena to hidden causes and so allowed the goddess no real existence. Such a solution, however, could not be a convincing summary of experience: nothing is a more devout act of faith than the intellectualist's (or the scientist's) belief in a rational universe. One thinks of the problem of the buried treasure and the man who comes upon it "accidentally." Naturally there are causes for the treasure, as well as for its burial in that particular spot; and there is a parallel chain of causes for the man's coming there at that particular time. Yet for the nexus between these facts and the effect of the discovery on the man's own career (spiritually as well as materially) what is to be said? What can time the discovery so that it will not be deeply injurious in the man's life? Yet if chance enters here, where may it not penetrate? The mediaeval philosopher took account of this exigency indirectly in his theory of hidden causes, the *causa per accidens*, and the omnipotent rational Deity; and yet, even with this explanation, enough emphasis hardly falls on the experience of apparent chance. To this more tangible element the poet, therefore, gave full recognition in personifying chance, — that is to say, in accepting the personified figure of the pagans, — and in making the figure subservient to the rational God. In this way complete account was taken of both experience and faith, and reason itself was satisfied.

While, therefore, the pagan idea managed to keep a fairly large number of devotees, a compromise with Christianity was effected for others, and a genuinely Christian figure was created, retaining the title and the apparatus of the pagan cult. Leading poets arrived independently at this conception, and some lesser ones followed in their train. For much of the development Boethius was responsible, and his suggestions were far-reaching. At the time of the Renaissance, therefore, the goddess was still available in one form or another, and obviously in her pagan guise she was especially acceptable at that time. There is evidence to show that even in our own day she has persisted with some followers, although, of course, under the influence of certain recrudescent forms of materialism, the personification is less apt to be popular now than the mere abstraction.

Whether the goddess was ever actually believed in as something more than a symbolic creature, at least after the Roman period, it is really impossible to say. But we do know that there were people in the Middle Ages who could in terms of a deity conceive of what we call forces; and we know also how generally available the figure of Fortuna was, attempting in her libertine fashion to suit everybody. How far we are really entitled to unite the one fact with the other, and to conclude that just so far an actual faith in the capricious deity extended, I should not dare to conjecture. One may fairly assert, however, that all the evidence points to the conclusion that there was some faith of that kind in some quarters. What was substantially positive in this, and what was in harmony with her own truth, Christianity made her own.

CHAPTER II

TRADITIONAL THEMES OF FORTUNE IN MEDIAEVAL LITERATURE

IN the preceding chapters I have found it convenient
to define three distinct mental attitudes toward Fortuna, — the pagan, the attitude of compromise, and the
Christian, — and have thus practically defined three separate figures of the goddess: the independent ruling power,
the power which shares the universe with some other force,
and the power completely subservient to another god. In
this chapter I need not discriminate sharply among these
three figures, because it is my purpose to study the com-
posite portrait of Fortuna in the Middle Ages, to observe
the establishment and growth of the tradition, not chronologically but *en masse*, in order to see precisely what was
the nature of that tradition. In other words, here we are
not so much concerned with the philosophy of Fortune as
with her paraphernalia.

The method of study which I shall pursue will be: (1)
to establish the conception of Fortuna as a goddess; (2) to
observe the epithets and technical terms of her cult; (3)
to depict her general appearance and character as we find
them described; (4) to determine the limits of her powers
and the field of her activities; (5) to notice, in connection
with all these topics, the literary formulae which are
regularly used in expressing them, or, as I have already
called these formulae, the "themes" of the tradition.
One result of this study will be to enable us to put to-

gether a typical mediaeval account of Fortuna, so that we may criticize any particular mediaeval discussion either as purely traditional or as strikingly original. We may also draw some conclusions as to the nature of the development that gave rise to such elaborate properties and accoutrements.

I

THE GODDESS

Mere personification, or the attribution of a proper name, does not imply that Fortuna is strictly a goddess.[1] She is a goddess only while she remains in power as such, that is, while she actually bestows. What she bestows, what we take as the abstraction "fortuna," — good fortune, wealth, riches, and the like, — is often personified, and this figure may easily be confused with the divinity. This abstraction, when personified, is particularly marked by the qualities of the gifts. It is typical of persons endowed with these qualities, and hence may conveniently be called a "type." On the other hand, a symbol as a unit of allegory does not attempt to represent the original idea by reproducing its characteristics; the goddess should not require identification by these means. Fortuna is not particularly fortunate while she is meting out her gifts. In this way she is more easily distinguishable from a type than is such a figure as Justice, who to a certain extent must be just. Fortuna is, then, purely symbolic. She may not suffer what as a goddess she inflicts, whereas the type must continually suffer reversals of that kind.

[1] See *Smith College Studies in Modern Languages*, III, 188–190; and above, pp. 17, 30.

Between the two figures of symbol and type, however, there is continual danger of confusion; and, when it occurs, it means that the author did not have a clear idea of the deity. Yet there may be confusion in slight details, which are worth our attention because, using them as a starting-point, we can test the complete descriptions of the goddess with more security. Thus even in Ovid we find,

Nostra per aduersas agitur fortuna procellas;[1]

and in Chaucer,

She goth upright and yet she halt.[2]

In one of the Vatican pictures she is represented on the sea, with a boat, a sail, and an oar, "car la fortune vient du commerce maritime"; but clearly "wealth" is what is implied by the artist.[3] Again, she is found, involved in difficulties, in an emblem picturing a naked figure lifted from the sea by a mailed figure. The inscription, "Fortuna forti subleuanda Industria," [4] implies that she was sinking before her rescue. In all these cases the symbolism can best be explained by interpreting Fortuna as "possessions," "riches," and so on. The abstract "fortune" suffers adversity; that is, our riches are in poor condition, are sinking, are beaten by the winds, are lame. So much for this confusion of type and symbol.

[1] *Tristia*, V, xii, 5. Cf. Cousin's *Livre de Fortune*, pl. 171: "La Fortune exposée a tous les Vents."
[2] *Book of the Duchesse*, l. 622. Cf. Alexander Montgomerie, *Ane Invectione against Fortun*, l. 36 (*Poems*, ed. Cranstoun, 1887, p. 130): "Sho stottis at strais, syn stumbillis not at stanis."
[3] Barbier de Montault, *Traité*, I, 163, § 5.
[4] Achille Bocchi, *Symbolicae Quaestiones* (1574), symb. li.

For our present purposes, the name Fortuna must represent the goddess. With this name we have many qualifying epithets and adjectives, implying her nature. Here is a list of some which form a customary part of the tradition:

amara	invidiosa
aspera	laeta
belle	laide
benigna	lubrica
blind	mala
bona	meretrix
caeca	mobilis
crudel	noiosa
double	parjur
dulcia	perfida
fallace	perversa
favorevole	ria
fera	ruinosa
fickle	surda
incerta	traitor
inconstans	tristia
infortune [1]	ugly
ingrata	vaga
inimica	varia
iniqua	variable
instabilis	volubilis [2]

[1] See the play on the verb *fortuner* in Watriquet de Couvin's *Dis de Fortune*, ll. 49 ff. (*Dits*, ed. Scheler, p. 75): *desfortunez, fortunez, enfortunez, renfortunez, desfortune.*

[2] Cf. Canter, pp. 72 ff. With these we may note the words which, because of themes, are usually involved: *assalt, assaut; casus; colpa, coupe; estable, stable; fidem, faith; fiel; firm; ludum; miel; moë, moue, mowe; traboccare, trabuchier,* etc.

At least one or more of these words or its cognate enters into every literary discussion of the goddess,[1] and, following in her train, many of them pass from one language into another. These and many others are the technical vocabulary of her cult; and the rimes probably kept many of them going in pairs. Gathering a number of these expressions about her like robes, the goddess sweeps on down through the ages.

VENTURA

Ventura, or *Aventure,* is a name that at one time threatened to replace the name Fortuna. As we have elsewhere noticed,[2] Ventura receives a treatment similar to that of Fortuna herself. Like Fortuna, she turns a wheel, and exalts and debases; [3] she guides; [4] and she is confused with Fate or Destiny.[5]

Aventure was particularly well received in France. She is depicted in the Christian conception of Watriquet

[1] For long lists of epithets, see Pliny, *Natural History,* ii, 22, 'Inuenit tamen inter," etc., quoted above, p. 11; Dreves, *Analecta Hymnica,* xxi, 103 (no. 152, st. 5); Henricus Septimellensis, *Trattato* (1730), p. 16; A. Medin, *Lamenti,* p. 43, ll. 13 f; etc.

[2] *Smith College Studies in Modern Languages,* IV, 12 ff. Cf. also the *Roman de Fauvel,* ll. 2254–85. Also see Baudouin de Condé, *Dits et Contes,* I, 301–302, ll. 967–968.

[3] Brunetto Latini, *Il Favoletto,* ll. 71 ff; *Poeti del Primo Secolo,* I, 515; Lorenzo de' Medici, *Poesie* (1801), I, 169; Van Duyse, *Het Oude Ned. Lied,* II, 1572 ff.

[4] *Poeti del Primo Secolo,* I, 513; Herzhoff, *Personif. lebl. Dinge,* etc., pp. 11 f. (finds Aventure is most often connected with "amener," "mener," etc.; notice his references).

[5] Chaucer, *Knight's Tale,* A. 1465 (cf. l. 1490); *Troilus and Criseyde,* v, 1540, "And thus he dryeth forth his aventure" (cf. the usual "dree his wierd").

de Couvin's *Mireoirs as Dames*.[1] Sometimes she goes hand in hand with Fortune,[2] or she may supersede her.[3] At one time Aventure was apparently the more familiar term for "the casual," and was scarcely felt as a proper name. When the word got outside of French literature, it seems to have meant merely "chance" or "the chances" — a good commentary on its significance in French. The idea came to be that Fortune deals in *aventures*.[4] Clearly, then, Fortune controlled these *aventures*, and so survived any danger of being overcome by the upstart.

EÜRE

As a substitute for Fortune, or at least as a companion, *Eüre* or *Maleüre*, gained great popularity in France. This figure is also endowed with power by Watriquet de Couvin, who helped to give Aventure such great vogue:

> Eürs sui en terre apelez,
> Qui sert à ma dame Fortune,
> Qui ne crient au monde fors une,
> Qui seur lui ait poor ne force
> Ne vertu, jà tant s'i efforce,
> Car elle defforce les fors,
> Les fiers orgueilleus, et met fors

---

[1] Lines 59 ff. (*Dits*, pp. 3 ff.). Cf. this description with that of Fortuna.

[2] *Renart le Nouvel* (*Roman du Renart*, ed. Méon, IV, 255), l. 3247; G. de Machaut, *Le Dit de l'Alerion*, ll. 4275, 4281 (*Œuvres*, ed. Hoepffner, II, 385); Alain Chartier, *Œuvres*, p. 612; Charles d'Orléans, *Poésies*, I, 188. See also Chaucer, *Clerk's Tale*, E. 812; Jubinal, *Contes, Dits*, etc., I, 195 ("Fortune est aventure").

[3] Simund de Freine, *Roman de Philosophie*, l. 61 ("Fortune ceo est aventure").

[4] Gower, *Mirour de l'Omme*, l. 18270; Lydgate, *Troy Book*, i, 1420 ff.; Dunbar, *To Dwell in Court, My Friend*, ll. 11 f. (*Poems*, II, 98); Cranstoun, *Satirical Poems*, I, 44, ll. 172–173.

Du leur et soi monstre con forte
Quant l'un grieve et l'autre conforte, etc.[1]

In Nicole de Margival's *Panthère d'Amours*, Eürs and
Meseürs stand at the entrance to Fortune's house. The
author explains that when Fortune is angry Eürs has no
power.[2] By the time of Guillaume de Machaut, Eüre,
now become Bonneürté, is fairly independent:

La dame a nom Bonneürté
Qui tient en sa main Sëurté
En la partie de Fortune;
Car il n'est personne nesune
Cui Fortune peüst abatre,
Se la dame le vuet debatre.

Bonneürté controls even Nature. Her duties include the
bestowal of prosperity in general, the acquisition of
friends for her favorites, victory over their enemies, and
so on.[3] The cult of Eüre or Maleüre was surprisingly
large;[4] but here again Fortune was for some reason found

[1] *Dis de l'Escharbote*, ll. 48 ff. (*Dits*, pp. 398–399). See a reference to
Eürs also in his *Mireoirs as Dames*, ll. 132 ff. (*ibid.*, pp. 5 f.).

[2] *Panthère*, ll. 1985 ff. Cf. Eur and Maleur as the trumpeters of Fortune
in Pierre Michault's *Dance aux Aveugles*, pp. 30 ff. (cf. p. 42).

[3] Guillaume de Machaut, *Le Jugement dou Roy de Navarre*, ll. 3851 ff.
(*Œuvres*, ed. Hoepffner, I, 270.) See also his *Remede de Fortune*, ll. 2779 ff.
(*ibid.*, II, 102): "Have no regard for Fortune; seek Bonneürté, who gives
Glory, Delight, Reverence," etc. Lines 2801 ff. seem to imply that these
are "les biens de vertu."

[4] A few references, not in every case to the personification but to important uses of the word, may be given. In *Perceval le Gallois* (II, 202, ll. 6040 ff.)
the adjective "maléureus" is used. — *Eüre*: Adenes le Roi, *Li Romans de
Berte aus Grans Piés*, p. 51; *L'Escoufle*, p. 105, ll. 3510 ff.; Jean le Seneschal,
Les Cents Ballades, p. 53, l. 1 ("eür de Fortune"); G. de Machaut, *Poésies*,
ed. Chichmaref, I, 52 (xxxviii, 11, Eürs, Fortune), 71 (lvi, 6, Grace, Eür,
Fortune), 113 (cxiii, Love, Fortune, Eürs), 150 (clxiv, Eürs, Fortune), 192
(ccxiii, Fortune, Eür). I have not been able in every case to give the
references to Machaut in the latest edition (published by the Société des

more satisfactory (perhaps because her name covered the conception of both fortune and misfortune), and she accordingly predominated. Neither Eüre nor Maleüre ever received the imaginative description which was lavished upon Fortuna, and they repeatedly threatened to lapse into pure abstractions or types. They did, however, contribute to the vocabulary of the Fortune tradition.[1]

II

DESCRIPTION

Fortune sometimes has two faces, one beautiful, the other ugly. In Boccaccio she has great stature and a

Anciens Textes Français); transferring these references and others to later editions would have postponed the publication of this volume longer than seemed really worth while. See also Froissart, *Œuvres*, III, 216–223 *passim* (Bon Eür); Charles d'Orléans, *Poésies*, II, 232. — *Meseür:* Watriquet de Couvin, *Tournois des Dames*, ll. 488, 1248 (*Dits*, pp. 247, 270); G. de Machaut, *Poésies*, ed. Chichmaref, I, 63 (xlviii, 11–12),

> Meseürs m'a mis et enserré
> En crueus las de Fortune si fort, etc. —

Maleüre: Deschamps, *Œuvres*, VI, 222 (mccxxiv); Koch, *Christine de Pizan*, pp. 68–69 (summary of *Le Livre de la Mutaçion de Fortune*; in it Maleur appears as a brother of Fortune); Christine de Pisan, *Œuvres*, I, 9 (viii, 15), and *Le Livre du Chemin*, p. 14, l. 320; Alain Chartier, *Œuvres*, pp. 365 (remedy of courage, refers to Seneca and to Boccaccio's "cas des nobles"), 584 (the same); Raynaud, *Rondeaux*, p. 2 ("De par Maleur qui tresfort me fortune").

[1] Jean de Garencières, *Vous m'avez*, ed. A. Piaget, in *Romania*, XXII, 477, st. ix, "Fortune la maleureuse"; Lydgate, *Troy Book*, i, 3169 f.,

> Right as ferforth as Fortune wil hym Ewre,
> What so be-tide of his aventure,

and iv, 5999, "grace and ewre and hap of olde fortune"; cf. Lydgate's *Pilgrimage of the Life of Man*, l. 131, "swyche grace & Eur." "Felicity" seems to be an English attempt to render Eüre: see Chaucer, *Troilus and Criseyde*, iii, 1691 (cf. l. 1714); Lydgate, *Troy Book*, ii, 3201–3204; iv, 276–278; Sir Gilbert Hay's *Manuscript*, I, 65 (*Buke of the Law of Armys*, pt. ii, cap. xv), "warldly fortune na felicitee"; *The Complaynt of Scotlande*, p. 13, ll. 31–32.

strange figure, her eyes are burning and seem to threaten, her face is cruel and horrible, her long thick hair hangs over her mouth.[1] Elsewhere we find that she changes her countenance toward us,[2] and this change is figured in two separate faces,[3] one of which may be black, the other white.[4] The idea of Fortune's change in mood is symbolized in her smile or frown.[5] When in bad humor she

[1] *De Casibus* (lib. vi, cap. i), p. 146. For her great stature, cf. Frezzi, *Quadriregio*, I, 134 (lib. ii, cap. x), ll. 4 ff.; *Roman de Fauvel*, ll. 2328–2331 (reminiscent of Boethius, *Cons. Philos.*, I, pr. i, and of the *Iliad*, iv, 439–444); Chaucer, *Hous of Fame*, ll. 1369–1375. Cf. plate 10, below.

[2] Boccaccio, *Teseide*, i, 138 (*Opere*, IX, 55); Lorenzo de' Medici, *Opere* (1825), I, 78; Lydgate, *Albon and Amphabel*, iii, 494–495; also *Troy Book*, iii, 2722, cf. 4079; iv, 1088–1089.

[3] See Boethius, *Cons. Philos.*, II, pr. i, 31; *Bocace des Nobles Maleureux* (Couteau, Paris, 1538), fol. xlvi^{vo}, drawing at head of bk. iii, ch. i; Cousin, *Livre de Fortune*, pl. 25; Henricus Septimellensis, *Trattato*, 1730, p. 4 (quotes Boethius's phrase); G. de Machaut, *Remede de Fortune*, ll. 2408 ff.; Pischedda, *Canti Popolari*, p. 39. Cf. plate 1, above.

[4] See Fortune as a negress, Du Sommerard, *Les Arts au Moyen Age*, Album, vol. II, ser. 4, plates 37, 40. With face half black and half white, Cousin, *Livre de Fortune*, pl. 27; Piaget, *Martin le Franc*, p. 178; Albertus Magnus, *Opera*, II, 85 (*Physicorum*, lib. ii, tr. ii, cap. xi, "dimidium nigrum & dimidium album propter eufortunium & infortunium"). See also Boccaccio, *Teseide*, vi, 1, l. 5; Frezzi, *Quadriregio*, I, 149, l. 15; Lorenzo de' Medici, *Poemi*, ed. Carabba, p. 120; *Roman de Fauvel*, ll. 2163–2164; Watriquet de Couvin, *Mireoirs as Dames*, ll. 59 ff. (*Dits*, p. 3, Aventure); *Pierre de la Broche* (Monmerqué and Michel, *Théâtre Français*, p. 209, st. 4); De Guilleville, *Rommant des Trois Pelerinaiges* (c. 1500), fol. lxvii (Fortune is half white and half black). See also Lydgate, *Assembly of Gods*, l. 316; Pierre Michault, *La Dance aux Aveugles*, p. 30.

[5] Smile: *Bocace des Nobles Maleureux* (Couteau), fol. cxxiii, drawing. Cf. Hildebert de Lavardin, *De Exsilio Suo* (Migne, vol. CLXXI, col. 1418), "risere ... fata"; Trissino, *Tutte le Opere*, I, 303 (*Sofonisba*, l. 52), and *Italia Liberata*, ii, 244; Ariosto, *I Cinque Canti*, II, lxii; Charles d'Orléans, *Poésies*, II, 130; etc. — Frown: Lydgate, *Siege of Thebes*, l. 4250, and *Troy Book*, iii, 4221; v, 532; Sir William Mure, *Works*, I, 16 (l. 26, "Let fortoune froune, the world invy, hir smyle will me reviue"). Sometimes the sad face is weeping: see Henricus Septimellensis, *Trattato*, 1730, p. 16; G. de Machaut,

makes a face (*moë*) at us.[1] Fortuna is blind,[2] or more often blindfolded,[3] to show that she has no regard for merit. Yet sometimes her eyes appear, and very expressively, as when one of them weeps and the other laughs.[4]

Her hands, too, betray her nature. She is light-fingered in her ability to take back again; she has many hands.[5] As her face is divided in significance, so her hands, right and left, apparently mean good and evil fortune respectively.[6]

Remede de Fortune, ll. 990 ff. (cf. the variation in a picture of a *divided* face, ll. 1161 ff.).

[1] Philippe de Beaumanoir, *Jehan et Blonde*, l. 2509 (*Œuvres*, II, 79); *Girart de Rossillon*, l. 448; *Le Petit Traittiet* (Pierre Michault's *Dance aux Aveugles*, p. 233); Chaucer, *Troilus and Criseyde*, iv, st. 1; Lydgate, *Troy Book*, ii, 24, 4262–4263.

[2] Boethius, *Cons. Philos.*, II, pr. i, 31; Henricus Septimellensis, *Trattato*, 1730, p. 16; A. Medin, *Lamenti*, p. 43, ll. 13 f.; Boccaccio, *Ameto* (*Œuvres*, XV, 122); Du Sommerard, *Les Arts au Moyen Age*, Album, vol. II, ser. 4, pl. 40; etc.

[3] Du Sommerard, *Les Arts au Moyen Age*, Album, vol. II, ser. 8, pl. 30 (drawing of Boethius from a MS. of 1492; also in Molinier's *Manuscrits et Miniatures*, p. 289); *Roman de la Rose*, ll. 6196 ff.; Bourdillon, *Early Editions of the Roman de la Rose*, p. 110, §40; Scarlattini, *Homo Symbolicus*, II, 70 ("ligatos . . . oculos"); Piaget, *Martin le Franc*, p. 178, n. 2. Cousin has seventeen blindfolded figures; the bandage is thin in most cases, showing Fortune's eyes. See also Weinhold, *Glücksrad und Lebensrad*, pl. 1; Boll, *Die Lebensalter*, Abb. 4; and Pierre Michault, *La Dance aux Aveugles*, p. 30.

[4] See the burning eyes, Boccaccio, *De Casibus* (lib. vi, cap. i), p. 146. Note the contrast in the expressions of the eyes, G. de Machaut, *Remede de Fortune*, ll. 1161 ff.; *Roman de Fauvel*, ll. 1917 ff.

[5] "Levi manu," Poliziano, *Prose Volgari*, p. 240, ll. 49–50; "who can evade the hands of Fortune?" Boccaccio, *De Casibus*, p. 135; she has "a hundred hands," *ibid.*, p. 146 (also *Bocace des Nobles Maleureux*, fol. cxxiii). See the drawing in Durrieu's Munich MS., pl. xviii (six hands); and plate 10 in the present book.

[6] See the classical idea in "ambigua manu," Wright, *Satirical Poets*, I, 301 (John of Altaville). In Alanus de Insulis, Fortuna shifts her hands on the wheel to rest them (*Anticlaudianus*, VIII, i, Migne, vol. CCX, col. 560). In

Other features in the description of Fortuna we shall observe in a later chapter — as, for instance, her forelock and baldness when she appears as Occasio.[1] Sometimes, however, she has flowing hair.[2] She has wings, because she is fleeting.[3] In art her posture may have some significance. We find her standing on a ball,[4] and on a

Durrieu's drawing (see note above) one of the left hands is on the wheel. See Boccaccio, *Filocopo*, ii, iii (*Opere*, VII, 85, 262); G. de Machaut, *Remede de Fortune*, ll. 1057 ff. In Watriquet de Couvin's *Mireoirs as Dames*, l. 94, Aventure puts her right arm on the author's neck. See Cousin's plate 199, where Fortune's left hand is on Death's right arm, which moves the wheel.

[1] See below, pp. 116 f.

[2] See Fregoso, *Dialogo di Fortuna*, title-page; cf. Boccaccio, cited above, p. 43, n. 1 (see plate 10, below), and see many of Cousin's drawings.

[3] See Bocchi, *Symbolicae Quaestiones*, symbols xxiii, cxi; Solorzano, *Emblemata*, p. 32; Pontano, *Carmina*, I, 66 (*Urania*, ii, 1032); Cousin, *Livre de Fortune*, plates 15, 21, 31, 33, 67, 69, 77, 115, 123, 135, 167, 171, 173, 175, 177 (she has no feet in plate 21; cf. Adrian Junius, *Emblemata*, 1565, p. 32); Frezzi, *Quadriregio*, I, 134, l. 2. See wings on the feet of Occasio, Alciati's *Emblemata* (Paris, 1536); cf. Cousin's plates 17, 115.

[4] See Cousin's *Livre de Fortune*, plates 1, 15, 81, 105, 115, 151, 173, 175, 193, 199; in some of his other drawings (69, 123, 129, 141, 147) Fortune either sits on a globe or has one in her hand or near her; in plate 31 her elbow rests on one. At least one of his drawings is said to have come from Roman sculpture (see his preface, pp. 3–4, and cf. p. 33, nos. 141, 143, 145), and obviously the others belong to a period earlier than 1568. For the globe, see also Alciati's "In Occasionem" (emblems, Augsburg, 1531, sig. A8, — ed. Green, *Fontes Quatuor*, 1870 — and see a slightly different representation in the Padua edition, 1626, p. 179), and his "Ars Naturam Adjuvans" (Venice, 1546, sig. Fii, — ed. Green, as above, — and Lyons, 1551, p. 107, ed. Green, *Flumen Abundans*, 1871); Fregoso's *Dialogo* (1531), title-page; Adrian Junius's *Emblemata* (1565), p. 32; Bocchi, *Symbolicae Quaestiones*, 1574, symb. 111 (cf. 23, 132); *Mirrour of Maiestie* (1618), ed. Green and Croston, 1870, pl. 23 (after p. 63); Picinelli's *Mundus Symbolicus* (1680), I, 155 (lib. iii, cap. xix, 46, description). Schoonhoven (*Emblemata*, 1618, emb. 5) represents Fortune with one foot on a globe and the other on an upright wheel (Cousin's figure, 115, "Fortuna Volubilis," has one on a globe and the other on a flat wheel, with a little ball in one hand and a little wheel in the other, each ball and each wheel being equipped with wings). Solorzano (*Emblemata*, 1653,

wheel,[1] positions of course symbolic of her unsteadiness. She has an unpleasant reputation for being unclean, with a more or less constant reminiscence of the "whited sepulchre."[2] Other points of her description will occur as we go on.

As to her garments, her costume is characteristically changeable and differs from one writer to another. Boccaccio gives her "mollisque cutis, roseus color, ac purpurea uestis." Also he refers to her robe of many colors.[3] Lydgate takes this touch in his *Fall of Princes:*

> Her habite was of manifolde colours,
> Watchet blewe of feyned stedfastnes,
> her gold alleyed lyke sunne in watry showres
> meint with light grene for change & doublenes
> A pretens red drede meint with hardines,
> White for clennes like sone for to fayle
> Feynte blacke for mourning, russet for trauayle.[4]

In his *Assembly of Gods* we find her gown of "gawdy grene chamelet" of changeable colors.[5] Another description, this time of Aventure's costume, is given by Watriquet de Couvin in his *Mireoirs as Dames:* [6]

> Ses vestemens n'iert pas entiers,
> Mais de parçon mout tres diverse:

---

p. 32) shows her with each foot on a globe, two wings on each foot, and a wheel in her hand.

[1] Instances are given in note 5, pp. 148 f., below.

[2] See the origin of the idea in Boethius, *Cons. Philos.*, II, pr. v, 85 ff. See Henricus Septimellensis, *Trattato*, 1730, p. 16 ("surda"); Fregoso, *Dialogo di Fortuna*, cap. iv, sig. A7[vo] ("verme ha sempre dentro"); Chaucer, *Book of the Duchesse*, l. 629.

[3] *De Casibus*, III, i, p. 60. The robe of many colors is found on p. 146 (VI, i).

[4] VI, i, st. 7 (fol. cxliii[vo] of 1554 ed., cxxxiv of 1558 ed.).

[5] Lines 320–321. See *Roman de la Rose*, ll. 6146 ff. Note the *Morte Arthure* (allit.), ll. 3250 ff., and the *Kingis Quair*, stanzas 159–160.

[6] Especially lines 84 ff. The full description is found in lines 75 ff.

Noire iert à l'esclen lez et perse,
Blanche au destre con fleurs de lis,
Du resgarder yert fins delis.
Vermeille ot la face con rose:
Onques ne vie plus belle chose
Ne plaine de si grant bonté.

In manner Fortune is naturally both kind and unkind; we hear of her placid face [1] and her bland air,[2] as well as of her stormy appearance [3] and her truculent [4] and threatening [5] attitude.

In character she is proud,[6] subject to wrath,[7] and consequently vindictive and malign.[8] In effecting her will she is deceitful and dishonest.[9] Does she ever feel shame and pity?[10] She sometimes flatters,[11] but she is in general

[1] Boccaccio, *De Casibus*, p. 39 ("pauxillum placido vultu").

[2] Boethius, *Cons. Philos.*, II, pr. i, 7; Hildebert, Migne, CLXXI, col. 1419; Petrarch, *Africa*, i, 134; Lydgate, *Minor Poems*, ed. MacCracken, I, 28, st. 6. Also Cousin, pl. 105.

[3] Boccaccio, *Filocopo*, ii (*Opere*, VII, 132).

[4] Pulci, *Morgante Maggiore*, xxii, 186.

[5] Gower, *Cronica Tripertita*, ii, 6.

[6] Charles d'Orléans, *Poésies*, II, 154–155; *Roman de la Rose*, l. 6575.

[7] Boccaccio, *De Casibus*, pp. 96, 153; Masuccio Salernitano, *Il Novellino*, p. 263; Benoît de Ste. Maure, *Roman de Troie*, II, 274–275, ll. 13094 ff.

[8] Boccaccio, *De Casibus*, pp. 15–16, *Filocopo*, iii (*Opere*, VII, 247), *Donne Famose*, p. 198 (cap. lxiii); Petrarch, *Africa*, vii, 338; Alain Chartier, *Œuvres*, p. 394 ("bat ses paulmes, quant il meschiet à grans Seigneurs"); the anonymous *Débat de Lomme Mondain et du Religieux* (Pierre Michault's *Dance aux Aveugles*, p. 314); Villon, *Œuvres*, ed. Lacroix, p. 90; Chaucer, *Monk's Tale*, B. 3740 (cf. *Melusine*, l. 201, she is glad to do ill); Chaucer, *Troilus and Criseyde*, iv, st. 1.

[9] A. Medin, *Lamenti*, p. 43, ll. 13 f. ("mendace"); Boccaccio, *Fiammetta*, viii (*Opere*, VI, 198), "gli antichi inganni della fortuna"; Ariosto, *Rime e Satire*, p. 55 (canz. iii); Pontano, *Carmina*, II, 393 (*Eridanus*, II, xxxi, 25–26, "insidias"); *Roman de la Rose*, l. 6578.

[10] Boethius, *Cons. Philos.*, I, pr. iv, 63–64; Boccaccio, *De Casibus*, p. 165. PITY: Petrarch, *Africa*, vii, 880 ff.; Pulci, *Morgante Maggiore*, xxi, 82; Gower, *Vox Clamantis*, ii, 179–182; Machiavelli, *Capitolo di Fortuna* (*Opere*, VII, 367).

[11] Boethius, *Cons. Philos.*, II, pr. i, 13; Henricus Septimellensis, *Trattato*,

such an envious creature that authors are fond of dwelling on this idea. She envies any man's prosperity and deprives him of it.[1] In satisfying her desire she is thoroughly unjust and favors the undeserving.[2] She is therefore quite irrational.[3] Inconstant she is of course; this trait is made so much of, indeed, and is treated in such a variety of ways that it will form our next general topic.

Certain relatives of Fortune are mentioned. Alanus de Insulis makes Nobility the daughter of Fortune; [4] ac-

1730, p. 13 ("blandifero"); Boccaccio, De Casibus, pp. 96, 269; Teseide, v, 55. See above, p. 47, n. 2.

[1] Boethius, Cons. Philos., II, pr. iii, 36–37; Boccaccio, Decameron, IV, i (Opere, II, 153); De Casibus, pp. 43 ("felicis impaciens"), 98; also Filocopo, i, ii, iii (Opere, VII, 69, 152, 262), and Fiammetta, i (ibid., VI, 4, 12); Petrarch, Bucolicum Carmen, p. 154, l. 381; Masuccio, Il Novellino, pp. 378, 442; Alberti, Opere, V, 360 (egl. 1); Pulci, Morgante Maggiore, xx, 45; L'Escoufle, p. 133, ll. 4466 ff.; Philippe de Beaumanoir, Jehan et Blonde, ll. 549, 1629 ff. (Œuvres, II, 20, 52); Christine de Pisan, Œuvres, I, 8 (vii), 9 (viii, 15 f., "Meseur"); Gower, Mirour de l'Omme, ll. 26422 ff.; Lydgate, Siege of Thebes, ll. 887 f., and Troy Book, i, 750 f.; Melusine, ll. 3986 f.

[2] Boethius, Cons. Philos., I, met. v, 33–34; Baehrens, Poetae Latini Minores, IV, 148, no. 145; Petrarch, Bucolicum Carmen, p. 135, ll. 81 ff.; Roman de la Rose, ll. 6188 ff.; Alex. Montgomerie, Ane Invectione against Fortun, ll. 10 ff. Contrast Guido Cavalcanti, in Poeti del Primo Secolo, II, 326 (the Christian Fortune, who refutes all this slander).

[3] For the remedy of prudence, and the opposition of Reason against Fortune, see Smith College Studies in Modern Languages, III, 197, 207, 217–218, etc. The idea of the remedy is, of course, the opposition of reason to Fortune's unreason. See drawings in Bourdillon's Early Editions of the Roman de la Rose, p. 110, §40 (Raison crowned, pointing to blindfolded Fortune), and Cousin's Livre de Fortune, pl. 83, "La Raison et la Fortune sont rarement d'Accord." See Reason crowned and also Fortune (xv-century drawing in MS. of a French version of Petrarch's De Remediis), in Du Sommerard's Les Arts au Moyen Age, Album, vol. II, ser. 4, plates 37, 38, 39. For the remedy of prudence, see Weinhold, Glücksrad und Lebensrad, p. 4, inscription. In the Chevalier Errant the traveller visits Fortune after leaving Reason: Gorra, Studi di Crit. Lett., pp. 44–45. Cf. plate 2, above.

[4] Anticlaudianus, VII, viii (Migne, vol. CCX, col. 557). Cf. Roman de la Rose, l. 6591 ("gentillesce"). Petit de Julleville (Histoire de la Littérature

cording to another view her father was Justice,[1] and from Fregoso we learn that her parents were Human Judgment and Opinion.[2]

III

FICKLENESS

As we have seen in the description of Fortuna, much detail is given to symbolizing her inconstancy. On the whole, there is an average ratio of about five to three between the passages in which she appears unfavorable and those in which she is kindly; and very likely this average gives a little too much credit to favorable Fortuna, for the goddess is chiefly called on in cases of objection to her manner of doing things. Hence our usual optimistic interpretation of the abstract "fortune" cannot come from the name of the goddess.

Fortune is highly variable and scarcely knows her own mind. She is in doubt;[3] she is sometimes asleep, but wakes up when she pleases;[4] she goes along changing her style,[5] or turning her face like a weathercock.[6] Her inconstancy is so universal a theme[7] that we must study the various motifs which symbolize it.

Française, Moyen Âge, II, 200) notes that the *Roman de Fauvel* makes Vaine Gloire a bastard daughter of Fortune. Cf. Cousin, pl. 27 (described on his p. 20).

[1] See Cousin's *Livre de Fortune*, pl. 131. Cf. the Roman cult, Fortuna Primigenia, daughter of Jupiter. See the *Roman de Fauvel*, ll. 2166 ff.; and cf. below, p. 61. [2] *Dialogo di Fortuna*, sig. B 3vo.

[3] Boccaccio, *De Casibus*, p. 164; Gower, *Cronica Tripertita*, iii, 189 ff.

[4] Villon, *Œuvres*, ed. Lacroix (*Poésies Attribuées*), p. 180.

[5] Petrarch, *Rime*, ed. Albertini, II, 224 (*Trionfo della Morte*, i, 135); *Poesie Ital. Ined.*, III, 375, last line.

[6] Cranstoun, *Satirical Poems*, I, 326, ll. 31–32.

[7] See Boccaccio, *De Casibus*, p. 7; Petrarch, *Vite d. Uomini*, I[1], 319; Gower, *Cronica Tripertita*, ii, 29, and *Confessio Amantis*, iii, 2440 ff., vii, 3431 ff.;

Since Fortuna is deceitful, there is probably no faith in her; [1] he is a fool who trusts in her. [2] For her wheel cannot stop: [3] she would cease to be Fortuna if she ceased to be changeable. [4] Her moves are sudden and, of course, unexpected. [5]

Her changeableness leads inevitably to a comparison with the moon. As the moon varies from day to day, and as it controls the shifting tides, so Fortuna ceaselessly changes her aspect and turns the tide of mankind. [6] Her

Lydgate, *Troy Book*, ii, 311; v, 2432. In *Floire et Blanceflor*, ll. 2252–2254, Fortune changes seven times between "prime" and "none." In Cousin's plate 53 she holds a chameleon in her left hand.

[1] Petrarch, *Africa*, v, 16 f. ("dum fortuna fidem tenuit"), 134 ("Fortuna mihi nota fides"); also *Vite d. Uomini*, I[2], 567; Boccaccio, *Rime*, xxxv, 1 (*Opere*, XVI, 64, "crede la fortuna"); Frezzi, *Quadriregio*, I, 149, ll. 10 ff.

[2] Jubinal, *Contes, Dits*, etc., I, 198; G. de Machaut, *Poésies*, ed. Chichmaref, II, 497, l. 1; Charles d'Orléans, *Poésies*, I, 74; *Melusine*, ll. 272–273; Chaucer, *Troilus and Criseyde*, iv, st. 1; Lydgate, *Troy Book*, ii, 2300–2303, 3201–3202, 3206 (cf. i, 3190). For a "Note on Folsifie," see G. C. Keidel, *Mod. Lang. Notes*, X, 146 ff.

[3] Boethius, *Cons. Philos.*, II, pr. i, 56 ff.; Poliziano, *Le Stanze*, etc., ed. Carducci, 1863, p. 384, l. 36 (Fortune's wheel will stop before Lorenzo de' Medici's fame ceases); *Roman de la Rose*, l. 6434; Lydgate, *Troy Book*, iv, 1078.

[4] Boethius, *Cons. Philos.*, II, pr. i, 57 f.; Chaucer, *Troilus and Criseyde*, i, 848–849; Voigt, *Florilegium Gottingense* (*Roman. Forschung.*, III, 311), no. 333.

[5] Orderic Vital, in Bouquet's *Recueil*, XII, 723, C–D; Henricus Septimellensis, *Trattato*, 1730, p. 13 ("quare subito"); Boccaccio, *Decameron*, V, i (*Opere*, III, 27, 29); also *Filocopo*, iii (*ibid.*, VII, 286), and *De Casibus*, p. 271; Sannazaro, *Opere*, p. 428; Boiardo, *Orlando Innamorato*, III, vii, 59; Chrestien de Troyes, *Erec und Enide*, ll. 2785 ff.; Robert of Avesbury, ed. Hearne, p. 258 ("auferet hora brevis"); Chaucer, *Troilus and Criseyde*, iv, 384–385.

[6] See *Carmina Burana*, ed. Schmeller, p. 1. Cf. Novati, *Carmina Medii Aevi*, p. 44, st. vi; Dante, *Paradiso*, xvi, 82–84; Pulci, *Morgante Maggiore*, xi, 8; Pischedda, *Canti Popolari*, p. 39; *Poesie Ital. Ined.*, IV, 301, 310; Simund de Freine, *Roman de Philosophie*, ll. 115 ff. (cf. his *Vie de St. Georges*, ll. 107 ff.); *Roman de la Rose*, l. 4799 (eclipse of Fortune), cf. l. 5371; G. de

frailty is also indicated by a comparison with glass: she is both frail and brittle in temperament.[1] Her fickleness, too, includes her treachery. Her face may smile, but she

Machaut, *Remede de Fortune*, ll. 956 ff.; also his *Poésies*, ed. Chichmaref, II, 477, l. 89, and his *Livre du Voir-Dit*, p. 355, ll. 8732 ff.; Christine de Pisan, *Œuvres*, I, 13 (xii); Charles d'Orléans, *Poésies*, II, 220 (ccxxii); Gower, *Vox Clamantis*, ii, 151–152 (cf. *Carmina Burana*, p. 1); Lydgate and Burgh's *Secrees of the Old Philisoffres*, p. 39, ll. 1208–1209; also Lydgate's *Reson and Sensuallyte*, ll. 47–48; Alex. Montgomerie, *Ane Invectione against Fortun*, l. 10. Lydgate is influenced by Fortuna in his pictures of Lucina: see his *Balade made at the Departyng of Thomas Chaucyer on Ambassade in to Fraunce* (*Modern Philol.*, I, 333); and his *Troy Book*, ii, 5613 ff.,

> Now ful of liȝt, now hornyd pale is sche,
> Lady of chaunge and mutabilite,
> Þat selde in on halt hir any tyme.

For the Fortune-moon theme, cf. Boll, *Die Lebensalter* (relation of the planets to the seven ages, and the seven ages to Fortune's wheel). See Gower, *Cronica Tripertita*, iii, 228, "Est rota fortune quodamodo regula lune." Cf. Furnivall, *Political, Religious, and Love Poems*, p. 265. Also in Wackernagel's *Glücksrad und die Kugel des Glücks* (in his *Kleinere Schriften*, I, 251), the relation of the wheel to the moon is discussed. Tatlock (*Astrology and Magic in Chaucer's Franklin's Tale*, Kittredge Anniversary vol., pp. 341–342) quotes Roger Bacon as saying that the moon is of most power in nigromancy. I have heard of a modern Basque proverb, "Wind, women, and fortune change like the moon."

[1] See Werner, *Beiträge*, p. 3, no. 2, l. 18 ("fragilis"); Boethius, *Cons. Philos.*, II, met. iii, 15 ("fortunis caducis"); Baehrens, *Poetae Latini Minores*, IV, 148, no. 145, l. 13 ("fragilis"); Chaucer, *Troilus and Criseyde*, iii, 820 ("brotel wele"); Lydgate, *Troy Book*, iii, 4225; Hoccleve, *Regement of Princes*, l. 61; Solorzano, *Emblemata*, p. 32, emb. v, inscription, "Fortuna Vitrea Est" (see the following commentary, p. 38, which quotes from Tertullian's *Apologeticus*, I, xxxiii, and refers to Lipsius and to Schoonhoven's emblem No. 60); Cousin, *Livre de Fortune*, pl. 55, "La Fortune de Verre." See the cap of glass which Chaucer's Fortune fits on her victim, *Troilus and Criseyde*, v. 469; and *Monk's Tale*, B. 3562. Cf. the ice-figure in *Carmina Burana*, p. 1 ("dissolvit ut glaciem"); for Fortune's "slippery solace," which dissolves like ice in fire, see John Stewart of Baldynneis, *Roland Furious*, xi, 125–126 (*Poems*, II, 83); and note the house of ice in the *Panthère d'Amours* of Nicole de Margival (see below, pp. 133 f.).

stings just the same, and thus she resembles a serpent [1] or (even better) a scorpion.[2]

As we thirst for her gifts,[3] so Fortune gives us sweet and bitter to drink, by turns honey and gall.[4] She bor-

[1] See the serpent in the symbolism of Fortuna Panthea, noticed in *Smith College Studies in Modern Languages*, III, 136. Scarlattini (*Homo Symbolicus*, I, 10) has an emblem of a youth dedicating himself to Fortune ("haec uero adolescentis collo Leonis caput inserebat, tum etiam caput serpentis, & monstruosi praeterea animalis cujusdam"). Cf. Henricus Septimellensis, *Trattato*, 1730, p. 13 ("Est fortuna mihi serpente Neronior omni," etc.); Froissart, *Œuvres*, III, 213 f., ll. 26–27 ("pointure de vipere Ou bas estage de sa roe"); Christine de Pisan, *Œuvres*, I, 8 ("Ta pointure très venimeuse").

[2] See Chaucer, *Book of the Duchesse*, l. 636, and Skeat's note (Oxford Chaucer, I, 479) referring to the *Ancren Riwle* and to Vincent of Beauvais; see also the *Merchant's Tale*, E. 2057–2058; *Pierre de la Broche* (Monmerqué and Michel, *Théâtre Français*, p. 211), "Escorpie de venin plaine . . . oint devant et point derriere"; Rutebeuf, *Œuvres*, I, 98, l. 109 ("oins devant & poins derrière"); G. de Machaut, *Remede de Fortune*, ll. 931 ("viper"), 990 (she anoints and stabs). Cf. Lydgate, *Troy Book*, ii, 3314, "Feyth in hir face & fraude ay in þe tail."

[3] See Boethius, *Cons. Philos.*, II, met. ii, 18; Boccaccio, *De Casibus*, p. 151; cf. the *Pearl*, l. 132 ("Hyttez to haue ay more & more").

[4] Cf. William of Malmesbury's "hydromellum" (*Gesta Regum*, I, 230, §189), which according to his story was offered to the goddess of the pagans. For Fortune's drink for mankind, see Henricus Septimellensis, *Trattato*, 1730, p. 4 ("mellea felle," etc.); Petrarch, *Rime*, ed. Albertini, II, 220 (*Trionfo della Morte*, i); Boccaccio, *Filocopo*, iv (*Opere*, VIII, 14); Alberti, *Opere*, III, 200 (*Il Teog.*, i). See Bembo, *Rime*, p. 184; Baudouin de Condé, *Li Prisons d'Amour*, l. 880 (*Dits et Contes*, I, 298). See the streams of Fortune in Alanus de Insulis: "Very sweet water hath the one, and honeyed cups it giveth. With its honey it seduceth many, and they that drink the waters do thirst for them the more," etc. (*Anticlaudianus*, VII, viii, Migne, vol. CCX, col. 558). See, further, *Roman de la Rose*, ll. 6002 ff.; G. de Machaut, *Remede de Fortune*, ll. 2412 ff. 2516, 2518; Alain Chartier, *Œuvres*, pp. 632–633 (the two streams troubled by Fortune); René d'Anjou, *Œuvres Complètes*, III, 9 ("fontaine de Fortune"); Chaucer, *Monk's Tale*, B. 3537 ("fortune hath in hir hony galle"); Lydgate, *Pilgrimage of the Life of Man*, l. 25. Cf. with all this the two fountains in Sicily, "the one of which had the property of turning barren things into fruitful, the other of turning fruitful things into barren" (*Gesta*

rows from Jupiter the two urns of good and evil,[1] and makes them her own.[2] Lydgate, following *Les Échecs Amoureux*, gives Fortune two tuns in her cellar, one containing prosperity, one adversity: the former, which is delicious, creates false delight and increases thirst; the latter is full of bitterness.[3] Since the Fortune of this poem is practically a goddess of love, the tuns are easily transformed to love-tuns, and so they are in Gower.[4] Perhaps related to this idea is the theme of Fortune's buckets, which, however, seems rather to derive from scales[5] or from the see-saw effect of rising and falling personages on the wheel.[6] Yet there is some suggestion as to

Romanorum, ccliii, in the Latin): Herrtage, *The Early English Versions of the Gesta Romanorum*, London, 1879, EETS., Extra Series, No. 33, p. 537.

[1] See *Iliad*, xxiv, 527 f.; *Roman de la Rose*, ll. 6836 ff.; Gower, *Confessio Amantis*, vi, 330 ff.; Lydgate, *Pilgrimage of the Life of Man*, ll. 176–177. Cf. Cousin's plate 125; and see the two vats held by the king in J. Sauer's *Symbolik*, p. 273.

[2] In *Pierre de la Broche* (Monmerqué and Michel, *Théâtre Français*, p. 211) Fortune is called "Vessiaux plains de mal et d'amer." Boethius puts the reference to Jove's vessels into the monologue of Fortune (*Cons. Philos.*, II, pr. ii, 38 ff.; and note the following "quid si a te non tota discessi?"). The *Roman de la Rose* makes Fortune taverner of Jupiter and his tuns (see lines 6836 ff., tuns of wine and wormwood).

[3] See Lydgate, *Reson and Sensuallyte*, ll. 50 ff., and for further parallels see Sieper's note, II, 78. In Reisch's *Margarita Philosophica*, lib. viii, cap. xvi, there is a drawing of Fortune holding two goblets, one inverted with the contents spilling out.

[4] *Confessio Amantis*, vi, 325 ff., cf. 76 ff. (the tuns and the drunkenness of love; Cupid is butler). See Froissart, *Œuvres*, I, 21 (*Le Paradys d'Amours*, ll. 677–678); Lydgate, *Fabula Duorum Mercatorum*, ed. Schleich, ll. 446–447; Gavin Douglas, *King Hart*, canto I, last line (*Works*, I, 100), "Dame Venus tun."

[5] Cf. the golden scales in *Paradise Lost*, iv, 997 ff.

[6] Cf., for example, Lydgate's *Siege of Thebes*, l. 1132 ("The ton ascendeth, that other hath a fal"). For the see-saw, cf. Cousin's *Livre de Fortune*, pl. 33.

the contents of the buckets.[1] The figure seems to have
been well known and is certainly often used.[2]

Naturally, when one has once enjoyed the favors of
Fortune and then feels her frown, one's "song is turned
to pleyning" and one fitly acquires the name "Chauntepleure." [3] In such adversity the keenest prick of suffering
comes from remembering happier things, and so we have
the theme of "a sorrow's crown of sorrows." [4] Moreover,
the cruelty of Fortune is in proportion to her former

[1] See G. de Machaut, *Remede de Fortune*, ll. 969 ff. ("Li uns est pleins, li
autres vuis").

[2] See Cranstoun, *Satirical Poems*, I, 326, ll. 15–16 (". . . Lyke draw-well
bukkets dowkand vp and doun"). Cf. Shakespeare's *Richard II*, IV, i,
183 ff.:

> On this side my hand, and on that side yours.
> Now is this golden crown like a deep well
> That owes two buckets, filling one another,
> The emptier ever dancing in the air,
> The other down, unseen and full of water:
> That bucket down and full of tears am I,
> Drinking my griefs, whilst you mount up on high.

Cf. also Goethe's "goldnen Eimer" (*Faust*, ll. 449 f.):

> Wie Himmelskräfte auf und nieder steigen
> Und sich die goldnen Eimer reichen!

Notice the two buckets in the picture of Galeazzo Visconti (14th century),
in A. S. Cook's article on "The Last Months of Chaucer's Earliest Patron,"
Connecticut Acad. of Arts and Sciences, *Trans.*, XXI (1916), 17.

[3] See Chaucer, *Anelida and Arcite*, l. 320, and *Book of the Duchesse*, l. 599.
See also Rutebeuf, *Œuvres*, I, 105, l. 40 (and note *ibid.*, III, 91 ff.); *Roman de
Fauvel*, l. 2774. P. Meyer, in *Romania*, XIII, 510–511 (12), describes the
poem *La Pleure-chante*.

[4] See Boethius, *Cons. Philos.*, II, pr. iv, 4 f.; Dante, *Inferno*, v, 121 ff.
(not connected with Fortune); *Pierre de la Broche* (Monmerqué and Michel,
Théâtre Français, p. 211), "Quar hom qui n'a plus richece," etc.; Chaucer,
Troilus and Criseyde, iii, 1625 ff.; Gower, *Vox Clamantis*, ii, 61 ff.; Gavin
Douglas, *Eneados*, bk. xi, prol. (*Works*, IV, 6, ll. 11–12; reference to Boethius);
The Complaynt of Scotlande, p. 71, ll. 7 ff.

kindness: the higher we are exalted, the farther we fall.[1]

This lady Fortune is so changeable that her variations are to all intents and purposes instantaneous; hence most appropriately the rhetorical formula "now — now" is often used in describing her or her activities.[2] This device, or the conception which prompts it, naturally gives rise to considerable use of contrast and antithesis, even without the particular formula;[3] and this in turn leads to

---

[1] QUANTO-TANTO: see Dreves, *Analecta Hymnica*, XXI, 103 (no. 152, st. 3); Henricus Septimellensis, *Trattato*, 1730, p. 27 ("Nam graviore ruit turris tumefacta ruina," etc.); Abélard and Héloïse, epistle iv (Migne, vol. CLXXVIII, col. 194), "quanto universis in te . . . tanto hinc," etc.; Boccaccio, *De Casibus*, pp. 250-251, 255 ("in tantum illi laetior arrisit," etc.); Frezzi, *Quadriregio*, I, 148 ff., ll. 27 ff.; Aeneas Sylvius, *Opera Omnia*, p. 761, B ("quanto altius . . . tanto periculosius," etc.); Guicciardini, *Opere Ined.*, I, 272 ("quanto più . . . tanto più"), 391 ("che o . . . o che"); Philippe de Beaumanoir, *La Manekine*, ll. 1088 f., 4648 (*Œuvres*, I, 36, 144); Watriquet de Couvin, *Dis de l'Escharbote*, ll. 141 f. (*Dits*, p. 401); Jubinal, *Jongleurs et Trouvères*, pp. 177 ff., ll. 16 ff.; Alain Chartier, *Œuvres*, p. 394 ("si haut si bas").

[2] See Henricus Septimellensis, *Trattato*, 1730, pp. 16 (now cheerful, now lamenting, etc.), 17; Alanus de Insulis, *Anticlaudianus*, VIII, i (Migne, vol. CCX, col. 560), now in better gown, now in poor garb, etc.; *Gesta di Federico*, l. 1674; Boccaccio, *De Casibus*, p. 146 (now threatening, now flattering, etc.); *Chevalier Errant*, §vi, in Gorra's *Studi*, p. 46 (now she makes a poor cleric a pope, etc.); Benoit de Ste. Maure, *Roman de Troie*, IV, 320, ll. 29050 ff.; *Grant Mal fist Adam*, ed. Suchier, p. 62, st. 123; Simund de Freine, *Roman de Philosophie*, ll. 119 f.; Alain Chartier, *Œuvres*, pp. 267 ("ores eslongne . . . ores"), 394; Gower, *Mirour de l'Omme*, ll. 22154-22156; also *Confessio Amantis*, prol., 569-570, and *Vox Clamantis*, ii, 123, 154; Lydgate, *Troy Book*, ii, 2019; also *Temple of Glas*, App. I (continuation of Mss.), ll. 366 ff. (Schick's ed., p. 64); Gavin Douglas, *The Palice of Honour* (*Works*, I, 9, ll. 6-14); Pinkerton, *Ancient Scotish Poems*, II, 263, l. 23.

[3] See in general the themes of tragedy, poverty and riches, white and black, smiling and tearful, etc. See Boccaccio, *De Casibus*, p. 146 (visits high and low, palace and hut); Sannazaro, *Opere*, p. 383, son. lviii ("acerba," "dolce"); Pulci, *Morgante Maggiore*, xxi, 82 ("savj matti"); *Roman de la Rose*, ll. 3990 ff.; G. de Machaut, *Poésies*, ed. Chichmaref, II, 416, ll. 47 ff.;

the adoption of paradoxes to express the particular dis-
taste the author in question feels at Fortune's fickleness.[1]

The goddess who sometimes seems kind to us, but who
is really treacherous, resembles a step-mother. She has
fed us perhaps from her breast,[2] but later she turns
against us. She is interested in us only from selfish
motives, and she thus becomes fittingly a *noverca*.[3]

But such mobility of character and such caprice in
favor and affection stamp Fortune as something still
worse. As all men sooner or later share in her favors,[4]

also his *Remède de Fortune*, ll. 990 ff.; Christine de Pisan, *Œuvres*, 1, 19
(xviii, 11, "Dueil pour solas"); Gower, *Vox Clamantis*, ii, 121 ff.; Lydgate,
Temple of Glas, App. I (continuation of Mss.), ll. 365 ff. (with and without
nunc — nunc); the *Pearl*, l. 130.

[1] Alanus, *Anticlaudianus*, VIII, i (Migne, vol. CCX, col. 559), harsh in
her blandishments, cloudy in light, rich and poor, gentle and cruel, sweet and
bitter, laughing and weeping, fixed yet moving, blind yet seeing, constant in
fickleness, firm in motion, faithful in falsity, fickle in truth, etc.; *Roman de la
Rose*, ll. 5972 ff.; G. de Machaut, *Remede de Fortune*, ll. 1129 ff. ("Fortune est
amour haïneuse, Bonneürté maleüreuse," etc.). Cf. the paradoxes of love,
Roman de la Rose, ll. 4307 ff. See S. L. Wolff, *Greek Romances in Elizabethan
Prose Fiction*, p. 437; cf. p. 234, where he calls the oxymoron a "flashy"
literary device.

[2] NURSE: Boethius, *Cons. Philos.*, II, pr. ii, 8 ff.; *Roman de la Rose*, ll.
4906 f.; G. de Machaut, *Remède de Fortune*, ll. 2612 ff., and *Poésies*, ed.
Chichmaref, II, 497, l. 19; Deschamps, *Œuvres*, VI, 56 (mcxxxiv); Pierre
Michault, *La Dance aux Aveugles*, p. 46; Bocchi, *Symbolicae Quaestiones*,
symb. xxiii (right breast exposed; cf. the similar picture of the Fortune of
Antium on coins, Roscher, col. 1547). See Cousin, pl. 189.

[3] NOVERCA: Henricus Septimellensis, *Trattato*, 1730, pp. 4, 15; Alanus
de Insulis, *Anticlaudianus*, VII, vii (Migne, vol. CCX, col. 556); Boccaccio,
De Casibus, p. 78; *Filocopo*, iii (*Opere*, VII, 254-255); *Pierre de la Broche*
(Monmerqué and Michel, *Théâtre Français*, p. 210), "marrastre et mere";
Roman de la Rose, l. 4912; Deschamps, *Œuvres*, VI, 57, l. 10 ("mere de tous");
Gower, *Vox Clamantis*, II, ii.

[4] COMMON: Wright, *Satirical Poets*, I, 21 (Nigel Wireker), "non est
uitare"; Adam de la Halle, *Jeu de la Feuillée*, ll. 774 ff.; Chaucer, *Troilus and
Criseyde*, i, 843-844; iv, 391-392.

and as she has apparently no serious motive in life, but "playeth with free and bonde," she is no more or less than a harlot.[1]

IV

POWER

In enumerating the various traits of Fortuna's character I have dwelt particularly on her inconstancy in dealing out her gifts. Let us now consider what is the nature of these gifts and what are the limitations of her realm of activity.

There are many allusions to Fortune's might and her desire to show it.[2] Sometimes, indeed, she seems to be in complete control of human life, whether man makes any resistance or not. One poet tells us that

> Fortuna tutto può, che dà 'l potere,
> Nè senza il suo voler si volta foglia;

---

[1] Boccaccio, *Decameron*, II, vii (*Opere*, I, 189), X, viii (*ibid.*, V, 86, "amato dalla fortuna"); and *Donne Famose*, p. 193 (cap. lxii, "FLORA MERETRICE ROMANA. Gli antichi paiono provare che Flora fu una donna romana, alla quale quanto tolse il vituperoso guadagno, tanto le aggiunse di nominanza la favorevole fortuna"). See Henricus Septimellensis, *Trattato*, 1730, p. 15 ("meretrix"); Aeneas Sylvius, *Storia di Due Amanti*, p. 29 ("libidine è socia della fortuna"); Fregoso, *Dialogo di Fortuna*, sig. A7^{vo} (cap. iv); Machiavelli, *Capitolo di Fortuna* (*Opere*, VII, 368); *Floire et Blanceflor*, l. 2264 ("druërie"); G. Paris, *Chansons*, p. 112 (cxiv, 6), "ma maistresse"; Chaucer, *Monk's Tale*, B. 3746–3747 ("kiste So likerously"); Gower, *Vox Clamantis*, ii, 131; Lydgate, *Troy Book*, v, 1020; Hoccleve, *Regement of Princes*, ll. 1387 ff.; *Melusine*, ll. 3461 f. (Fortune not privy with me); Dunbar, *Quhome to sall I Complane my Wo*, l. 58 (*Poems*, II, 102), "freyndly smylingis of ane hure"; Laing, *Scottish Worthies*, p. 54, "She lovly lul'd me in her lape."

[2] See the yoke of Fortune, Boethius, *Cons. Philos.*, II, pr. i, 48; also Alberti, *Opere*, II, 10 (*Della Famose*, proem.). See Henricus Septimellensis, *Trattato*, 1730, p. 16 (the most powerful in the world); Guido Cavalcanti, in *Poeti del Primo Secolo*, II, 329; Lydgate, *Troy Book*, i, 776–777 ("schewen her myght"), iv, 2683 ff. (no remedy); Petrarch, *Vite d. Uomini*, I², 411 ("sig-

THE GODDESS FORTUNA

that pleasure and displeasure follow according to her will, that she rules the heavens, that the world is under her law, and so on.[1] Chaucer holds that "fortuna may non angel dere,"[2] but the Church at least appears to be subject to her influence. Ecclesiasts find themselves on her wheel, and Fortune raises and puts down both priest and bishop.[3]

Usually, however, Fortune's powers have to do with more secular matters, and we find her particularly associated with the world[4] (which, adopting her qualities, becomes more than ever temporal and "mundane") and

noria della fortuna"); Boccaccio, *De Casibus*, p. 271 (spares no age); also *Decameron*, IV, i (*Opere*, II, 161, what Fortune grants); *Filostrato*, VIII, xxvi (*ibid.*, XIII, 252, what Fortune plans), and II, li (*ibid.*, 48, control of life; cf. *Decameron*, X, ix, *ibid.*, V, 113); Ariosto, *Orlando Furioso*, XXI, xx (Fortune scatters all defence against her; cf. Gower, *Vox Clamantis*, ii, 177 ff.).

[1] Bracci, *Canti Carnascialeschi*, p. 324. See also Petrarch, *Bucolicum Carmen*, p. 135, ll. 81 f. ("fortuna gubernat Res hominum"); Aeneas Sylvius, *Storia di Due Amanti*, p. 80 ("universale regolatrice"); Boiardo, *Orlando Innamorato*, I, xvi, 1 ("Tutte le cose sotto de la luna . . . Son sottoposti," etc.).

[2] *Monk's Tale*, B. 3191.

[3] A. Medin, *Ballata della Fortuna*, in *Il Propugnatore*, new ser., II¹ (1889), 121 f., st. xxvii ("La santa Chiesa la Fortuna mena," etc.). See Guicciardini, *Opere Ined.*, I, 203 (cccxlvi); *Floire et Blanceflor*, ll. 2259 f. ("les vesquiés . . . les boins clers"); G. de Machaut, *Remède de Fortune*, ll. 1179 ff. (power over emperors, popes, and kings); David Lindsay, *Works*, ed. Laing, I, 74 (*Papyngo*, l. 359, "Nocht sparing Papis, Conquerouris, nor Kyngis"). See also, in art, Lydgate's *Fall of Princes*, ed. 1554, picture at end of the prologue (two figures on the wheel wearing bishops' mitres, with a kneeling ecclesiast at the left); also that at beginning of the sixth book (fol. cxliii, a bishop on the wheel); Bocchi, *Symbolicae Quaestiones*, symb. cxi (Fortune bestowing the papal crown on Clement VII). Cf. the remarkable wheel (if that is what it is) with Christ transfigured in the centre, Moses and Elias on each side of him, and the three apostles, Peter, James, John, at the base of the picture, in the cathedral at Chartres (xii century), Didron, *Histoire de Dieu*, p. 119; and cf. above, p. 19, n. 2; also Heider, *Mittheilungen*, p. 122.

[4] Cf. Boethius, *Cons. Philos.*, II, met. iii, 13. Notice the title of one of Benivieni's poems, "De la Vanita Inganni et Superbia del Mondo" (*Opere*,

the court.[1] Both the world and the court are fickle. The court is of course a smaller world, a specialized microcosm, and thus forms a suitable background for the changes of Fortune's favor.

As Fortuna is very much at home at court, so she deals particularly in royal favors, bestowing kingship, empire, and crown, and taking them back at will.[2] This is a favor-

p. 153[vo]). See Chambers, *Early English Lyrics*, p. 167, l. 37, "Ne tristou to this world" (see also p. 360, note on a variant of this verse and on a drawing of Fortune's wheel, with a stanza of French poetry on a similar theme); Lydgate, *Fabula Duorum Mercatorum*, ll. 622 f. (the world is "unstable . . . nat abydyng . . . variable"); *Schir William Wallace*, vi, ll. 97 ff. ("nothing till hewynly gouwernance"); Douglas, *The Palice of Honour* (*Works*, I, 9, l. 4, "Inconstant warld and quheill contrarious"). Description of the world seems associated in terminology with the description of Fortune.

[1] See Walter Map, *De Nugis Curialium*, ed. Wright, p. 2, "Si quod Boecius de fortuna veraciter asserit de curia dixerimus, recte quidem et hoc, ut sola sit mobilitate stabilis"; cf. p. 1, "Scio tamen quod curia," etc., and p. 238, "Curia fortuna non est; in motu tamen immobiliter est," etc. See Alain Chartier, *Œuvres*, pp. 267 ("en Cour la trouveras"), 394 (note the title of the piece, "Le Curial"); Deschamps, *Œuvres*, V, 289 (mxxi), VI, 171 (mcxci, 29), 260, ll. 15 ff.; Gower, *Confessio Amantis*, v. 2247 ff., 2268–2269; David Lindsay, *Works*, I, 68 (*Papyngo*, ll. 192 ff.; Fortune does not seem to be in the forest, see l. 197); Cranstoun, *Satirical Poems*, I, 7, ll. 73 ff; Sibbald, *Chronicle*, I, 348, ll. 1 f. See Dryden's *Miscellany* (5th ed., 1727, VI, 283, *Eccho to the Cavalier's Complaint*).

[2] See Lucan, *Pharsalia*, viii, 207; Boethius, *Cons. Philos.*, II, met. i, 3; *Carmina Burana*, p. 47 (lxxvii, st. 3); Hildebert de Lavardin, *De Exsilio Suo* (Migne, vol. CLXXI, col. 1419, "Has ludit fortuna . . . regesque," etc.); Boccaccio, *De Casibus*, p. 135 ("quis regum"); Sannazaro, *Opere*, p. 46; *Floire et Blanceflor*, ll. 2258, 2965 ff.; *Roman de Fauvel*, ll. 23 ff.; Jean de Condé, *Dits et Contes*, II, 360, ll. 179 ff.; Dinaux, *Trouvères*, II, 38; Chaucer, *Monk's Tale*, B. 3538–3540, 3557–3558; Gower, *Mirour de l'Omme*, ll. 22057 ff.; also *Confessio Amantis*, prol., 769 ff., and vii, 3172–3173 (king on the wheel); Lydgate, *Siege of Thebes*, ll. 1975 ff.; and *Troy Book*, ii, 1864 ff.; v, 530 ff., 1032 ff., 3549 ff.; Furnivall, *Political, Religious, and Love Poems*, p. 265 ("þis wondir wel under þis trone" reads as if describing a drawing); James I, *Kingis Quair*, st. 9, l. 5; Metcalfe, *Legends of the Saints*, II, 250 (xxxvi, 943–944); Cranstoun, *Satirical Poems*, I, 32, l. 26.

ite theme with poet and artist alike,[1] and plays a prominent part in the "formula of four" (*regnabo, regno, regnavi, sum sine regno*), which we shall study in connection with the wheel.[2] The point here is that Fortune controls royal offices.

Since Fortuna rules affairs at court, it is natural that she should be figured as a queen. She is crowned, and is empowered to rule her realm.[3] This is another favorite theme in art.[4] As a queen she is, of course, furnished with subjects and servants, who attend upon her will.[5]

[1] In drawings, see Lydgate's *Fall of Princes*, ed. 1554, fol. cxliii (figure of the wheel, — cf. the picture at end of the prologue, and see plate 10 below); Aubry, *Roman de Fauvel*, pl. xvi (Fortune offering two crowns); Cousin, *Livre de Fortune*, plates 117 (three crowns and three scepters on the wheel), 181 (Fortune taking away with one hand a king's crown and with the other his scepter); Villard de Honnecourt, *Album*, xlii (six figures); Du Sommerard, *Les Arts du Moyen Age*, Album, vol. II, ser. 4, plates 38, 39 (a crowned figure at the top; cf. ser. 8, pl. 30); Barbier de Montault, *Traité*, I, 162–163, §3 (in sculpture at Amiens there are eight figures on each side and a king at the top; again, at Beauvais there are five on each side, one at the top, and one prostrate underneath); Bocchi, *Symbolicae Quaestiones*, symb. xxiii (Fortune upholding a royal coat of arms).   [2] Below, pp. 164 ff.

[3] See Boethius, *Cons. Philos.*, II, pr. i, 55; Leyser, *Historia Poetarum*, p. 864 ("regendam"); Henricus Septimellensis, *Trattato*, 1730, p. 17 ("tunc regina verenda"); Poliziano, *Le Stanze*, etc., ed. Carducci, 1863, p. 388, ll. 25–27; Baudouin de Condé, *Dits et Contes*, I, 34, ll. 73–75; Charles d'Orléans, *Poésies*, I, 58 ("princesse"); *Roman de Fauvel*, ll. 1877 ff. ("double couronne"), 2339 ("je suis roine"); Lydgate, *Troy Book*, v, 635 ("stormy quene"); Christine de Pisan, *Livre du Chemin*, p. 96, l. 2205 ("royne de tout meseur"). Cf. plates 5, 6, 8, in this volume.

[4] See Fortune crowned, *Carmina Burana*, p. 1; Aubry, *Roman de Fauvel*, pl. xvi; crowned deity, Didron, *Annales Archéol.*, I, 433 f. (Bibl. Amiens, Ms. 216); enthroned and crowned, Du Sommerard, *Les Arts au Moyen Age*, Album, vol. II, ser. 4, plates 37, 38, 39, 40 (from Ms. of Petrarch's *De Remediis* in French); Weinhold, *Glücksrad und Lebensrad*, p. 14 (drawing on Ms. of the *Trésor* of Brunetto Latini); Cousin, pl. 27 (cf. pl. 129), and see pl. 173.

[5] Boccaccio refers (*De Casibus*, III, i, p. 60) to her "ancillarum longior ordo." See Charles d'Orléans, *Poésies*, II, 150 ("subgiet de Fortune"); Boe-

This point brings our study to a rather remarkable conception. Fortune, we have seen, is queen, with a complete retinue; she is the mother of mankind, a daughter of Jove, and there has even been an idea that the men of ancient Rome thought of her as Jove's mother.[1] She stands on a ball or on a wheel, and her wheel has been compared with the moon.[2] Our summary even thus far may suggest a similarity to the figure of the Blessed Virgin as she has often been depicted in art. Anyone who studies the poetry dedicated to the Virgin would do well to see whether there has not been some influence, on one side or the other, between the poetry of Fortuna and that of the Virgin. For example, we read in one poem to Our Lady:

> Li soleux est ta couverture:
> La lune, souz les piez pozée,
> Se nos sénéfie à droiture
> Que sor nos serez essaucée
> Et seur fortune & seur nature.

---

thius, *Cons. Philos.*, II, pr. ii, 17; Innocent III, *De Contemptu Mundi*, I, xvii (Migne, vol. CCXVII, col. 709), "fortuna servos constituit." — FORTUNE'S COURT: Aeneas Sylvius, *Opera Omnia*, p. 614; Koch, *Christine de Pizan*, p. 68, last half (Dame Richece at the first door, Espérance at the second, Poverty at the third); Pierre Michault, *La Dance aux Aveugles*, pp. 30–33 (Eur and Maleur are trumpeters, Destiny gives prizes); Furnivall, *Originals and Analogues*, p. 164 ("magna omnis fortuna seruitus magna est"); Lydgate, *Minor Poems*, ed. MacCracken, I, 128, ll. 35–36; Charles d'Orléans, *Poésies*, I, 121 (Dangiers apparently obeys Fortune); Gower, *Mirour de l'Omme*, passage ll. 22081 ff. (Fortune has two handmaids, Renomée and Desfame, with horns which they blow to spread tidings). See Fortune's companions, Concupiscentia-carnis, Couetyse-of-eyen, Pruyde-of-parfit-Lyuynge, *Piers Plowman*, C. xii, 173–176 (Skeat's ed., I, 331). Deschamps (*Œuvres*, IX, 358, ll. 11148 ff.) makes Diligence mistress of Fortune.

[1] See H. Dessau (*Hermes*, 1884, XIX, 453–455), refuting this idea. He shows that *Jovi puer* means *filia Jovis*. Cf. above, p. 49, n. 1.

[2] See p. 50, n. 6, above.

Tu iez chatiaux, roche hautainne
Qui ne crienz ost ne sorvenue;
Tu iez li puis & la fontainne.[1]

And so the parallels continue. The Virgin is a fortress and a lofty rock, and Fortune's house is often on a towering rock. To be sure, the significance of the symbolism in the two cases is entirely different; but, despite the contrast in meaning, a greater effect may have been gained in the representation of Our Lady by use of some of the symbols already familiar in the cult of the pagan deity. The similarity of some of Murillo's pictures of the Blessed Virgin to some of the drawings of Fortuna is striking indeed. Incidentally I may mention that, in the poem of the *Wallace*, the hero has a significant vision of a lady, "full brycht and scheyne," who gives him a wand of red and green, blesses his face and eyes with a sapphire, and chooses him as her love. She tells him that his people are in pain but that he will return to them. She gives him a book divided into three parts, the first part in letters of brass, the second in gold, the third in silver, and then "on to the cloud ascendyt off his sycht." A clerk who interprets the dream observes,

I can nocht witt quhat qweyn at it suld be,
Quhethir fortoun, or our lady so fre.
Lykly it is, be the brychtnes scho brocht,
Modyr off him that all this warld has wrocht.[2]

---

[1] Rutebeuf, *Œuvres*, II, 157. For the figure of a woman standing on the moon, see the book of Revelation, xii, 1. The parallelism with Fortuna must not be pressed too hard.

[2] *Wallace*, vii, 90–132. This lady reminds one of the magnificent "duches" who descended from the clouds to King Arthur (*Morte Arthure*, allit., ll. 3250 ff.).

Manifestly the author of the *Wallace* felt, whether he showed good taste or not, that there was some point in confusing the goddess with the Virgin, in mixing the profane with the sacred.[1] The exact degree of the dignity of Fortuna, however, can be determined only by a further study of her powers. We have seen that she is royal, that she sometimes controls the Church, and that she is the bestower of gifts to mankind. What is the nature of these gifts?

Fortuna is, of course, primarily the giver.[2] She gives, but, we must remember, she takes away again;[3] and yet she does no injustice, for, after all, the possessions are hers.[4] These possessions are of various kinds; but first and foremost there is a general notion that Fortune deals in the mundane, the temporal, in goods of mortal con-

---

[1] The point that the author of the *Wallace* wished to make is, clearly, that Wallace was not sure whether his hopes (to which he was led by the visionary lady) were dependable or not.

[2] See Boccaccio, *Genealogia de gli Dei*, p. 11 ("tutte quelle cose, che s'appartengono à mortali"); also *Decameron*, II, ii (*Opere*, I, 120); *Fiammetta*, cap. v (*ibid.*, VI, 115), "larghezze," and cap. vi (p. 142), "quello che la fortuna t'ha riserbato"; and *Filocopo*, lib. v (*ibid.*, VIII, 234), "i beni della fortuna"; Sannazaro, *Opere*, p. 46 ("liberale in donare"); Petrarch, *Vite d. Uomini*, I², 795 ("bene cosa che possa dare la fortuna"); Gareth, *Rime*, II, 243, son. ccv ("mercede"); G. de Machaut, *Le Dit de l'Alerion*, ll. 2288 ff. (*Œuvres*, ed. Hoepffner, II, 318). See Boccaccio's hundred-handed goddess, *De Casibus*, p. 146 (VI, i).

[3] Poliziano, *Prose Volgari*, p. 240, l. 50 ("fertque refertque"); Lorenzo de' Medici, *Opere* (1825), I, 84; Ariosto, *Orlando Furioso*, III, xxxvii; Charles d'Orléans, *Poésies*, I, 212; *Roman de la Rose*, ll. 18804–18805; Gower, *Cronica Tripertita*, i, 93.

[4] Boethius, *Cons. Philos.*, II, pr. ii, 12 ff. See Michault Taillevent, *Regime de Fortune*, bal. vi (Alain Chartier's *Œuvres*, p. 715). For the reverse of the idea (Fortune being nothing, having nothing to give), see Gower, *Vox Clamantis*, ii, 301–302; and *Mirour de l'Omme*, ll. 14296 ff. (cf. Seneca, epistle lix, 18, referred to in Macaulay's note to the *Mirour*, p. 428).

cern.[1] These we may subdivide appropriately as (1) dignities — honor, fame, glory, and the like;[2] (2) riches,
which are of course the mundane gifts *par excellence*.[3]

[1] No VIRTUE IN THEM: Wright, *Satirical Poets*, I, 234 (Nigel Wireker),
"vitiorum Semina sunt, scelerum patula, mortis iter . . . toxica mortis";
Carmina Burana, p. 47 (lxxvi *a*, 4); Alanus de Insulis, *Anticlaudianus*, VIII,
ii (Migne, vol. CCX, § 401); Pontano, *Opera Omnia*, II, 147 (*De Fortuna*, i);
Gareth, *Rime*, II, 243, son. ccv; Christine de Pisan, *Livre du Chemin*, p. 11,
ll. 254 ff. — MUNDANE GOODS: Dante, *Inferno*, vii, 79 ("li ben vani"); Boccaccio, *Filocopo*, ii (*Opere*, VII, 145); also *De Casibus*, p. 146 ("rerum mor-
talium ministra"); Guido Cavalcanti, in *Poeti del Primo Secolo*, II, 318;
(Boccaccio *Ameto*, *Opere*, XV, 122, "beni mondani"); Frezzi, *Quadriregio*, I,
146, l. 4 ("ben temporal"); Poliziano, *Prose Volgari*, p. 104 ("cose umane");
Simund de Freine, *Roman de Philosophie*, ll. 863 f. ("not worth a prune");
Roman de la Rose, ll. 4870–4871, 4897; Deschamps, *Œuvres*, I, 241 (cxxi, 1,
"biens temporelz de ce monde"); II, 124, l. 29 ("faulx biens"), 141, l. 18
("biens de pardurableté"); Gower, *Confessio Amantis*, prol., 560 ff.; Lydgate,
The Churl and the Bird, st. 30; G. de Machaut, *Poésies*, ed. Chichmaref, II, 476,
ll. 78 f. (Fortune gives a prune, green or "meüre," as she likes); Sannazaro,
Opere, p. 45 ("le mondane prosperità").

[2] See Boethius, *Cons. Philos.*, II, pr. ii, 5; Honorius of Autun, *Speculum
Ecclesiae* (Migne, vol. CLXXII, col. 1057, C), "gloria hujus mundi"; *Gesta di
Federico*, l. 2761 ("laus et honor"); Guido Cavalcanti, in *Poeti del Primo
Secolo*, II, 326 ("estate"); Boccaccio, *De Casibus*, pp. 41 ("natos egregios"),
151 ("gloriae"); Pucci, *Poesia Popolare*, ed. Ferri, p. 125 (lordship, and for
knowledge of Boethius see p. 285); Fregoso, *Dialogo di Fortuna*, sig. B4ᵛᵒ (cap.
viii); G. de Machaut, *Le Jugement dou Roy de Navarre*, ll. 2258 ff. (*Œuvres*,
ed. Hoepffner, I, 214, "honneur"); also *Poésies*, ed. Chichmaref, II, 556, ll.
17 ff.; Taillevent, *Regime de Fortune*, bal. ii (Alain Chartier's *Œuvres*, p. 711),
glory, honor, fame, wealth; Deschamps, *Œuvres*, X, p. xliv (bal. xxxvi, 5 ff.);
Chaucer, *Anelida and Arcite*, l. 43 ("triumphe and laurer-crouned"); Lydgate, *Serpent of Division*, p. 54, ll. 18 f.; and *Troy Book*, ii, 2035 f.; v. 1493 f.
Cf. Sibbald, *Chronicle*, II, 399, ll. 23–24 (only virtue wins true honor).

[3] Boethius, *Cons. Philos.*, II, pr. ii, 5. See Hildebert de Lavardin, *De
Fortunae Bonis* (Migne, vol. CLXXI, col. 1044): "Bona sunt opulentia, prae-
latio, gloria. Ad opulentiam referuntur praedia, clientelae, peculium, the-
saurus, ornatus. In praediis uero aedificia et agri numerantur," etc. Croesus was subject to Fortuna, — a stock example: see Boethius, *Cons. Philos.*,
II, pr. ii, 32 ff. (not the usual account, but how Croesus was saved by rain);
Henricus Septimellensis, *Trattato*, 1730, p. 14; Alanus de Insulis, *Anticlau-*

Our abstract "fortune" of to-day is in some uses dominated by this latter idea.

Some deliberate thought has, however, been expended on a more definite catalogue of Fortune's bounties; in fact, they are listed and published dogmatically, as it were, and the list is accepted. Frère Lorens, in his *Somme des Vices et des Vertus* (1279), sets forth the gifts of God as divided into those of nature, of fortune, and of grace. Nature bestows the properties of the body — fairness, strength, prowess, nobility, eloquence; and the properties of the soul — clear intelligence and subtle wit.[1] Fortune gives us "hautesces, honors, richesces, delices, prosperitez."[2] This list establishes for us the difference be-

dianus, VIII, i (Migne, vol. CCX, col. 560); *Poesie Ital. Ined.*, II, 62 ("uom ricco"); Guido Cavalcanti, in *Poeti del Primo Secolo*, II, 319; Boccaccio, *Teseide*, iv, 68 (*Opere*, IX, 142), and *Amorosa Visione*, cap. xxxi (*ibid.*, XIV, 125 ff.); Petrarch, *Bucolicum Carmen*, p. 135, l. 104; Frezzi, *Quadriregio*, I, 271 (lib. iv, cap. iv), ll. 25 ff.; Masuccio, *Il Novellino*, p. 226 (rich and poor); Bembo, *Opere*, I, 101–102 (*Degli Asolani*, lib. ii, debate about Fortune and love of wealth); Machiavelli, *Opere*, VII, 324 (*Decennale Secondo*); Fregoso, *Dialogo di Fortuna*, sig. B4^vo (cap. viii); Chrestien de Troyes, *Eric und Enid*, ll. 4801 ff. ("Povre estiiez: or seroiz riche"); *Roman de la Rose*, l. 5927; Gorra, *Studi*, p. 60 (summary of Ms. fr. 1164, Bibl. Nat., *Rommant de Fortune et tous les Estas du Monde:* teaches that riches do not make a man happy; a satire on all stages of society including the religious); G. de Machaut, *Poésies*, ed. Chichmaref, II, 497, l. 2; Deschamps, *Œuvres*, V, 209 (bal. dccccclxxii interprets Boethius's Fortuna; cf. I, 316, bal. clxxxi, "En Boece . . . trouverezvous," etc.); VI, 9, l. 15 ("tresors"); X, p. xxiii (bal. xvi, 6 f.); Christine de Pisan, *Œuvres*, I, 208 (i, 15, 16), 214 (vii, 5); Chaucer, *Pardoner's Tale*, C. 779 ("This tresor hath fortune un-to us yiven"). In Lydgate's *Assembly of Gods*, ll. 316–317, Fortune sits next to Plutus. See the drawing of Fortune leading Plutus, in Cousin's *Livre de Fortune*, pl. 65.

[1] See the translation in Dan Michel's *Ayenbite*, ed. Morris, pp. 24 ff.

[2] See F. W. Eilers, in *Essays on Chaucer*, pt. V, p. 512. Cf. Guilielmus Peraldus, quoted in K. O. Petersen's *Sources of the Parson's Tale*, p. 42: "Bona uero fortune sunt bona exteriora que sunt in potestate hominum, que ab hominibus possunt auferri, ut sunt diuitie, delicie, dignitates, laus seu gloria et gratia humana." Cf. Aeneas Sylvius, *Opera Omnia*, p. 614.

tween the gifts of Nature and those of Fortune, and forms
the beginning of a steady tradition.[1] A little extension of
Fortune's powers, however, is found in Boccaccio, who
speaks of "diuitias, honestum coniugium,[2] dilectissimam
prolem, spectabiles amicitias, clientelas, & huiusmodi
fortunae bona."[3] Deschamps includes among the offer-
ings of Fortuna "beauté de corps, jeunesce," and a variety of riches — "chiens et oisiaux, grans chevaulx pour
jouster, Plaisans joyaulx," and the like.[4]

We must remember that Fortuna, when she is unfavorable, not only withholds these treasures but sends
actual suffering, specifically *injuria;* [5] and that she sends
what is due from her — failure as well as success — in her
special functions as goddess of love, war, and so on.[6]

[1] Where Laurentius found this analysis, I do not know. It is not likely, of
course, that it originated with him. See the three gifts referred to by Lorenzo
de' Medici, *Poemi*, ed. Carabba, pp. 79–80; Pontano, *Opera Omnia*, II, 129
(*De Fortuna*, i); Gorra's *Studi*, pp. 75–76 (*Chevalier Errant*, §vii); Chaucer,
Parson's Tale, §27 (450–455). Cf. Aeneas Sylvius, *Opera Omnia*, p. 601.

[2] Cf. Chaucer, *Merchant's Tale*, E. 1311 ff. Skeat (Oxford Chaucer, V,
355) relates this reference to Albertano of Brescia, *Liber de Amore Dei*. Cf.
Selmi's edition of Albertano's *Trattati Morali*, p. 269 and note: "La casa e le
ricchezze son dati dai padri et dalla madre; ma da Domenedio propriamente
è data la buona moglie e savia." The passage, as Skeat notes, is not from
Ecclesiasticus, to which Albertano refers it, but from Proverbs xix, 14.

[3] *De Casibus*, p. 170.

[4] Deschamps, *Œuvres*, III, 386 (bal. dxliv). Cf. Raynaud, *Rondeaux*, p.
90, "Beauté, bonté ne grant lignaige," etc.

[5] Alberti, *Opere*, II, 33 (*Della Fam.*, i), III, 369 (*Deifira*); Petrarch, *Rime*,
ed. Mestica, p. 84 (canz. vi [xi], 86, Fortuna ingiuriosa"), and *Africa*, v, 90;
Boccaccio, *L'Urbano* (*Opere*, XVI), p. 49; Pulci, *Morgante Maggiore*, xxii, 15;
Gower, *Cronica Tripertita*, ii, 331; *Piers Plowman*, B. vi, 221 (A. vii, 207),
"any freke that fortune hath appeyred."

[6] See below, pp. 89 ff. See the gifts of "Pees, vnytee, plentee and ha-
boundance" from Juno and Ceres, which Fortune cannot remove: Lydgate's
"balade for a momyng," in Brotanek's *Englischen Maskenspiele*, p. 308, l. 58.
Cf. the "quanti varii e istranissimi casi" that Fortune prepares: Da Prato,
Paradiso d. Alberti, II, 171. Cf. Boethius, *Cons. Philos.*, II, pr. v, 37–38.

As Fortune may not only give but withhold high estate, so she may also cause a man to suffer particular kinds of debasement. He may actually be led to prison by her deceit. The prison theme is particularly important because it has a beginning in the great work of Boethius. Without exaggerating the importance of the *Consolatio*, it is fair to suspect that, when a mediaeval man in prison complained of Fortune, he was induced to think of blaming the goddess by remembering what Boethius did under similar circumstances. This theme is, moreover, a great favorite and suggests the influence of Boethius by its very extensiveness.[1] A theme of similar nature is that of banishment or exile caused by Fortuna.[2]

Of course the greatest injuries one can receive from Fortune nearly all consist in the fall from a high position,

[1] See Henricus Septimellensis, *Trattato*, 1730, p. 24 (refers to Boethius); Guido Cavalcanti, in *Poeti del Primo Secolo*, II, 313 ("consolazione Di preda, e di prigione"); Boccaccio, *Donne Famose*, p. 75 (cap. xxvii); Petrarch's address to John of France, Barbeu du Rocher, in *Mémoires de l'Académie des Inscriptions*, etc., 2d ser., III, 214 ff.; Burchiello, *Sonetti*, p. 59 (pp. 29, 43, refer to Boethius); Sannazaro, *Opere*, pp. 351 (son. xxvii), 428; Lorenzo de' Medici, *Opere* (1825), III, 38; Trissino, *Italia Liberata*, III, 156; Gorra, *Studi*, p. 57 (Ms. fr. 12460, Bibl. Nat., dated 1345); *Le Donnei des Amants*, in *Romania*, XXV, 505, ll. 278 ff.; Froissart, *Œuvres*, I, 304–306 (*La Prison Amoureuse*); Alain Chartier, *Œuvres*, p. 610; Villon, *Œuvres*, ed. Lacroix, p. 112; Christine de Pisan, *Œuvres*, II, 199 (*Livre du Dit de Poissy*, ll. 1324 f.); Charles d'Orléans, *Poésies*, I, 43–55, 56–57, etc. (*Poème de la Prison*), 151; Chaucer, *Knight's Tale*, A. 1085 f.; *Monk's Tale*, B. 3591 ff. (Barnabo killed in prison); Furnivall, *Originals and Analogues*, Appendix (after p. 550); Pinkerton, *Ancient Scotish Poems*, II, 235 f. I have a reference to the *Dunbar Anthology*, pp. 180 ff., for a poem written before June 25, 1483, by Anthony Woodville, Lord Rivers, when in prison.

[2] See Hildebert de Lavardin, *De Exsilio Suo* (Migne, vol. CLXXI, col. 1418, § lxxv); Petrarch, *Vite d. Uomini*, I², 825; Alberti, *Opere*, II, 256 (*Della Fam.*, iii); Giov. Fiorentino, *Il Pecorone*, II, 21 (xvi, 1); *Le Donnei des Amants*, in *Romania*, XXV, 505, l. 283; Charles d'Orléans, *Poésies*, I, 82.

from a state of happiness in general, as well as from a state of honor. "High to low" is the great theme in the middle ages as well as in classical times. Since this change in man's fortune is what really constitutes the mediaeval idea of tragedy, we may call this the "tragic theme." Dante thus describes tragedy for us: "In principio est admirabilis et quieta, in fine siue exitu est foetida et horribilis." [1] Now it is clear that, if tragedy deals with mankind, the unpleasant ending must be brought about by the ultimate suffering of some human figure. To cause this suffering is the particular work of Fortuna. [2] We see her lowering man's estate again and again in the mediaeval authors; the victim thinks he is secure in his greatest glory and suddenly falls. [3] The more general theme

[1] *Tutte le Opere*, ed. Moore, p. 416 (epist. x, 197–199).

[2] Boethius, *Cons. Philos.*, II, pr. ii, 36 f. See Chaucer's definition of tragedy, *Monk's Tale*, B. 3181 ff., 3951 ff.; also see Lydgate, *Troy Book*, ii, 844 ff. Sedgewick, in his unpublished thesis on "Dramatic Irony" (Harvard, 1913, pp. 356 ff.), shows the use Shakespeare makes of the reversals of Fortune, especially in the historical plays. For a comparison with the use of this pagan Fortuna in Greek tragedy, see H. O. Taylor, *Classical Heritage of the Middle Ages*, pp. 41 f. (Æschylus and Sophocles).

[3] See Dreves, *Analecta Hymnica*, XXI, 103 (no. 152, st. 3); Wright, *Satirical Poets*, II, 112 (lxvi); Boccaccio, *Fiammetta*, ix (*Opere*, VI, 200); also *Filocopo*, ii (*ibid.*, VII, 131–132); *Teseide*, ii, 37, iv, 80 (*ibid.*, IX, 68, 146); and *De Casibus*, pp. 44 ("perpetuari arbitrantur"), 174; Petrarch, *Africa*, ii, 71 f.; Sannazaro, *Opere*, p. 52; Ariosto, *Rime e Satire*, p. 205, ll. 16 ff. (sat. iii); *L'Escoufle*, p. 105, ll. 3510 ff.; Chrestien de Troyes, *Roman du Chevalier de la Charrette*, p. 174; *Roman de Fauvel*, ll. 78 ff.; Philippe de Beaumanoir, *Jehan et Blonde*, ll. 1743 ff. (*Œuvres*, II, 56); Watriquet de Couvin, *Dits*, pp. 81 (ll. 129 ff.), 228 (ll. 936 ff.); G. de Machaut, *Poésies*, ed. Chichmaref, II, 477, ll. 115 ff.; Deschamps, *Œuvres*, V, 289 (mxxi); VII, 56, ll. 20 f.; Christine de Pisan, *Œuvres*, I, 13 (xii, 5–7); *Awntyrs of Arthure*, st. xxi, ll. 254 ff.; Chaucer, *Troilus and Criseyde*, v, 1459 ff.; also *Monk's Tale*, B. 3325 ff.; Gower, *Mirour de l'Omme*, ll. 10937 ff., 13028 ff., 26357 ff.; Lydgate, *Siege of Thebes*, ll. 889 f. Cf. Hoccleve, *Regement of Princes*, ll. 1135 ff.; Robert Lindsay of Pitscottie, *Cronicles*, I, 32, ll. 16 ff. Contrast Boccaccio, *Decam-*

than this, the theme not of "falling" but of the transition from happiness to wretchedness, is also very widely used.[1]

So far we are not sure whether Fortune acts justly or not in these cases that have been called tragedies. If the suffering of the chief figure in the scene comes accidentally, then we may indeed consider this a weak and sentimental kind of tragedy. No doubt that is how the term was understood in the Middle Ages, as the quotation from Dante indicates. But mediaeval authors wrote better stories than those of pure chance. We find many allusions to the wanton pride of the hero before his fall, a circumstance that makes the action of Fortuna more rational. Here she does not really put down the meritorious; she castigates pride, which was at this time considered as the greatest sin of all, as a vice involving every other.[2] The goddess may unreasonably exalt a man, but it is his own business to avoid self-satisfaction. Certain men, we learn, Fortune did succeed in making proud (and in this case she is not so definitely the Christian figure); or they became proud through their own fault — whereupon

eron, II, iv (Opere, I, 134). The opposite theme of "low to high" is, of course, not uncommon: see Boethius, Cons. Philos., II, met. i, 4; Dreves, Analecta Hymnica, XXI, 102 (no. 152, st. 1); Carmina Burana, p. 47 (lxxvi a, 4); Cranstoun, Satirical Poems, I, 325 ff. (Ane Complaint vpon Fortoun); etc.

[1] I list only a few instances of its use: Boccaccio, Filocopo ii, iii, iv (Opere, VII, 131, 315, and VIII, 185, 187); Petrarch, Vite d. Uomini, I², 825; Ariosto, Orlando Furioso, VIII, xl–xliv; Roman de la Rose, ll. 6132 ff.; Deschamps, Œuvres, V, 75; etc.

[2] See the circle of Pride in Dante's Purgatorio. Lucifer's fall was especially attributed to Orgueil: see De Guilleville's Pelerinage de l'Ame, ll. 4455 ff. (notice "trebucher," l. 4464). Pride seems to have been considered the mental attitude of consciously or unconsciously measuring one's self with God.

she cast them down.[1] The remedy, of course, is to seek God and virtue, and not to prize the gifts of Fortune.[2]

The tragic theme is elaborated by means of numerous examples, and thus we arrive at what we may call genuine tragedies. The beginning of these, however, is found in the mere listing of the names of those who have suffered at the hands of Fortune. It is unnecessary to copy out the catalogues. We need only remark that the men cited were famous figures in the literature and history of the Middle Ages, and that some of them were Biblical.[3]

[1] For pride, and Fortune's method of dealing with it in mankind, see Petrarch, *Bucolicum Carmen*, p. 165, l. 141; Boccaccio, *De Casibus* (see *Smith College Studies in Modern Languages*, III, 210–211); Ariosto, *Rime e Satire*, p. 92 (cap. ix); Rutebeuf, *Œuvres*, II, 175, ll. 157 ff., especially 174 ff.; Watriquet de Couvin, *Dits*, pp. 73 (l. 11), 261 (ll. 967 ff.); Baudouin de Condé, *Li Prisons d'Amours*, ll. 989–990, 2588 (*Dits et Contes*, I, 302, 358); Jean de Condé, *Dits et Contes*, III, 154, ll. 78–79, 85 ff.; Jubinal, *Jongleurs et Trouvères*, p. 177, ll. 7 ff.; also Jubinal, *Contes, Dits*, etc., I, 128; Deschamps, *Œuvres*, I, 237 (cxviii, 5); II, 286 (xxviii, heading, "Comment aucun ne se doit eslever en Orguel pour service de Grant Signeur"); III, 134, ll. 40 ff.; VI, 101 (mclxiii, 6 ff.); Christine de Pisan, *Œuvres*, III, 29 (xv), 36 (lx); Chaucer, *Monk's Tale*, B. 3375 ff., 3773 ff.; also *Nonne Preestes Tale*, B. 4593–4594, and *Parson's Tale*, § 27 (445, 470); Gower, *Mirour de l'Omme*, ll. 21985 ff., 22017 ff.; Lydgate, *Serpent of Division*, pp. 13 (extract from Jehan de Tuim, ll. 6 ff.), 55 ff., also *Troy Book*, II, 6540 f. (the phrase is "þe hiʒe goddis," not Fortune). See a drawing described in *Roman du Renart*, ed. Méon, I, p. x (Regnard at the top of the wheel, at his right Orgueil, at his left Guille).

[2] Jean de Condé, *Dits et Contes*, III, 153, ll. 51 ff.

[3] See Boethius, *Cons. Philos.*, II, pr. ii, 32 ff.; II, pr. vi, 32 ff., and met. vi; Henricus Septimellensis, *Trattato*, 1730, p. 15; Dreves, *Analecta Hymnica*, XXI, 103 (no. 152, st. 3); *Carmina Burana*, p. 47 (lxxvii, st. 3); Alanus de Insulis, *Anticlaudianus*, VIII, i (Migne, vol. CCX, col. 560); Petrarch, *Rime*, ed. Albertini, I, 142 (son. lxx); II, 246 (*Trionfo della Fama*, ii, 15 ff.); A. Medin, *Ballata della Fortune*, in *Il Propugnatore*, new ser., II¹ (1889), 101 ff.; Aeneas Sylvius, *Opera Omnia*, pp. 601–602, 613–614, 761–762 (includes the examples of Carolus Magnus, Pipinus, and Arturus); Guido Cavalcanti, in

The complete development of this theme is found in Boccaccio's *De Casibus,* which is devoted entirely to summarizing the tragedies caused by Fortune. This work excited favorable comment and appreciation in its own time and had many translators and imitators.[1] As we should expect, Boccaccio makes the most elaborate use of the theme: he refers to the sin which the victim has committed,[2] in fact he often discusses it; he summarizes the victim's life, and he draws attention to the part Fortuna plays. No wonder Cassandra, in Chaucer's *Troilus,* attempts to divert Troilus with accounts of mishaps like his own, and no wonder she knew plenty of them:

Poeti del Primo Secolo, II, 318 ff.; Boccaccio, *Amorosa Visione (Opere,* XIV), caps. xxxiv–xxxvii, and *Lettere (ibid.,* XVII), p. 62; Alberti, *Opere,* III, 204 (*Il Teog.,* ii), and see references at II, 4 ff. (*Della Fam.,* proem.); Ariosto, *Orlando Furioso,* XIII, lxviii; Guicciardini, *Opere Ined.,* I, 272; Ghirardacci, *Historia di Bologna,* III, 511 ff. (Sapienza and Fortune claiming the man); Adam de la Halle, *Jeu de la Feuillée,* ll. 788 ff. (contemporary figures; *Smith College Studies in Modern Languages,* IV, 10, n. 48); *Roman de Fauvel,* ll. 2355 ff., 2403 ff., etc.; *Roman de la Rose,* ll. 5870 ff., 6197 ff. (Fortune is unjust, but the gods allow it in order to torment the wicked more later); Philippe de Beaumanoir, *Œuvres,* I, 267–268 (the *Manekine* is written in prose as an example); Froissart, *Œuvres,* I, 216 f.; G. de Machaut, *Remede de Fortune,* ll. 1001 ff.; Alain Chartier, *Œuvres,* p. 268; Villon, *Œuvres,* ed. Lacroix, p. 132; Deschamps, *Œuvres,* VII, 192 ff. (pp. 197–199 have examples from the Old Testament); Piaget, *Martin le Franc,* pp. 179 f. ("d'abaisser l'orgueil"); Koch, *Christine de Pizan,* p. 69 (part iii of the summary of *Le Livre de la Mutacion* mentions Richard II and Peter of Lusignan); Chaucer, *Book of the Duchesse,* l. 717; Gower, *Vox Clamantis,* ii, 315 ff., and *Balades,* p. 354, xxi (Troilus, Palamedes); Sir Gilbert Hay's *Manuscript,* I, 65 (*Buke of the Law of Armys,* pt. ii, cap. xv), ll. 1 ff. (the Nine Worthies); *Morte Arthure,* allit., 3394 ff.; *Gude and Godlie Ballatis,* p. 215, ll. 20 ff.; Cranstoun, *Satirical Poems,* I, 325 ff. (examples of low to high and high to low; a modern case is that of the Earl of Morton); Lydgate, *Serpent of Division,* p. 13.

[1] See, for example, Lydgate's *Fall of Princes* and Chaucer's *Monk's Tale;* note also the verses in the introduction to the Ziegler edition of *De Casibus.*

[2] See *Smith College Studies in Modern Languages,* III, 210.

Thou most a fewe of olde stories here,
To purpos, how that fortune over-throwe
Hath lordes olde.[1]

The literary type of the tragedy caused by Fortuna was firmly established and well recognized in the Middle Ages. In such a type it is natural that we should have a use of the *vbi sunt* formula: "mais où sont les neiges d'antan!" [2]

So much, then, may be said of Fortune's power over high estate from which man may fall. Incidentally, this fall may also involve a fall from a position of wealth; but the theme of the control of Fortune over wealth includes still another motif which deserves separate attention. This is embodied in the contest of Fortune and Poverty. First, since Fortune gives riches, she also bestows poverty when she is in an unfavorable mood.[3] Therefore adverse Fortuna and Poverty go together, they become companions; indeed, Poverty assists Fortuna.[4] The type Poverty,

[1] *Troilus and Criseyde*, v, 1459–1461. Cf. Machiavelli, *Dell' Asino d'Oro*, v (*Opere*, VII, 349),

> Come l'antiche genti alte e famose
> Fortuna spesso or carezzò, ed or morse.

Lydgate, *Serpent of Division*, p. 65, ll. 20 ff., refers to Chaucer's version.

[2] See Boethius, *Cons. Philos.*, II, met. vii, 15 f.; Carducci, *Cantilene e Ballate*, pp. 106–108 ("Dov'è Nembrotto il grande," etc.); Gower, *Mirour de l'Omme*, l. 22160. See *Modern Language Notes*, VIII, 94 ff., 253 ff.; XXVIII, 106 ff.; for other instances, cf. Lowes's *Convention and Revolt in Poetry*, Boston, 1919, pp. 100 ff., and Ramiro Ortiz's *Fortuna Labilis*, Bucharest, 1927.

[3] Frezzi, *Quadriregio*, I, 134 (lib. ii, cap. x), ll. 16 ff.; Aeneas Sylvius, *Opera Omnia*, p. 569, C; Villon, *Œuvres*, ed. Prompsault, p. 476, ll. 67–68; Hoccleve, *Regement of Princes*, ll. 15 ff.; Lydgate, *Troy Book*, v, 2097 ff.; *Bocace de Nobles Maleureux* (Couteau), fol. xlvi[vo], heading to bk. iii, ch. i (drawing [figure of a beggar?] below the wheel); Bourdillon, *Early Editions of the Roman de la Rose*, p. 110, §40 (drawings).

[4] Boccaccio, *Teseide*, iv, 23 (*Opere*, IX, 127); *Roman de la Rose*, ll. 8060 f., 8078–8079; G. de Machaut, *Poésies*, ed. Chichmaref, II, 644 (x, 8–9); *Piers Plowman*, B. xi, 60 f. (C. xiii, 14 f.).

PLATE 3

THE STRUGGLE WITH POVERTY

which suffers the blows of the goddess, does not accept adverse Fortuna's companionship so meekly. Boccaccio in his *De Casibus* describes a meeting between this figure and Fortuna:

The fable is told by Andalus, who relates how Poverty was sitting at the crossroads, dressed in a coat with a hundred holes [note Fortune's hundred hands, above, p. 44, n. 5] and deep in melancholy, when Fortune smiling proudly passed by. Rising with a harsh and bitter countenance, Poverty demanded, "Foolish one, why smilest thou?" Fortune replied, "I am looking with wonder at thee and thy dearth, thy pallor, fleeing thy friends, and arousing dogs." Poverty, angered by the words and hardly withholding her fists, answered: "Lo, Fortuna, foolish judge, part-goddess, why dost thou slander me? I deny that my estate is caused by thee; for I am here by my own free-will. Let us compare our powers." Fortune responded derisively: "See what an obstinate spirit this wretched woman has because I have reduced her. It will take still more to sink her pride." A little pleased with this, Poverty said: "We have already won part of the victory, for this trifler is stirred. But you mistake if you think I shall move to soften you with flattery. I have renounced all your gifts by my free-will. You think to debase me, but you raise me on high without knowing it; for he who does not wish to have riches is exalted in thought, considering the lofty possessions he would not own if he served the worldly." Fortune replied with ill-patience, reminding Poverty of her power. "I believe you really do wonderful things," said Poverty, "as I have often seen. Let us try our strength. If you talk about kings, I have been nurse to the Emperor of Rome and I was not then clad better than now." Nearly desperate, Fortune answered, "Certainly this woman will make me mad with her presumption!" Poverty will fight her, and insists that they fight on one condition — that she who conquers shall put such law as pleases her upon the conquered. "What judges shall we have, what pledges?" sneered Fortune. "No man will be hostage for you. What prize can you give?" "You must fight me for myself alone, since I have nothing else," answered Poverty. Fortune said she could lead Poverty to prison and keep her chained there; that way, however, Poverty would only feed at Fortune's expense. She would have Poverty flayed. Poverty having no armor, Fortune immediately flung herself upon her adversary; but Poverty finally made Fortune fall swooning, put her knee on her breast, bound her tightly, and did not let her recover until she confessed that she was conquered. "You know my power," said Poverty; "now feel my graciousness. I had intended to break your wheel, but I have pity. You must keep the law I impose on you. You have control over fortune and misfortune; I want half the lordship, and I order that you bind Misfortune to a stake in a public place, so that he cannot pass any threshold or follow anybody unless some one looses him from his bondage. If you agree to this, you are free." Fortune was released and kept faith.[1]

Poverty is proof against the turns of Fortune and is therefore wholly admirable.[2] But in all adverse circumstances there is another consolation besides that afforded by Poverty in Boccaccio: it is in such situations that we discover our true friends, and a friend in need is a friend indeed. This theme of the "friend in need," which is very important and widespread, furnishes the substance of Chaucer's "balade" on the subject of Fortune.[3]

[1] *De Casibus*, III, i, pp. 60 ff. Cf. the complimentary speech to Poverty, *ibid.*, p. 25: "Tibi stabilitas, tibi immunitas, tibi si qua est quies, in mundanis concessa est. Tu artificiosa, tu ingeniosa, tu studiorum omnium laudabilium mater egregia es: te fortuna despicit, quam tu uiceuersa contemnis."

[2] See Henricus Septimellensis, *Trattato*, 1730, p. 27 (poverty is a lion of defence, a prop of faith); Pierre Michault, *La Dance aux Aveugles*, p. 103 ("Quant povreté est voluntaire," etc.); Schönbach, in *Sitzungsb. der Kaiserl. Akad. der Wissenschaften*, CXLII, no. vii, p. 101 (the poor are free from the vicissitudes of Fortune's wheel; refers to F. Vogt, in *Zeitschrift des Vereins für Volkskunde*, III, 349–372, and IV, 195–197); Durrieu, *Boccace de Munich*, pl. ix (Poverty wrestling with Fortune). See plate 3 in the present volume.

[3] See St. Augustine, epist. iii (Migne, vol. XXXIII, col. 65), "At si in potestate fortunæ est, ut hominem amet homo," etc.; Gerbert of Aurillac, epist. xii (Migne, vol. CXXXIX, col. 204), "Hoc quidem ita," etc.; Boethius, *Cons. Philos.*, II, pr. viii, 18 ff.; Hildebert de Lavardin, *Epistola ad Amicum* (Migne, vol. CLXXI, cols. 1420–1423; Brunetto Latini, *Il Favoletto*, ll. 71 ff. (Ventura); Petrarch, *De' Rimedii*, ed. Dassaminiato, I, 229, cap. l, motto ("Non tecum qui sunt, ueri sunt semper amici, etc."); Frezzi, *Quadriregio*, I, 148 f., ll. 32 ff. (whole passage); Wace, *Roman de Brut*, ll. 1991 ff.; *Roman de Fauvel*, ll. 2849 ff.; *Roman de la Rose*, ll. 4719 ff., 4881,

This theme brings us almost to the close of our description of Fortune's powers and capabilities and the accompanying formulae. But the discussion would be incomplete unless we examined the extent of her powers in regard to the boundaries between the field of her activities and the domain of other gods. What is the difference between the gifts of Fortune and the gifts of Nature, Astrology, and Fate? We have already given some attention to the bounties of Fortune and those of Nature,[1] and have observed that Nature confers gifts relating to the body and the soul. This is already hinted at in the works of the Church Fathers, where Nature is said to control outer nature and physical man.[2] A distinction between Nature and Fortune seems to have persisted throughout the Middle Ages.[3] In Alanus de Insulis, Nature appears to be chiefly in control of "external nature" as we understand the phrase to-day;[4] and this idea, to-

4968, 8054 ff.; *Pierre de la Broche* (Monmerqué and Michel, *Théâtre Français*, p. 213), "Son ami peut-on au besoin Essaier"; Deschamps, *Œuvres*, I, 289 f.; IX, 3 ff.; X, p. xxii (bal. xv); Chaucer, *Fortune;* and *Monk's Tale*, B. 3431–3436; Hoccleve, *Works*, I, 197, n. 1; Dunbar, *To Dwell in Court, My Friend*, l. 12 (*Poems*, II, 98).

[1] Above, pp. 65 f.

[2] See *Smith College Studies in Modern Languages*, III, 184; 198, n. 101.

[3] Pontano, *Opere Omnia*, II, 129 (Fortune not nature); Pico della Mirandola, *Opera*, I, 353 (*In Astrologiam*, lib. iv, cap. ii); Rutebeuf, *Œuvres*, II, 157, l. 96 ("seur fortune & seur nature"); Jean de Condé, *Dits et Contes*, III, 152, ll. 29, 32; also pp. 126–127, ll. 113 ff.; G. de Machaut, *Le Dit de l'Alerion*, l. 2502 (*Œuvres* ed. Hoepffner, II, 325); also *Poésies*, ed. Chichmaref, I, 170 (clxxxviii); Froissart, *Œuvres*, II, 417 (cf. 414); Deschamps, *Œuvres*, VI, 56 (mcxxxiv); Alain Chartier, *Œuvres*, p. 534; Lydgate, *Troy Book*, iii, 2060 ff., and *Assembly of Gods*, ll. 316 ff. (description of Fortune, next to whom sits Pan); David Lindsay, *Works*, ed. Laing, I, 40, ll. 1046–1049; Sibbald, *Chronicle*, III, 478, l. 18 (Fortune "stayde Dame Nature's will").

[4] *De Planctu Naturae* (Migne, vol. CCX, col. 476; gifts mentioned, col. 478).

gether with the theory of Nature's control over man's physical and mental endowments, seems to continue.[1]

Originally, also, Fortune was different from Astrology.[2] Fortune is fickle, but the stars are arranged in accordance with the primal and enduring plan of a fixed destiny. They send down their influence according to their revolutions. The Church Fathers would say that, since Fortune and Astrology are both ministers of the Divine will, they are simply different modes of expression of that will; [3] but the poets, when aroused, do not seem particular about discriminating between these different modes of

[1] See Boethius, *Cons. Philos.*, II, pr. v, 29; Dante, *Paradiso*, viii, 139 ff. (which can best be interpreted by taking Fortune to mean the giver of one's environment, one's worldly surroundings, and Nature the giver of one's talents); Boccaccio, *Decameron*, VI, ii (*Opere*, III, 129); also *Teseide*, vi, 31 (*ibid.*, IX, 196, "bellezza . . . gentilezza Di real sangue"); Ariosto, *Rime e Satire*, p. 110 (cap. xvi); Pontano, *Opera Omnia*, II, 163ᵛº f. (Nature gives talents); *Roman de la Rose*, ll. 5327 ("cors . . . forces . . . sagesces"), 16092 ff., 19705 ("Nature . . . de tout le monde a la cure"); G. de Machaut, *Le Dit de l'Alerion*, ll. 4275 ff. (*Œuvres*, ed. Hoepffner, II, 385). Gower (*Confessio Amantis*, ii, 3250 ff.) disagrees and makes abstract "fortune" equivalent to the prenatal destiny of a child and its physical endowments. See Cousin's *Livre de Fortune* (p. 41), "Naturam autem, dei potestatem ordinariam. Fortunam uero, eius uoluntatem." G. de Machaut (*Le Jugement dou Roy de Navarre*, ll. 3851 ff., *Œuvres*, ed. Hoepffner, I, 270) makes Bonneürté superior to Nature; in Simund de Freine's *Roman de Philosophie*, ll. 331 ff., Nature controls Fortune's acts.

[2] I am aware that astrology, as it is generally used and as I have sometimes used it here, is a pseudo-science and not a person; but, taking the hint from De Guilleville's *Pelerinage*, I use the personified figure to cover conveniently the idea of planetary influence as it was considered in the Middle Ages.

[3] See Albertus Magnus, *Opera*, IV, 67 (*Ethicorum*, lib. i, tr. vii, cap. vi, quoted in *Smith College Studies in Modern Languages*, III, 199, n. 109); Pico della Mirandola, *Opera*, I, 353 (*In Astrologiam*, lib. iv, cap. ii, "Fortuita à Coelo non Esse"), and II, 373 (*De Rerum Prænotione*, lib. v, cap. viii, "Fatum . . . id est, syderum constitutionem cum quid aut nascitur, aut concipitur, aut inchoatur").

expression; with them either Fortune or Astrology, or both, may be to blame for their sufferings.[1] And we find spreading a general idea that Fortune's gifts after all come from the stars. Pontano tells us, "Bona fortunae a coelo et stellis promitti."[2] And Gower,

> The chances of the world also,
> That we fortune clepen so,
> Among the mennes nacion
> Al is thurgh constellacion.[3]

There is no doubt that the people of the Middle Ages actually believed in planetary influence.[4] Fortune, there-

[1] See Fortune and the stars: Petrarch, *Rime*, ed. Mestica, p. 187 (canz. xv [xxviii], 93); Boccaccio, *Ameto* (*Opere*, XV, 190); Giusto de' Conti, *La Bella Mano*, cap. iii (*Lirichi Antichi*, p. 178); Benivieni, *Opere*, p. 103ᵛᵒ (*Bucolica*, egl. 6); Burchiello, *Sonetti*, p. 59; Sannazaro, *Opere*, pp. 344 (son. xviii), 353 (canz. v); Pulci, *Morgante Maggiore*, xxviii, 150; Boiardo, *Orlando Innamorato*, I, xxii, 12; Lorenzo de' Medici, *Poemi*, ed. Carabba, p. 72; G. de Machaut, *Poésies*, ed. Chichmaref, II, 415, st. 2; *Le Petit Traittiet* (Pierre Michault's *Dance aux Aveugles*, p. 241, Mars and Saturn join with Fortune); Lydgate, *Fall of Princes*, heading of book iii (one should blame one's own sins and not the stars or Fortune); Sibbald, *Chronicle*, III, 330, st. i.

[2] *Opera Omnia*, II, 189ᵛᵒ; cf. 191ᵛᵒ, "Qua è re liquido cernitur, fortunam, rerum quae à stellis geniturae promittuntur tempore, executricem esse, uel effectum esse ipsum potius." Almost the Christian figure!

[3] *Confessio Amantis*, vii, 639; cf. prol., 525 (man is the cause of all woe). See Tatlock, *Scene of the Franklin's Tale Visited*, p. 25.

[4] See especially Wedel's *The Mediaeval Attitude toward Astrology*, 1920 (Yale Studies in English, No. 60); and Thorndike's *History of Magic and Experimental Science*, N. Y., 1923, *passim*. For Chaucer's belief in astrology, see Lounsbury's *Studies*, II, 497 ff., where an attempt is made to show Chaucer's incredulity; and, for a more persuasive account, suggesting Chaucer's real faith in astrology of the more legitimate kind, see Tatlock's paper in the Kittredge anniversary volume, pp. 339 ff., and his *Scene of the Franklin's Tale Visited*. On p. 23 of the latter work he points out the part the heavens play in *Troilus and Criseyde*, ii, 680–686, iii, 617–628, and shows that in the *Legend of Good Women* (ll. 2584–2599) Hypermnestra got her "looks, character, and fate" from the planets. Also Curry in *Philol. Quarterly*, IV, 1 ff., should be consulted. Cf. the *Knight's Tale*, A. 1086 ff., 1108-1109, 2033–2038, 2450–2452 (Fortune, Fate, Destiny). See *Piers Plowman*, C. xv, 30 ff.

fore, is indeed "executrice" of the "wierdes" that are written in the stars.[1]

The distinction between Fortune and the Fates, or between Fortune and Destiny, is more difficult to settle. The abstract word "fate" as embodying the will of God was in the earliest mediaeval times accepted by the philosophers and the Church Fathers;[2] but as early as Boethius Fate tended to become a changeable, almost a whimsical, force,[3] and to approach Fortuna in manner if

---

[1] See Chaucer, *Troilus and Criseyde*, iii, 617 ff., and *Man of Law's Tale*, B. 190 ff., 295 ff.; De Guilleville, *Rommant des Trois Pelerinaiges*, fol. lxx^{vo}; James I, *Kingis Quair*, st. 147; Deschamps, *Œuvres*, IV, 332 (dcccxiv); Boccaccio, *Comento sopra Dante (Opere*, XI), pp. 157 ff.; Lydgate, *Temple of Glas*, ll. 1100 ff.; Jean de Meun's *Plaisant Jeu du Dodechedron de Fortune* (Lyons, 1581), a scheme of fortune-telling mixed with astrology. In Spanish fields, see Post's *Mediaeval Spanish Allegory*, pp. 54 f., apropos of an allegory in the *Decir* of Francisco Imperial: "The eight stars are the seven planets and Fortune. The planets in turn bestow their beneficent influences . . . Fortune, as the universal mistress, sanctions and completes their gifts by her own indulgence . . . and endows him with the graces of the twelve other faces, which are the signs of the zodiac." For connection between the planets, the seven ages, and the wheel of Fortune, see Boll's *Lebensalter*. Cf. Bocchi, *Symbolicae Quaestiones*, symb. cxxxi. And see pp. 173 f., below.

[2] See Boethius, *Cons. Philos.*, IV, pr. vi; Albertus Magnus, *Opera*, II, 91–94 (*Physicorum*, lib. ii, tr. ii, caps. xix–xxi). Cf. Pontano, *Opera Omnia*, II, 139vo: "Itaque fatum ipsum digerere, explicare, administrare, disponere ordine suo, suoque loco, ac tempore, quae uidelicet prouidentia ipsa in sese congesta, ac prospecta habeat, et qua etiam ratione et uia gerenda sint," etc.

[3] See the wheel figure, *Cons. Philos.*, IV, pr. vi, 61 ff. This was accepted by the fathers: see Albertus Magnus, above, note 2. On the other hand, contrast Martianus Capella, *De Nuptiis*, i, §§ 88–89, "Tunc etiam . . . Haec mox ut Fata," etc., quoted in *Smith College Studies in Modern Languages*, III, 164–165 (Fortune is called Nemesis; cf. Cousin's *Livre de Fortune*, pl. 129). For Fate and the wheel, see Petrarch, *Bucolicum Carmen*, p. 141, l. 15 (cf. Seneca's *Thyestes*, ll. 617–618, "Prohibetque Clotho stare fortunam, rotat omne fatum"); Petrarch, *Africa*, ii, 293; Brant, *Narrenschiff*, ed. Simrock, p. 86, l. 10, "Da Clothòs hand das Rädchen dreht" (Brant knew Boethius — see his edition of the *Cons. Philos.*, 1501, with the St. Thomas commentary);

not in figure. Mediaeval writers never seem to be quite clear about the distinction between Fate and Fortune; they either blame both figures, or at least confuse the operations of the two.[1] Boccaccio records some attempt among the poets to identify Fortuna with the second sister of the three Fates: "Sono appresso di quelli, che uogliono Lachesi esser quella, che noi chiamiamo Fortuna."[2] But it is obvious that Fortune was not lost among the Fates; rather, the Fates submitted to her.[3]

Laing, *Scottish Worthies*, p. 64; Wackernagel, *Glücksrad und die Kugel des Glücks*, in his *Kleinere Schriften*, I, 249–250 (refers to Hemmerlin von Zürich). See also "fatal chaunce" in Lydgate's *Troy Book*, i, 3606, and in his *Daunce of Machabree*, p. 337, col. 1, st. 1.

[1] See Wright, *Satirical Poets*, I, 301 (John of Altaville); Henricus Septimellensis, *Trattato*, 1730, p. 4; *Gesta di Federico*, ll. 1251 f.; Boccaccio, *Teseide*, ix, 78 (*Opere*, IX, 331); also *Ninfale Fiesolano*, I, xxxiv (*ibid.*, XVII, 14); Petrarch, *Bucolicum Carmen*, p. 165, l. 159; Burchiello, *Sonetti*, p. 26; Aeneas Sylvius, *Storia di Due Amanti*, p. 80; Sannazaro, *Opere*, pp. 46 (*Arcadia*), 367 (son. xliv), 404 (son. lxxx), 422 (*Farsa*); Giov. Fiorentino, *Il Pecorone*, II, 168 (xxiv, 2); Pontano, *Carmina*, I, 38 (*Urania*, ii, 58 ff.), 91 (*ibid.*, iii, 507); Bracci, *Canti Carnascialeschi*, p. 33; *Roman de Fauvel*, ll. 2269 ff. (gives Fate or Destiny as Fortune's second name); *L'Escoufle*, p. 135, ll. 4536–4537 ("Com Fortune l'a destinée"); Benoît de Ste. Maure, *Roman de Troie*, IV, 296, l. 28615; Froissart, *Œuvres*, II, 109, ll. 3684 ff.; Alain Chartier, *Œuvres*, pp. 392, 607 f.; Gower, *Vox Clamantis*, i, 1517 f., 1527 (cf. 1541–1547, 1986 ff., and ii, 158–159, 293–296); also *Confessio Amantis*, v, 4830, and *Mirour de l'Omme*, l. 16006; Lydgate, *Siege of Thebes*, ll. 1233–1235, cf. 1248; also *Troy Book*, ii, 3201 ff., cf. 3218 ff.; iii, 1975 ff. (Fortune and Fate debate), 2898 ff., 4922; iv, 4270 ff.; also his "balade" to the Duchess of Gloucester, *Anglia*, XXVII, 388 (2), cf. 393 (27); Barbour, *The Bruce*, iv, 650 (one must "dre" one's fortune); James I, *Kingis Quair* (see reference to Fortune, st. 160, l. 4, and cf. st. 191, ll. 1–4); Sibbald, *Chronicle*, III, 330, st. i. And see Cousin's *Livre de Fortune*, plates 167 ("La Fortune Fatale"), 195 (the three Fates, "Fortunae et Fatorum Ministrae").

[2] *Geneologia de gli Dei*, p. 11; see also his *Comento sopra Dante* (*Opere*, XI), p. 159. Cf. Gower, *Vox Clamantis*, vii, 1385 ff.; James I, *Kingis Quair* (see reference to Fortune in st. 24, and cf. st. 25, ll. 2–4, "the secund sistere").

[3] In Cousin's plate 195 they are called her "servantes."

This glance at Fortune's relations with other gods concludes our study of the material dealing with the extent and limits of her power. She is queen; she frequents the court; she controls all mundane affairs and gives all worldly gifts; she is responsible for tragedy in the higher as well as in the more primitive sense of the word; she threatens to dominate the Fates. Only with Nature and Astrology does she seem to share her influence. The problem of one's endowment becomes, therefore, a question of "nature's livery or fortune's star." [1]

V

ACTIVITIES

This section will be devoted to the themes that have to do with Fortune's activities and methods of action, and the themes that are related to these topics although not directly connected with them.

Fortune goes on a course of her own. That is, she goes her own way; and, although her route may not be so direct as that of Destiny, it is characteristic of Fortune. We may follow her, she may intercept our paths, she may flee from us. [2]

As the will of Fortuna was made known by lots at Praeneste, so she is never quite disassociated from *sortes*. In fact, the term appears frequently in accounts of her,

---

[1] Further information concerning Fortune's powers will appear in the chapter on her special functions and smaller cults.

[2] R. Lindsay, *Cronicles*, I, 32. She is a sort of will-o'-the-wisp. See Ovid, *Tristia*, I, ix, 13, and V, xiv, 29–30; Novati, *Carmina Medii Aevi*, p. 44, st. vi; Petrarch, *Africa*, vii, 301 ff.; G. de Machaut, *Poésies*, ed. Chichmaref, II, 479, ll. 180 ff.; Chaucer, *Legend of Good Women*, l. 1340; Lydgate, *Troy Book*, iii, 4053 f. Cf. Occasio, below, pp. 115 ff.

generally as a synonym for her work or for the gifts she bestows.[1]

Fortune enjoys exalting and debasing mankind as a game.[2] She also plays games with human beings, in which they may either win or lose according to their fortune. Of these games the most common are dice [3] and

[1] See Boethius, *Cons. Philos.*, II, pr. iv, 58; Dreves, *Analecta Hymnica*, XXI, 103 (no. 152, st. 4); *Carmina Burana*, p. 2 (i, st. 2); Henricus Septimellensis, *Trattato*, 1730, pp. 13, 16; Wright, *Satirical Poets*, II, 256; Petrarch, *Africa*, v, 12 ff., and *Rime*, ed. Albertini, I, 237 (son. cxvii); Boccaccio, *De Casibus*, poem by Pontano, opposite index; Sannazaro, *Opere*, p. 387; Alberti, *Opere*, III, 215 (*Il Teog.*, ii), 277, 328; Lorenzo de' Medici, *Opere* (1825), I, 221, III, 35; Poliziano, *Le Stanze*, etc., ed. Carducci, 1863, p. 143, ll. 164 f.; Boiardo, *Orlando Innamorato*, I, viii, 24; Raynaud, *Rondeaux*, p. 25; Gower, *Vox Clamantis*, i, 1529–1534, 1539; ii, 209–211, 331, 623–625; iii, 1; vii, 1400 ff.; also *Cronica Tripertita*, i, 145 f., iii, 434 f., *Mirour de l'Omme*, l. 22091, and *Confessio Amantis*, v, 5309; Lydgate, *Troy Book*, i, 1066 f.; ii, 1802; v, 2182 f.; James I, *Kingis Quair*, st. 145 ("Onely to hir that has the cuttis two," etc.). In Schoonhoven's second emblem, "Sapiens suprà Fortunam," Fortune seems to be identified with Sors.

[2] Boethius, *Cons. Philos.*, II, pr. ii, 27 ff.; Prudentius, *Psychomachia*, l. 525; Jerome's commentary on Ecclesiasticus (Migne, vol. XXIII, col. 1085, B); *Gedicht auf die Zerstörung Mailands*, l. 45; Hildebert de Lavardin, *De Exsilio Suo* (Migne, vol. CLXXI, col. 1419); Wright, *Satirical Poets*, I, 338 (John of Altaville); Boccaccio, *Decameron*, II, vii (*Opere*, I, 205); also *De Casibus*, p. 27 ("lubricum ludum"); *Donne Famose*, p. 10 (cap. iii); and *Lettere* (*Opere*, XVII), pp. 33, 62; Petrarch, *Vite d. Uomini*, I[2], 657, and *Africa*, vi, 390; Poliziano, *Prose Volgari*, p. 274; Pulci, *Morgante Maggiore*, vii, 59; Ariosto, *Orlando Furioso*, VIII, 1; XVI, lxviii; Barbazan, *Fabliaux*, I, 139, ll. 129 ff.; G. de Machaut, *Poésies*, ed. Chichmaref, II, 506, ll. 43 ff.; Chaucer, *Troilus and Criseyde*, v, 1134; Lydgate, *Fabula Duorum Mercatorum*, st. xcvi.

[3] See Chaucer, *Knight's Tale*, A. 1238, and *Monk's Tale*, B. 3851; Gower, *Mirour de l'Omme*, ll. 14306, 22024, 22102–22103, and see the passage 22081 ff.; also *Confessio Amantis*, iii, 788, v, 2437; Lydgate, *Beware of Doubleness*, ll. 73 ff. (Skeat, *Chaucerian and other Pieces*, p. 292); *Gude and Godlie Ballatis*, p. 215. Cf. Skeat's note in the Oxford Chaucer, V, 143–144, n. 124. See Cousin, pl. 174.

chess.¹ Jean de Meun also refers to Fortune's game of shuttlecock,

> Ainçois s'en joë à la pelote,
> Comme pucele nice et sote,
> Et giete à grant desordenance
> Richece, honor et reverance; ²

and to the game of "boute-en-corroie." ³ Deschamps draws her into a game of bowls.⁴

Fortune, subduing mankind, makes sure of her prey by catching her victim in a net. Perhaps this idea is related to the conception of a Fortune of the sea; for man is apparently symbolized as a fish struggling in the weltering sea of life and finally caught by the goddess.⁵

Similarly, Fortune catches men on limed twigs, or snares them as if they were birds. They flutter about in the air until attracted by the luring branches, and then they are stuck in the lime; or she entices and entraps them.⁶ Once having captured men, she puts her bridle

---

¹ *Roman de la Rose*, ll. 6675, 6732; G. de Machaut, *Remède de Fortune*, l. 1191; *Les Échecs Amoureux* and Lydgate's *Reson and Sensuallyte*; Furnivall, *Originals and Analogues*, App. (after p. 550), l. 110; Chaucer, *Book of the Duchesse*, ll. 618 f., 652 ff.; Lydgate, *Fall of Princes*, prol., st. 26; and III, i, st. 34 (1554 ed., fol. lxx; 1558 ed., fol. lxvi); also *Troy Book*, ii, 1894, and v, 1406. See the game of chess with God, in Gautier's *Miracles* ed. Poquet, cols. 7–10.   ² *Roman de la Rose*, ll. 6580–6583.

³ Lines 6881 ff.   ⁴ *Œuvres*, V, 354 (mlxi, 25 ff.).

⁵ See Boccaccio, *Filocopo*, iv (*Opere*, VIII, 17); Sacchetti, *Novelle*, III, 266–267; Charles d'Orléans, *Poésies*, II, 135; Cousin, *Livre de Fortune*, plates 43, 105. Cf. the chain of Fortune, below, p. 98, n. 1.

⁶ Cf. Fortuna Viscata in ancient Rome, noticed in *Smith College Studies in Modern Languages*, III, 154; Petrarch, *Rime*, ed. Albertini, II, 337 (son. xx); Lorenzo de' Medici, *Poesie* (1801), I, 226; Charles d'Orléans, *Poésies*, II, 64; Chaucer, *Knight's Tale*, A. 1490, and *Monk's Tale*, B. 3603–3604; Lydgate, *Troy Book*, ii, 1869 ff.; *Wallace*, ii, 144; Cranstoun, *Satirical Poems*, I, 27, ll. 729–730. See Cousin's drawing, "La Fortuna avec les Gluaux," *Livre de Fortune*, pl. 139; and De Guilleville's tree full of nests, below, pp. 138 f.

on them and thenceforth they are subject to her sway.[1] But mankind may resist Fortune and oppose the pagan remedy of fortitude to her cruelties.[2] One may even take courage and defy or curse her.[3] We remember that "Fortune aids the bold."[4]

[1] Petrarch, *Rime*, ed. Mestica, p. 374 (son. ccxxvii); ed. Albertini, II, 318 (canz. iii); Ariosto, *Orlando Furioso*, XXIII, xcii; De Jennaro, *Canzonière*, p. 375, no. 102; *Roman de la Rose*, l. 6515 (she uses a hangman's noose); Alex. Montgomerie, *Ane Invectione against Fortun*, l. 40 (*Poems*, 1887, p. 130). See Alciati's emblems, Augsburg, 1531, sig. A 7; and, for a different figure but with the same accompanying verse (which calls the figure Nemesis), see the Paris editions of 1534, 1535, p. 17 in each case. All three drawings are printed in H. Green's *Fontes Quatuor*. Cf. Cousin, pl. 177.

[2] Boccaccio, *Decameron*, X, x (*Opere*, V, 133, 135); also *Filostrato*, proem. (*ibid.*, XIII, 6); Frezzi, *Quadriregio*, I, 277 (lib. iv, cap. vi), ll. 22 ff.; Lorenzo de' Medici, *Poemi*, ed. Carabba, p. 101; Froissart, *Méliador*, II, 238–239; Gower, *Mirour de l'Omme*, ll. 15289 ff. Cf. the use of strength against her: Boethius, *Cons. Philos.*, II, pr. i, 56 f.; Wright, *Satirical Poets*, I, 31 (Nigel Wireker); Cousin, *Livre de Fortune*, pl. 93, "La Patience triomphe de la Fortune."

[3] Boccaccio, *Decameron*, VI, ii (*Opere*, III, 130); X, i, ii (*ibid.*, V, 16, 22); also *De Casibus*, p. 68; Sannazaro, *Opere*, pp. 427, 436; Benoît de Ste. Maure, *Roman de Troie*, IV, 75, l. 24496; Charles d'Orléans, *Poésies*, I, 59; Chaucer, *Clerk's Tale*, E. 898; Gower, *Cronica Tripertita*, iii, 435, and *Confessio Amantis*, viii, 1066, 1584–1585; Lydgate, *Troy Book*, ii, 407 ff., 3915; *Wallace*, viii, 320; Dunbar, *Fenȝeit Freir*, l. 95 (*Poems*, II, 142); David Lindsay, *Squyer Meldrum*, l. 826 (*Works*, ed. Laing, I, 185); G. de Machaut, *Poésies*, ed. Chichmaref, I, 254, l. 33.

[4] Cf. *Aeneid*, x, 284; Ovid, *Metam.*, x, 586; Claudian, epistle iv, l. 9; Livy, *Historia*, lib. iv, cap. 37. See *Gesta di Federico*, ll. 1693, 2710, 2817; Boccaccio, *Decameron*, VI, iv (*Opere*, III, 137, Fortune aids the fearful here); also *Fiammetta*, vi (*ibid.*, VI, 152), *Filocopo*, iv (*ibid.*, VIII, 159), and *Ameto* (*ibid.*, XV, 159); Boiardo, *Orlando Innamorato*, II, x, 2; Ariosto, *Orlando Furioso*, XIII, lxvii; Pontano, *Carmina*, II, 392 (*Eridanus*, II, xxxi, 9–10); Guicciardini, *Opere Ined.*, I, 330, 373 ("come è in proverbio," Fortune helps those who help themselves); Jean le Seneschal, *Les Cent Ballades*, p. 17, ll. 13 f.; Sieper, *Les Échecs Amoureux*, p. 65; G. de Machaut, *Livre du Voir-Dit*, p. 90, l. 2106; Chaucer, *Troilus and Criseyde*, iv, 600 (cf. ll. 1587–1589, also *Les Échecs Amoureux* and G. de Machaut, just referred to); Gower, *Vox Clamantis*, vi, 969; and *Confessio Amantis*, vii, 3347–3348, 4902–4903. Contrast

Yet sometimes she remains hostile, and we have a war between her and man. She is often mentioned specifically as an enemy,[1] and still oftener the war with her is either alluded to or described.[2] We hear of her blows and of the wounds she causes;[3] and there are direct references to her

Froissart, *Œuvres*, II, 387, ll. 20–21. See inscription on Picinelli's drawing, in his *Mundus Symbolicus*, I, 155 (lib. iii, cap. xix, 46); cf. Schoonhoven, *Emblemata*, 1618, p. 15.

[1] Alanus de Insulis, *Summa de Arte Praedicatoria*, cap. xiii (Migne, vol. CCX, col. 137); Boccaccio, *Decameron*, III, vii (*Opere*, II, 74); also *Filocopo*, iv (*ibid.*, VIII, 134, 155, 162); *Teseide*, ii, 15, iv, 41, v, 10 (*ibid.*, IX, 61, 133, 153); *Rime*, canz. iv, 10 (*ibid.*, XVI, 118); *L'Urbano* (*ibid.*, XVI), pp. 9, 28, 45, 56; and *Lettere* (*ibid.*, XVII), p. 6; Sercambi, *Novelle*, ed. Renier, p. 406 (no. 108); Sannazaro, *Opere*, pp. 95 (*Arcadia*), 344 (son. xviii); Alberti, *Opere*, III, 277, 285; Boiardo, *Orlando Innamorato*, II, i, 4; Philippe de Beaumanoir, *La Manekine*, ll. 3325 f. (*Œuvres*, I, 105); G. de Machaut, *Poésies*, ed. Chichmaref, I, 170 ("Se Fortune ne le tient à amy"); Chaucer, *Monk's Tale*, B. 3868 ("adversarie"); Gower, *Confessio Amantis*, iv, 3408 ("fo"); Alex. Montgomerie, *Sen Fortun is my Fo* (*Poems*, 1887, p. 185); *Bannatyne MS.*, III, 655, l. 41; Ariosto, *Orlando Furioso*, I, x ("rubella"); XXII, lxx; Trissino, *Italia Liberata*, I, 340 ("ribella"); Machiavelli, *Capitolo di Fortuna* (*Opere*, VII, 370); Sacchetti, *Novelle*, III, 266.

[2] See Lactantius (Migne, vol. VI, col. 437); Alanus de Insulis, as in note 1 above; Carducci, *Cantilene e Ballate*, p. 109, ll. 1 ff.; Aeneas Sylvius, *De Viris Illustribus*, p. 38; Boiardo, *Orlando Innamorato*, I, xxi, 44; Alberti, *Opere*, II, 34 (*Della Fam.*, i); Gareth, *Rime*, II, 324; *Chevalier Errant*, § vi, summarized in Gorra's *Studi*, p. 53 (the battle between the barons and the followers of Fortune is guided by Coup de Fortune); Froissart, *Œuvres*, I, 84 (ll. 1090 f.), 141 (l. 1860); II, 265, 269; Christine de Pisan, *Livre du Chemin*, p. 7, l. 149; Alain Chartier, *Œuvres*, pp. 534, 747; *Le Petit Traittiet* (Pierre Michault's *Dance aux Aveugles*, p. 241); Charles d'Orléans, *Poésies*, I, 56–57, 133 ("armée de Fortune"); Furnivall, *Originals and Analogues*, p. 166 (sources of *Clerk's Tale*, "assalto della nimica fortuna"); *Awntyrs of Arthure*, st. xxi, l. 257; Gower, *Confessio Amantis*, vi, 1517, 1610; Dunbar, *In Asking sowld Discretion be*, l. 44 (*Poems*, II, 86); Gregory Smith, *Specimens of Middle Scots*, pp. 74–75 (*The Portous of Nobleness*); *Poésie Ital. Ined.*, III, 46 (Fortune, roused in wrath, comes crying vengeance).

[3] Boethius, *Cons. Philos.*, III, pr. i, 6; *Carmina Burana*, p. 47 (lxxvii, st. 1, "vulnera"); Boccaccio, *Decameron*, II, viii (*Opere*, I, 220); *Fiammetta*, ix,

weapons, which seem to be usually arrows, darts, or javelins.[1]

Such are the activities of Fortune, and we have traced her steps from game to earnest. These activities obviously suit her character perfectly; for she is just the envious, vindictive creature to throw dice with mankind and shout her laugh of triumph when she wins, to set traps for the sufferer, to snare the unwary, to wage petty warfare on the defiant.

VI

This study of Fortune's activities is by no means complete; other themes will be discussed in connections more appropriate to their particular significance, especially those which are concerned with her dwelling-place and her wheel.

All that we have noticed are used frequently by the

(*ibid.*, VI, 203); *Filocopo*, i (*ibid.*, VII, 55–56); *Rime*, canz. v (*ibid.*, XVI, 122); *Donne Famose*, p. 277 (cap. lxxxiii); *De Casibus*, pp. 26, 120, 145, 253; Alberti, *Opere*, III, 279; Lorenzo de' Medic., *Opere* (1825), III, 36; Pulci, *Morgante Maggiore*, xvii, 2 (I become a target); Boiardo, *Orlando Innamorato*, I, xvii, 11; Ariosto, *Orlando Furioso*, XXXVII, xi; XLIV, lxii; Bembo, *Rime*, p. 94, son. cix; *Roman de la Rose*, ll. 5900 f.; Alain Chartier, *Œuvres*, p. 627 ("bleca"); Chaucer, *Clerk's Tale*, E. 812.

[1] See Medin, *Lamenti*, pp. 69–70, ll. 118 ff. (notice "con furor fulminando"); cf. Molinier, *Essai sur Octovien de Saint-Gelais*, p. 279 ("de foudroyant tonnerre . . . sagiter"). See also Dante, *Paradiso*, xvii, 25 ff. (suggestion that arrows are Fortune's weapons); Faral, *Recherches*, p. 48 (darts); Boccaccio, *De Casibus*, pp. 246, 262 ("iacula," "tela"); Deschamps, *Œuvres*, IV, 238, ll. 47 f. (lance); Alain Chartier, *Œuvres*, p. 633 (fortune "archiere"); Charles d'Orléans, *Poésies*, II, 34 ("l'arc de Fortune"); Raynaud, *Rondeaux*, p. 57, l. 12 ("verges de Fortune"); Cousin, *Livre de Fortune*, plates 13, 15 (drawings of Fortune with arrows); Gower, *Vox Clamantis*, ii, 122 ("arma"). For Fortune's armor, see Lydgate's *Fabula Duorum Mercatorum*, l. 668 ("her habiriownys of steel"); *Carmina Burana*, p. 233 (no. 174, st. 3, "clypeum," shield).

mediaeval writers, but I have taken only the most common examples into consideration. Their customary setting should be observed in passing; for although it is not precisely a literary formula, yet it is so frequently employed in the accounts of Fortune that its importance must be noted here as the chief medium of expression for the tradition of the goddess. This favorite setting is the form of direct apostrophe, perhaps used, especially in the Middle Ages, as a substitute for the prayer of the ancient Roman. At any rate, it is an exceedingly prominent feature in the ritual of the mediaeval cult; [1] probably no other Roman divinity receives so many addresses in this form. And Fortune herself sometimes speaks in reply or in defence.[2]

Within settings like these come the long, detailed discussions that we have described. The apostrophe, the response of Fortune, the themes themselves, are as a rule delightfully consistent with the idea of a goddess. The confusion with type seldom occurs. Possibly such incongruities in the descriptions as that of two separate faces, or of a face part white and part black, or of one eye laughing and the other weeping, may result from introducing momentarily the idea of the abstraction; but Fortune's smile and frown, her characterization as step-mother and harlot, her amusements and games, are all part of a

[1] See Hildebert de Lavardin, *De Exsilio Suo* (Migne, vol. CLXXI, col. 1418); Henricus Septimellensis, *Trattato*, passim; Dreves, *Analecta Hymnica*, XXI, 102 (no. 152); *Carmina Burana*, pp. 1, 47 (lxxvi *a*); *Giornale Storico*, XIV, 33 (Christian Fortune); etc., etc.

[2] Boethius, *Cons. Philos.*, II, pr. ii; Henricus Septimellensis, *Trattato*, pp. 15–16, etc.; *Giornale Storico*, XIV, 33; Volpi, *Rime di Trecentisti Minori*, pp. 210 ff.; *Pierre de la Broche*, in Monmerqué and Michel's *Théâtre Français*, pp. 209 ff.; etc.

splendidly visualized image of the goddess. The astonish-
ing richness of these treatments in mediaeval literature,
compared with the accounts in classical times, certainly
becomes an argument worthy of attention for the survival of the goddess, at least in the mediaeval imagination.

CHAPTER III

FUNCTIONS AND CULTS

THE philosophy of Fortuna, the various themes and formulae used in describing her, and the literary discussions in general, have brought out characteristics of her nature; but as a rule, unless we have chosen for the moment to draw special conclusions, they have not made clear what are the particular duties of the goddess. We have seen from a study of her gifts what she has in her control, and from a study of her relations with Nature and Astrology what are some of her limitations. It will now be our purpose to discover what are her positive functions.

In considering ancient Rome, I have attained a satisfactory method of procedure, I think, by observing in what connections the goddess is mentioned.[1] There the names of the divisions of the great cult, or of the smaller functionary cults, were already furnished. One can work from the known to the unknown. Already informed as to what the goddess is supposed to do, one can look on while she is doing it. In the Middle Ages we shall have to work in the other direction and formulate the cults of Fortune from the chief activities with which we find her concerned.

In thus using the term "cult," I do not mean to imply that in mediaeval times any formal recognition was given to the separate aspects of the goddess. And yet there was

[1] *Smith College Studies in Modern Languages*, III, 131–177.

recognition of a kind, conscious or unconscious, on the part of the people. My formulation of these interests will have failed if it appears to be random; if, after examining it, the reader is unable to classify almost any allusion to the goddess as discovering her in one of these special functions. My purpose is to make clear that Fortune's duties *suggest themselves* from the passages in question, and that the whole sequence of references to her in the Middle Ages classifies itself automatically in separate lines of successive allusions to the goddess in one or another of these aspects.

The chief cults that I have found in the mediaeval field are these: (1) the Fortune of Love; (2) Fortuna the Guide; (3) Fortune of the Sea; (4) the Fortune of Combat; (5) the Fortune of Fame; (6) Personal Fortuna; (7) Fortuna Publica; (8) the Fortune of Time; (9) the Fortune of Death. All but the last two, it will be observed, cover the work otherwise assigned to Lachesis; the eighth and ninth invade the territory controlled by Atropos. One might object that these divisions comprehend the whole extent of human interest. Love, war, and the sea, someone might say, include about all that man cared for, outside of religion, in the Middle Ages. This is true in a measure. Fortune, when she dominates at all, does dominate in the crises of life, and she appears at important moments. But, after all, these divisions cover definite departments of life; they are not vague classifications including all sorts of related activities. Fortune appears quite specifically in charge of a vessel, she actually turns the tide of war, she borrows the hour-glass from Father Time. Furthermore, the cults "Personal Fortuna" and "Fortuna the Guide" have not so wide a scope even as that of war or of the sea. We should have no particular right to expect Fortune to *guide*, or to have a personal regard for, the individual. These cults, then, are specialized in their functions. A classification that simply divided life in general according to its activities and then related Fortune's work to those activities would indeed be at once haphazard and hazardous. That such is not the case in the divisions of Fortune's great cult which I have given will appear, I hope, in our present study.

We shall now take up these nine cults and analyze each of them to see its particular application to mediaeval life and its special meaning for us.

(1) THE FORTUNE OF LOVE

The personification, Love,[1] did not give up the control of his own affairs without a struggle. One must not suppose that he was entirely supplanted by Fortune. Sometimes, indeed, it seems as if Fortune got her power in love-affairs, not by replacing the God of Love, but by bestowing or withholding her gifts of riches and glory which would bring the lover to his lady more easily. Why, after all, should Fortune dabble in love-affairs anyway? Perhaps because the character of the God of Love is very much like hers. As early as the eleventh or twelfth century the similarity between Fortune and Love had been recognized in a poem by Hildebert de Lavardin, *De Infidelitate Fortunae et Amoris Mundi:*[2]

[1] Between the two figures, the masculine and feminine deities, I shall not distinguish. They are the same in function, and were confused in the Middle Ages. See Neilson, *Origins and Sources of the Court of Love*, pp. 26, 27, 36, etc.

[2] "Worldly love" rather than "love of the world." The poem is in Migne's *Patrologia Latina*, vol. CLXXI, cols. 1423–1424, and is described in *Notices et Extraits*, XXVIII², 352, no. xli.

Both Fortune and Love are faithless. They give no honey without some gall. Fortune raises men and sinks them again. Love blandishes and then burns men.

> Tempus, amor, fortuna rotam comitatur euntem,
>   Casus illa rotae, temperat illa uires.
> Stante rota fortuna fauet; cadit haec, premit illam.

Love changes and nourishes sighs; Fortuna begets fear. Joy is the beginning, grief the end, of both. Both turn darkness into day and day into darkness. Cares accompany them both, and with them go tears, labor, and groans. Their honey contains poison. Neither deity is true. Some men are broken by one, and some by the other.

But some writers make a distinction between Love and Fortune, representing one as obstructing the work of the other, or making them at odds somehow, or at least not in complete union.[1] So

> 'tis a question left us yet to prove,
> Whether love lead fortune, or else fortune love.[2]

And the lover asks Fortune, "Che hanno le cose d'Amore a fare con teco?"[3]

---

[1] See Boccaccio, *Decameron*, V, i (*Opere*, III, 21), and *Teseide*, v, 55 (*ibid.*, IX, 168); Lorenzo de' Medici, *Opere* (1825), I, 28 (son. xviii), 89 (sest. v), and *Poemi*, ed. Carabba, p. 21; *La Tenzone d'Amore e di Fortuna*, in Poliziano's *Stanze*, etc. (Carducci's text, ed. Donati, 1910), p. 230 (summarized in *Smith College Studies in Modern Languages*, III, 220); Ariosto, *Orlando Furioso*, XI, lv, and *Rime e Satire*, son. i; *L'Escoufle*, p. 153, ll. 5160 ff.; G. de Machaut, *Poésies*, ed. Chichmaref, I, 229 (cclxiii, 17 ff., where Fortune seems to be more concerned with her gifts; cf. p. 216, ccxliii); also *Œuvres*, ed. Hoepffner, II, 318 (*Dit de l'Alerion*, ll. 2282 ff.), and *Livre du Voir-Dit*, p. 367, xlvi (gifts); Christine de Pisan, *Œuvres*, II, 64, ll. 513 ff. (gifts); Alex. Montgomerie, *Poems*, 1887, p. 192, ll. 36 ff. ("Love maid my chose, bot Fortun maid my chance," etc.).

[2] *Hamlet*, III, ii, 212–213. Cf. Burchiello, *Sonetti*, p. 237:

> Chiariscimi, chi ha maggior potenza,
>   O Amor, o Fortuna, o Libertate.

[3] Boccaccio, *Fiammetta*, v (*Opere*, VI, 104 f.).

Fortune and Love become associated in work, however. They are both accused of causing trouble for lovers, and their names are linked.[1] In *Li Romanz de la Poire*, Amors, seated before the throne of Fortune, tells how lovers are treated by the goddess:

> Celui qui leaument eime, celui ai chier
> Et le voil hautement entor moi aluchier.
> Mes li fax qui me ment et me sert de trichier,
> De la roe vilment l'estuet jus trebuchier.
>
> Fortune sanz reproche fet tot quanque je loe.
> Cels que de mon dart toche, met en haut sor la roe,
> Et s'autres i aproche, Fortune le descroe
> Et estendu le coche tot envers en la boe.

Fortune then gives an account of her usual characteristics and tells how she casts men down. Those who are faithful in love suffer no injury.[2]

Here the Court of Love has become practically the Court of Fortune, and clearly Fortune is in chief power:

[1] *Poesie Ital. Ined.*, II, 166; III, 32; Cino da Pistoia, *Poesie*, ed. Ciampi, 1826, p. 60 (canz. v, Amor and Ventura); Boccaccio, *Teseide*, iv, 11 (*Opere*, IX, 123), and *Filostrato*, II, cxxxii (*ibid.*, XIII, 75); Petrarch, *Rime*, ed. Albertini, I, 103 (canz. vii, "Ne mai stato giojoso"), 167 (son. lxxxv, "Amor, Fortuna, e la mia mente schiva," etc.), 280 (canz. xvi, "or all' estremo," etc.); II, 28 (son. vi, "Non basta ben," etc.); ed. Mestica, pp. 316 (son. clxxxvii), 323 (son. cxciii); Sannazaro, *Opere*, pp. 341 (son. xii), 367 (son. xliv); Lorenzo de' Medici, *Opere* (1825), I, 10 (son. viii), 35 (son. xxv), 53 (canz. iii), 111 (son. lxx); also *Poesie* (1801), I, 67; Machiavelli, *Opere*, VII, 385; Poliziano, *Le Stanze*, etc., ed. Carducci, 1863, p. 248 (*Rispetti Spicciolati*, xxxviii); Benivieni, *Opere*, p. 81 (*Bucolica*, egl. 1); Alberti, *Opere*, V, 361 (egl. 1, "Amor ne inreta e tiene"); Trissino, *Tutte le Opere*, I, 361 (serv.); Boiardo, *Orlando Innamorato*, I, xii, 60, 77; *Roman de la Rose*, ll. 6896 f.; G. de Machaut, *Œuvres*, ed. Hoepffner, I, 88, ll. 820 ff.; also *Poésies*, ed. Chichmaref, I, 204; II, 434; and *Livre du Voir-Dit*, pp. 26, 77, 277, 309, 332; Deschamps, *Œuvres*, III, 371; IV, 178 (dccxiv, 12); Alain Chartier, *Œuvres*, p. 624; Raynaud, *Rondeaux*, pp. 81–82 (xciii), 104 (cxxi); Cousin, plates 67 and 69.

[2] See the whole passage, *Romanz*, ed. Stehlich, ll. 25 ff. For lovers on the wheel, see Chaucer, *Troilus and Criseyde*, iv, 323 ff.

Mout est Fortune sage et nos assez savon.
Ele quelt mon passage, grant seignorie avon,[1]

says Love. In the *Panthère d'Amours*,[2] and in the *Kingis Quair*,[3] Fortune seems to be in complete control. Cases of love are finally referred to her decision, and the Court of Fortune appears to be an established fact.

Perhaps Fortune earliest takes over the complete management of a love-affair in the case of Abélard and Héloïse, and here she assumes her powers with a burst of splendor. She has parted the lovers, as she often does, and so they suffer. Héloïse writes:

O si fas sit dici crudelem mihi per omnia Deum! o inclementem clementiam! o infortunatam fortunam, quae jam in me uniuersi conaminis sui tela in tantum consumpsit, ut quibus in alios saeuiat jam non habeat; plenam in me pharetram exhausit, ut frustra jam alii bella ejus formident. Nec si ei adhuc telum aliquod superesset, locum in me uulneris inueniret. Unum inter tot uulnera metuit, ne morte supplicia finiam. Et cum interimere non cesset, interitum tamen quem accelerat timet. O me miserarum miserrimam! infelicium infelicissimam, quae quanto uniuersis in te feminis praelata sublimiorem obtinui gradum, tanto hinc prostrata grauiorem in te et in me pariter perpessa sum casum! Quanto quippe altior ascendentis gradus, tanto grauior corruentis casus. Quam mihi nobilium ac potentium feminarum fortuna unquam praeponere potuit aut aequare?[4]

Here indeed are the slings and arrows of outrageous Fortune! From this time on, Fortuna is found meddling more or less in love-affairs.[5]

[1] *Romanz*, ll. 29–30.   [2] Lines 1918 ff.   [3] Stanza 144, ll. 6–7.

[4] Epistle iv (Migne, vol. CLXXVIII, col. 194). Héloïse later sees the hand of God in her suffering: "Ira Domini manum suam super nos uehementer aggrauauit, et immaculatum non pertulit torum qui diu ante sustinuerat pollutum."

[5] See, e.g., Boccaccio, *Filocopo*, i (*Opere*, VII, 6); also *Teseide*, viii, 96 (*ibid.*, IX, 292); *Filostrato*, II, lxxvii (*ibid.*, XIII, 57); *Ameto* (*ibid.*, XV, 144); Pe-

She is mentioned explicitly as taking a particular part;[1] she aids the bold;[2] she gives the guerdons of love;[3] she guides the lovers;[4] she brings them together and makes them fall in love;[5] she brings about the consummation of their love;[6] and she causes the birth of their children.[7] Boccaccio describes the methods of the goddess in the following complaint:

Thou dost give and thou dost take away. But while I was still young and knew not what a great part thou dost hold in the rule of love, thou, "delle passioni dell' anima donatrice," didst make me enamoured as thou didst wish; I fell in love with that youth, whom only thou put before mine eyes, at the moment I thought myself to

---

trarch, *Rime*, ed. Albertini, I, 272 (son. clii); II, 199 (*Trionfo d'Amore*, iv); Sercambi, *Novelle*, ed. Renier, p. 226 (no. 64); Masuccio, *Il Novellino*, p. 388; Alain Chartier, *Œuvres*, pp. 625–626, etc.

[1] Boccaccio, *Decameron*, X, viii (*Opere*, V, 76, 78); Alberti, *Opere*, III, 325; Lorenzo de' Medici, *Opere* (1825), I, 15 (son. xiii); also *Poemi*, ed. Carabba, p. 11 (*Selve d'Amore*, i); G. de Machaut, *Poésies*, ed. Chichmaref, II, 357, 510; Christine de Pisan, *Œuvres*, I, 25 (*Cent Balades*, xxiv, 13–14); Gower, *Confessio Amantis*, i, 2624 ff.; Lydgate, *Fabula Duorum Mercatorum*, ll. 439–441.

[2] Boccaccio, *Filostrato*, IV, lxxiii (*Opere*, XIII, 137). Cf. above, p. 83, n. 4.

[3] Jean le Seneschal, *Les Cent Ballades*, p. 162, ll. 25 ff.; Froissart, *Œuvres*, II, 406 (xxxv).

[4] Jean le Seneschal, *Les Cent Ballades*, p. 143, ll. 13 ff.; Gower, *Balades*, x, 2 (*Works*, I, 346).

[5] *Carmina Burana*, p. 189, no. 114, st. 4; Boccaccio, *Decameron*, IV, iv (*Opere*, II, 192); X, x (*ibid.*, V, 136); Masuccio, *Il Novellino*, p. 349 (gives a spouse); Giov. Fiorentino, *Il Pecorone*, II, 135 (xxii, 2); Aeneas Sylvius, *Storia di Due Amanti*, p. 29 (gives a spouse); Bembo, *Opere*, I, 53 (*Degli Asolani*, lib. i); Jean le Seneschal, *Les Cent Ballades*, p. 159; Chaucer, *Legend of Good Women*, ll. 1044 ff., 1609 f.; Gower, *Confessio Amantis*, i, 1859; also *Balades*, vi, 2 (*Works*, I, 343); Alex. Montgomerie, *Poems*, 1887, p. 173 (xxix, 11–12).

[6] Boccaccio, *Decameron*, VIII, vii (*Opere*, IV, 68); Chaucer, *Troilus and Criseyde*, iii, 1667 ff.; Lydgate, *Troy Book*, i, 2676 ff., 2758 ff.; cf. James I, *Kingis Quair*, st. 93; Alex. Montgomerie, *Poems*, 1887, p. 182, ll. 25–27.

[7] Alberti, *Opere*, III, 275, 302.

be furthest from loving. When thou feltest me bound indissolubly in heart, thou, unstable one, soughtest to make the pleasure of my love noisome to me. Sometimes hast thou subdued the spirit with vain and tricky deceits, and sometimes subjected the eyes to thee; for our love published abroad could do no harm. Oftener, as thou didst wish, ugly words of my lover came to mine ears, and some from me went to him, to create hatred between us. But is the virtue of the mind subject unto thee? Cannot our wisdom prevail over thee? What can aid against thee? Thou hast a thousand ways to harm thine enemies, all of them deceitful. I thought I was secure. If I were young, I might have defence now. Thou hast not kept to thine own fields, but hast put thy scythe into another's grain. What have the things of love to do with thee? Thou gavest me treasures, riches, fields — why not extend thy wrath to these bounties? Thou hast left me these which are of no avail to console me. If ever thou hast been pricked with the arrows of love, thou mightest offer counsel. All are happy but me. My name is a by-word among the people who once told the fame of my beauty. Begin to have pity on me, since I yearn to praise thee, to honor thỳ majesty. At the hour thou turnest back to greet me, I shall put up my statue with a tablet, saying, "This is Fiammetta, called by Fortune from deepest woe to greatest happiness." It will be seen by all.[1]

As we see here, Fortune is generally at the last unfavorable to one or both of the lovers. She is hard-hearted, envious, positively hostile, and torments them.[2] It was

---

[1] *Fiammetta*, v (*Opere*, VI, 103 ff.).

[2] Boccaccio, *Opere*, VIII, 274-275 (*Filocopo*, v); XIII, 2, 6 ("nemica"), 111 ("invidiosa"), 147 ("nemica"), 251 (all in *Filostrato*); XV, 135 (*Ameto*); XVII, 88 (*Ninfale Fiesolano*); Lorenzo de' Medici, *Opere* (1825), I, 11, 27, 38 ("iniqua, e ria"), 48 ("vieta, lo interrompe, e spezza"), 61 ("iniqua e dura"); also *Poemi*, ed. Carabba, p. 21; Luca Pulci, in Lorenzo de' Medici's *Poesie* (1801), II, 98; Poliziano, *Le Stanze*, etc., ed. Carducci, 1863, pp. 155 (ll. 366 f.), 225 ("contrapporre"); Alberti, *Opere*, III, 277 ("nemica"), 307, 324-325; Boiardo, *Orlando Innamorato*, I, xiii, 40, and xxv, 54 (allowed but one day of love); Gareth, *Rime*, II, 155 (son. cxxxii); Bembo, *Rime*, p. 87 (son. xcv); Marie de France, *Guigemar*, ll. 537 ff. (*Lais*, no. 1); *L'Escoufle*, pp. 234 f., ll. 7824 f. See especially *Roman de la Rose*, discussed in *Smith College Studies in Modern Languages*, IV, 6-9; Philippe de Beaumanoir, *Jehan et Blonde*, ll. 1629 ff. (*Œuvres*, II, 52-53, "l'outrageuse . . . pleine d'envie,"

she who was so cruel to Pyramus and Thisbe.[1] She is particularly noted for separating lovers.[2]

Thus Fortuna actually does or undoes the work of the God of Love. We may remember that in many ways her traits, as depicted in the preceding chapter, resemble those of the love deity. Fortune is blind, and slings arrows or darts at her victims.[3] These divinities, Fortune and Love, become sufficiently identified for Venus to take over the characteristics of her sister goddess, and by the time of *Les Échecs Amoureux* we find Venus turning a wheel and exalting and debasing mankind:

etc.); G. de Machaut, *Œuvres*, ed. Hoepffner, I, 84, ll. 725 ff.; also *Poésies* ed. Chichmaref, I, 81 ("contraire"), 171 ("dure"), 176 (cxcv), 182 (ccii); II, 419 (ll. 139 ff.), 557 (ll. 18 ff.), 638 (iii, 3 ff.); also *Livre du Voir-Dit*, pp. 67 (keeps the lovers apart), 264; Froissart, *Œuvres*, I, 142 (ll. 1880 ff.), 307 (ll. 2923 f.), 311 (ll. 3045 ff.); II, 18 (ll. 580 f.), 257 (ll. 37 ff.), 258 (ll. 56 ff.), 271 (ll. 75 ff.); Deschamps, *Œuvres*, I, 132 f. (xlv, "Dangier vient"); IV, 5 (ll. 19–20); V, 342, ll. 16 ff.; X, p. lxxxvii ("Denger me martire"); Christine de Pisan, *Œuvres*, I, 34 (*Cent Balades*, xxxiii, 19 f.); II, 135 (ll. 789 ff.), 144 (ll. 1101 ff.), 218 (ll. 1965 ff.); III, 159 (ll. 3128 ff., "preste . . . de destruire Les amans"); Alain Chartier, *Œuvres*, pp. 641, 678 ("dure et male"); Raynaud, *Rondeaux*, pp. 44 (xlviii, 4–5, "tourmente"), 133 (clvi, cf. clvii, clx), 142 (l. 8, "rigours"), 154–155 (clxxxiv), 157 (clxxxvii); Charles d' Orléans, *Poésies*, I, 55, 156; II, 87 (rond. xvi, also printed in the works of René d'Anjou, III, 202), 164 (by Madame d' Orléans); Jean de Garencières, *Vous m'avez*, ed. A. Piaget, in *Romania*, XXII, 477, st. ix; Lydgate, *Troy Book*, v, 2981; also *The Flour of Curtesye*, ll. 75–76 (Skeat, *Chaucerian and other Pieces*, p. 268); Child, *Ballads*, no. 150 (*Robin Hood and Maid Marian*), st. 6. Cf. above, p. 84, n. 1.

[1] Sercambi, *Novelle*, ed. Renier, p. 326 (no. 93).

[2] Boccaccio, *Fiammetta*, ii (*Opere*, VI, 44); *Filostrato* (*ibid.*, XIII, 153, 177); *L'Urbano* (*ibid.*, XVI), p. 43. Cf. Nicole de Margival, *Panthère d' Amours*, ll. 143 f.; G. de Machaut, *Poésies*, ed. Chichmaref, I, 209 (ccxxxii); II, 354–355 (ll. 69 ff.), 446 (ll. 99 f.); also *Livre du Voir-Dit*, pp. 67, 278; G. Paris, *Chansons*, pp. 88 ff. (xcii, cf. xciii); *Melusine*, ll. 3745–3747; Chaucer, *Troilus and Criseyde*, v, 1745 ff., and *Squire's Tale*, F. 576; Alex. Montgomerie, *Poems*, ed. Stevenson, 1910, p. 195 (*Wo Worth the Fall of Fortounis Quheill*).

[3] See the parallelism established in Pierre Michault's *Dance aux Aveugles*.

> Car elle [Venus] fait a son conuent
> Perdre leur bon Regnon souuent
> Et a plusieurs gloire et honneur
> Tant quelle fait serf le seigneur
> Et le plus hault monte descendre
> Et pour tout a briefz mos comprendre
> Elle fait auanchier fortune
> Oultre la maniere commune
> Et li fait destourner sa Roe
> Si que chil versent en la boe
> Qui estoient ou plus hault chief
> Et les Ramaine a tel meschief
> Quil ne sen peuent Jamais terdre.[1]

We may agree with Gower:

> For if ther evere was balance
> Which of fortune stant governed,
> I may wel lieve as I am lerned
> That love hath that balance on honde.[2]

In Lydgate, too, the confusion is striking.[3]

The association between Venus and Fortune might be studied even further. Fortune's house is often in the midst of a stormy sea; Venus "fleteth in a se,"

> To schewe þe trowble and adversite
> þat is in Love, and his stormy lawe,
> Whiche is beset with many sturdy wawe,
> Now calm, now rowe, who-so takeþ hede.[4]

---

[1] Sieper's ed., pp. 84–85 (fol. 50 b in MS. of the poem). Cf. Gower, *Confessio Amantis*, i, 42 ff. (love is represented as masculine), 2490–2495; viii, 2013 ff., 2355 ff., 2880. Note also Henryson's *Testament of Cresseid*, ll. 218 ff.

[2] *Confessio Amantis*, i, 42–45.

[3] See his *Complaint of the Black Knight* (Skeat, *Chaucerian and other Pieces*, pp. 258–259), ll. 420 ff., especially 453, 468 ff.

[4] Lydgate, *Troy Book*, ii, 2543 ff. Compare, too, the description of the house of Venus in Claudian's *De Nuptiis Honorii et Mariae*, ll. 49 ff., 86 ff., with that of Fortune; and see below, pp. 123 f.

This identification of the two figures of Fortune and Love only means that they had very much in common,[1] and that in one aspect Fortune was certainly regarded as concerned with the affairs of love.

[1] For the association of Love and Fortune in Elizabethan times, see Turbervile's poem on "A Controversie of a conquest in Love twixt Fortune and Venus" (*Epitaphes, Epigrams*, etc., 1567, ed. J. P. Collier, pp. 110 f.), and a comedy on "The Rare Triumphs of Love and Fortune," 1589 (Dodsley-Hazlitt, *Old English Plays*, 1874, vol. VI), both noted by J. H. Hanford in his article in the Kittredge anniversary volume, p. 449. See also Grimm, *Deutsche Mythologie*, III, 264, §728: "Eine sage von *frau Fortuna*, die eine art Venus ist, steht in den altd, bl. I, 297." For the wheel of Venus, see also Froissart, *Œuvres*, I, 59 (the wheels of *Li Orloge Amoureus*). Here the wheels are of a significance entirely different from that of the wheel of Fortune. They moderate each other: the Wheel of Desire is moderated by the Wheel of Temperance, and so on. See also Fortune's chain and that of Venus. See Chaucer's *Frankeleyn's Tale*, ll. 1355–1358. Cf. Seneca, *De Tranquillitate Animi*, x, 3: "Omnes cum fortuna copulati sumus; aliorum aurea catena est, aliorum laxa, aliorum arta et sordida. Sed quid refert? eadem custodia uniuersos circumdedit alligatique sunt etiam qui alligauerunt, nisi forte tu leuiorem in sinistra catenam putas." Also cf. Fregoso, *Dialogo di Fortuna*, v (sig. A 8[vo]):

> Che uno ordine infinito de le cose
> Concathenato la Fortuna sia
> Pieno d'hore infelice, & perigliose.[1]

Lydgate, *Troy Book*, ii, 5601 f., speaks of the chain of Venus. Cf. Jupiter's chain, Lydgate's "balade" to the Duchess of Gloucester, *Anglia*, XXVII, 388; and Satan's chain in Chaucer's *Envoy to Bukton*, ll. 9–14.

See the attribution of Fortune's characteristics to an *amie*, in Guillaume de Machaut's *Livre du Voir-Dit*, pp. 355 f., "You are changeable, unsteady, you have a double face, happy and weeping," etc.; cf. Poliziano, *Le Stanze*, etc., ed. Carducci, 1863, pp. 85–86 (*La Giostra*, ii, sts. 34–35). For the relation of the planet Venus to the seven ages and to the wheel of Fortune, see Boll's *Lebensalter*, pp. 120 ff. See Cousin's drawing, *Livre de Fortune*, pl. 67 (Fortune leading Amour); and Ripa's description of "Fortuna gioueuole ad Amore" (*Iconologia*, p. 170), "Donna la quale con la mano destra tiene il cornucopia, et la sinistra sarà posata sopra al capo di vn Cupido, che le scherzi d' intorno alla veste."

(2) FORTUNA THE GUIDE

The theme of "Fortune's course," mentioned in the preceding chapter,[1] suggests that to attain any gift of Fortune we must follow her though she flee. The same idea is found in the conception of Fortune as leading mankind on a way of her own choosing, and so giving men the various adventures they experience. Fortune, and not Reason, thus becomes the guide of life. It is presumed that her course will not be direct or easy to travel. Sections of the journey, as it were, are found in the various slight allusions to her in the process of so conducting affairs that man gets into certain pleasant or unpleasant situations. There are many such references, in which she is responsible in one way or another for *bringing* man into some particular place or set of circumstances.[2] A man who is walking comes into a wood by chance, or he is lost, or somehow the direction of his steps is taken out of his own hands.

[1] Page 80, above.

[2] See Dante, *Inferno*, xiii, 97 ff. ("là dove fortuna là balestra"); xxx, 146 ff.; xxxii, 76; Boccaccio, *Fiammetta*, i, iv, vi (*Opere*, VI, 4, 8, 68, 141); also *Filocopo*, iii (*ibid.*, VII, 303), v (VIII, 241); and *De Casibus*, p. 92 ("Tandem urgente in eius exitium fortuna uires"); Lorenzo de' Medici, *Opere* (1825), I, 18 (son. xvi); Poliziano, *Le Stanze*, etc., ed. Carducci, 1863, p. 86 (*La Giostra*, ii, st. 35); *La Compagnia del Mantellaccio*, p. 42 (appended to Burchiello's *Sonetti*); Frezzi, *Quadriregio*, I, 17 (lib. i, cap. iv), ll. 1 ff., the sufferer is lost; De Jennaro, *Canzonière*, p. 324, no. 78; Pulci, *Morgante Maggiore*, ii, 49; Boiardo, *Orlando Innamorato*, I, xvii, 6; Ariosto, *Orlando Furioso*, XXIII, xxii; XLVI, lxxi; Philippe de Beaumanoir, *La Manekine*, ll. 5496, 5513-5516 (*Œuvres*, I, 170); Jean le Seneschal, *Les Cent Ballades*, p. 90, ll. 24 ff.; Chaucer, *Somnour's Tale*, D. 2019 ff. (story of two knights' going forth; by fortune's will only one returns); Gower, *Confessio Amantis*, ii, 1477–1478; Lydgate, *Troy Book*, i, 3733 ff.; ii, 2235 ("And to what fyn Fortune wil hem lede"), 5256 f.; Alex. Montgomerie, *Poems*, 1887, p. 213, ll. 18–19.

But Fortune does more than this. The writers refer
quite definitely to her function as a guide. We read:

> Et uaga sunt mentis dubiae uestigia, tanquam
> Coeci palpantis. Quae uel qualis sit uia, cuius
> Est oculus baculus, & dux fortuna.[1]

Fortuna "guida," "ha condutto," "mena," "demainne,"
or "leads."[2] She is often found guiding one across the
sea, and this particular task of hers[3] leads us to the study
of the next cult.

[1] Leyser, *Historia Poetarum*, p. 953.

[2] Dante, *Inferno*, xv, 46 f.; Boccaccio, *Filocopo*, v (*Opere*, VIII, 332, "ha
portati ad essere in casa di"); also *Ninfale Fiesolano*, I, xxxiv (*ibid.*, XVII,
14), and *Donne Famose*, p. 392, cap. ciii; Petrarch, *Vite d. Uomini*, I², 829, II,
463; also *Africa*, i, 286–287; Frezzi, *Quadriregio*, I, 49 ("condutto"); Sannazaro, *Opere*, p. 94; Giov. Fiorentino, *Il Pecorone*, I, 208 (x, 1), 220 (xi, 1);
Sercambi, *Novelle*, ed. D'Ancona, p. 103 (no. xiii); ed. Renier, pp. 262 (no. 74),
370 (no. 101, "m'ha condutto a doverla dare a uno ragazzo"); Ferrario,
Poesie Pastorali, pp. 12 ("Fortuna prenderem per guida e scorta"), 184;
Benivieni, *Opere*, p. 109ᵛᵒ (*Bucolica*, egl. 8); Pulci, *Morgante Maggiore*,
xviii, 72; Boiardo, *Orlando Innamorato*, I, xii, 60; II, viii, 16, 34; xviii, 36; xix,
38; Alberti, *Opere*, III, 433 ("Così come la fortuna ti pigne così procedi");
Ariosto, *Orlando Furioso*, XVIII, lviii ("Fortuna il guida Per dargli onor che
Dardinello uccida"); XXIII, cix; XXV, lx ("Fortuna mi tirò fuor del cam-
mino"); Trissino, *Tutte le Opere*, I, 314, col. 2 (*Sofonisba*); Benoît de Ste.
Maure, *Roman de Troie*, IV, 235 (l. 27456), 314 (l. 28929, Ulysses); Barbazan, *Fabliaux*, I, 203, l. 1203; III, 311, l. 480; G. de Machaut, *Œuvres*, ed.
Hoepffner, II, 386 (*Dit de l'Alerion*, ll. 4301 ff.); Froissart, *Œuvres*, II, 22, ll.
715 f.; Deschamps, *Œuvres*, V, 411, ll. 23–24; Charles d'Orléans, *Poésies*, I,
114; II, 219 ("Quant assez m'aurez tort porté"); *Eger and Grine*, l. 1092;
Gower, *Confessio Amantis*, v, 314 (cf. viii, 1320); Lydgate, *Albon and Amphabel*, iii, 595, and *Troy Book*, ii, 3777; Metcalfe, *Legends of the Saints*, I, 269
(xvi, *Magdalena*, l. 454). Herzhoff (*Personif. lebl. Dinge*, etc., pp. 11 f.) finds
in his investigations that Aventure is most often connected with "amener,"
"mener," etc.: see his references. For Fortuna causing return, see Boccaccio, *Fiammetta*, vii (*Opere*, VI, 171 f.); Masuccio, *Il Novellino*, p. 410;
and Cousin's drawing, "Fortuna Redux," *Livre de Fortune*, pl. 143.

[3] Boccaccio, *Decameron*, V, i (*Opere*, III, 26; also *Teseide*, i, 12 (*ibid.*, IX,
13), and iv, 52–53 (IX, 136–137, "ella mi ha condotto a cotal porto");

(3) Fortune of the Sea

Dictys Cretensis, describing the wanderings of Ulysses, who after all was chiefly a romantic adventurer, says, "Adpulsusque ad Lotophagos atque aduersa usus fortuna deuenerit in Siciliam." [1] The sea-figure, comparing life to a sea and one's career to a vessel of which Fortune is in charge, is used with such great frequency in discussions of the work of Fortuna that it becomes a theme of unusual importance. In Boethius, for example, we find the following statements:

> Si uentis uela committeres, non quo uoluntas peteret, sed quo flatus impellerent, promoueres. . . . Fortunae te regendum dedisti, dominae moribus oportet obtemperes.[2]
>
> Nondum est ad unum omnes exosa fortuna nec tibi nimium ualida tempestas incubuit, quando tenaces haerent ancorae quae nec praesentis solamen nec futuri spem temporis abesse patiantur.[3]

Life is, therefore, a sea of trouble stirred up by Fortuna, and with our light skiff we venture on its waves.[4]

Ariosto, *Orlando Furioso*, XXX, xv; Bembo, *Opere*, I, 65 (*Degli Asolani*, lib. i).

[1] *Belli Troiani*, VI, v, 31–32.

[2] *Cons. Philos.*, II, pr. i, 52–56. Cf. Dinaux, *Trouvères*, IV, 625; G. de Machaut, *Remede de Fortune*, ll. 2577 ff.

[3] *Cons. Philos.*, II, pr. iv, 28–31. See also pr. ii, 22 ff. ("nunc . . . nunc"), and met. ii, 1 f., and iii, 9 ff.

[4] Hildebert de Lavardin, *De Exsilio Suo* (Migne, vol. CLXXI, col. 1419, "Inde ratem scando, uitam committo procellis"); Henricus Septimellensis, *Trattato*, 1730, p. 7 ("Obruor Oceano, sauisque reuerberor undis," etc.); *Gedicht auf die Zerstörüng Mailands*, ll. 26 ff.; Dante, *Il Convivio*, I, iii, 30 ff. ("quasi mendicando . . . Veramente io sono stato legno senza vela," etc.); *Le Règne de Fortune*, in Montaiglon's *Recueil de Poésies Françoises*, X, 79; G. de Machaut, *Poésies*, ed. Chichmaref, II, 497–498, ll. 21 ff.; Christine de Pisan *Œuvres*, II, 64, ll. 486 ff.; James I, *Kingis Quair*, st. 15, ll. 3–4 ("Ryght as the schip that sailith stereles," etc.); Dunbar, *Quhome to sall I Complene my Wo*, l. 59 (*Poems*, II, 102, "Quhair fals behechtis as wind hyne wavis"); Boc-

As in the case of Fortuna the Guide the goddess enjoys
leading people about, so here she takes a position at the
helm and guides the ship. She turns it, conducts it
through the storm, and brings it into a good or a bad
port.[1]

Sometimes her method of guiding the ship is by controlling the winds: one abandons the sails of one's ship to
Fortuna,[2] and she directs them.[3] Fortune is called "ven-

caccio, *Filocopo*, v (*Opere*, VIII, 274–275); Lorenzo de' Medici, *Opere* (1825),
I, 10 (son. viii, "Fortuna, ed Amor, che sta al temone"); Bembo, *Opere*, I,
73 f. (*Degli Asolani*, lib. i); Charles d'Orléans, *Poésies*, II, 230 ("L'eaue de
Pleurs, de Joye ou de Douleur").

[1] Dante, *Paradiso*, xxvii, 145 ff. ("Le poppe volgerà u' son le prore");
Petrarch, *Rime*, ed. Mestica, p. 349 (son. ccxv); Frezzi, *Quadriregio*, I, 280,
ll. 5 ff. ("tra la gran tempesta. . . . Conduce la sua barca con salute");
Masuccio, *Il Novellino*, pp. 257 ("ai loro moreschi liti"), 423 ("da . . . fortuna . . . al porto . . . accompagnato"); Alberti, *Opere*, V, 332 (*Lettere*, "a
questo porto"); Ariosto, *Orlando Furioso*, VIII, lix ("al lito infausto"); XX,
xlviii ("al nostro lito"); XXXVI, lxi ("che 'l legno ai liti inabitati"); Wace,
Roman de Rou, I, 27, ll. 476–477 ("al port de Lune"); Benoît de Ste. Maure,
Roman de Troie, IV, 285, ll. 28412 ff. (Menelaus arrives at Crete); Philippe
de Beaumanoir, *La Manekine*, ll. 1072 ff., cf. 1084 ff., 5495 ff. (*Œuvres*, I, 36,
170); Christine de Pisan, *Œuvres*, I, 182 (lxii, 8 ff.); Charles d'Orléans, *Poésies*,
I, 130 ("à douloureux port"); II, 222 ("venir à bon port"); Gower, *Confessio Amantis*, viii, 1320 (ship is led by Fortune); Dunbar, *Lucina Schyn-
nyng in Silence of the Nicht*, ll. 14 f. (*Poems*, II, 149, "Quhilk every worldly
thing dois turne and steir"); Chaucer, *Legend of Good Women*, ll.1044 (Aeneas
and Dido); Lydgate, *Troy Book*, ii, 3392–3393 ("And of fortune in her
[their] cours þei mette A Grekysche schip").

[2] Guido Cavalcanti, in *Poeti del Primo Secolo*, II, 318 ("Sostenitor delle
vele gonfiate . . . Eolo non può le mie vele impedire," etc.); Boiardo, *Orlando
Innamorato*, II, i, 7 ("a fortuna le vele abbandona").

[3] Ariosto, *Orlando Furioso*, XXII, x ("dove fortuna spinge"); David
Lindsay, *Satyre of the thrie Estaits*, ll. 582–583 ("Fortune turnit on thame hir
saill"); Paulo Maccio, *Emblemata*, pp. 172–173 (emblem xlii, verse and
inscription, "Quò fortuna uocat, si nauita uela retorquet," "Volentes ducunt
fata, nolentes trahunt"; with picture of a ship on the sea).

PLATE 4

BOETHIUS AND FORTUNE

tosa." [1] In the figure of the type, as we have seen,[2] Fortune is herself blown by the winds. In the symbolic figure she and the winds are apparently in close conspiracy with each other — both are mentioned as if concerned with the same work:

> E guidato dai venti,
> E la fortuna che volge in sua via.[3]

And then we read of the actual "winds of Fortune" which she sends to the ship;

> Oimè! Fortuna, non mi stare addosso;
> Abbia pietà di me, che più non posso.
> Tempera omai i tuoi venti crudeli,
> E non isconquassar più la mia barca.[4]

In control of the winds, she sends mist and fog. As early as the tenth century Gerbert of Aurillac complains, "Sed

---

[1] R. Holkot, *Opus super Sapientiam Salomonis*, lectio cviii ("uideas illam uentosam fluentem," quoting Boethius, II, pr. viii); Gower, *Mirour de l'Omme*, ll. 22106–22110,

> Ore es tout coye au sigle et nage,
> Menable et du paisible port;
> Ore es ventouse, plein du rage,
> Des haltes ondes tant salvage,
> Que l'en ne puet nager au port.

[2] See p. 37, above.

[3] *Poesie Ital. Ined.*, II, 55. See also Cino da Pistoia, *Poesie* (1826), p. 145 (son. lxxxi); Burchiello, *Sonetti*, p. 110 ("la mia vela sventola"); Sannazaro, *Opere*, p. 126 (*Arcadia*),

> Ma prega tu che i venti non tel guastino . . .
> Voto fo io, se tu, Fortuna, ajutici, etc.;

Giov. Fiorentino, *Il Pecorone*, I, 273 f. (xiv, 2); Pico della Mirandola, *Opera*, I, 397, xii (*In Astrologiam*, lib. vi, cap. iii, "Fortunamue petat pelago uentosque sequatur"); the anonymous *Débat de Lomme Mondain et du Religieux* (Pierre Michault's *Dance aux Aveugles*, p. 310); Lydgate, *Troy Book*, i, 1235 f. (cf. 1241, Neptunus); v, 628 ff.; Alain Chartier, *Œuvres*, p. 394.

[4] Giov. Fiorentino, *Il Pecorone*, II, 37 (xvi, 2). See Boccaccio, *De Casibus*, p. 214 ("ut aut omnem fortunæ spirantis auram"), and poem opposite the

inuoluit mundum caeca fortuna, quae premit caligine, an praecipitet, an dirigat me modo tendentem hac, modo illac." [1] Fortune brings dark clouds, rain, "cludy stormis," and tempests. [2] Storms, then, whether of wind or rain or clouds, are sent on occasion by the fickle goddess, whom Lydgate calls the "stormy quene"; [3] and she brings the unhappy vessel on a rock. [4]

index, by Pontano ("fortunæ quatitur procellis"); Benoît de Ste. Maure, *Roman de Troie*, I, 166, l. 3282 ("bon vent li a doné Fortune"); Charles d' Orléans, *Poésies*, II, 164,

> En la forest de Longue Attente,
> Par vent de Fortune Dolente,
> Tant y voy abatu de bois

(quoted by Raynaud, *Rondeaux*, p. 42, xlvii; for the first line, cf. René d' Anjou, *Œuvres Complètes*, III, 9, l. 11). See Christine de Pisan, *Œuvres*, I, 182 (lxii, 9); cf. Gower, *Mirour de l'Omme*, l. 22096 ("Plus que ly ventz perest changable"), and *Confessio Amantis*, v, 7556 ("such a wynd fortune hem sente"), viii, 600 ff. (at line 623 Neptune appears in power). Contrast Lydgate, *Troy Book*, v, 1 ff., where Fortune is in opposition to Juno, Eolus, and Neptune, who unite to make the sea calm. Fortune puts discord among the Greeks themselves.

　[1] Epistle xlvi (Migne, vol. CXXXIX, col. 215).

　[2] Ariosto, *I Cinque Canti*, III, lvi (fortune — storm?); see G. de Machaut's figure in his *Dit de l'Alerion*, ll. 1749 ff. (*Œuvres*, ed. Hoepffner, II, 300); Gareth, *Rime*, II, 45 (son. xxxvi); Sibbald, *Chronicle*, II, 55, xxii ("Thoucht scho with cludy stormis me assail").

　[3] *Troy Book*, v, 635; cf. ii, 3240 ("O stormy Fortune"). For the association of Fortuna with storms, see Lorenzo de' Medici, *Opere* (1825), I, 39, canz. ii; Bembo, *Rime*, p. 88, son. xcvii; Froissart, *Méliador*, II, 72, ll. 11790 ff. (after the storm; cf. l. 11846); Christine de Pisan, *Œuvres*, I, 4 (iii, 13 ff., "Fist en la mer trop tempesteux orage"); Gower, *Vox Clamantis*, ii, 132 ("uelut unda maris sic uenis atque redis" — cf. Boethius, *Cons. Philos.*, I, met. v, 45 ff.), 136 ("Turbinis et uento te facis esse parem"). See Alberti, *Opere*, III, 167 ("peritogli il naviglio"); Pulci, *Morgante Maggiore*. xxi, 165 ("ed or fortuna il tuo legno travaglia"); Sir William Mure, *Works*, I, 63 (*Dido and Aeneas*, I, 67, "Learne, noble warriours! Fortunes storme to beir"); Hoccleve, *Regement of Princes*, ll. 29–30 (Surety pitches her tent in poor estate to cover her from the "storm of descendyng"). Cf. the work of the Fata Morgana, Boiardo's *Orlando Innamorato*, II, viii, 61.

　[4] See De Guilleville's *Rommant des Trois Pelerinaiges*, fol. lxvii[vo], which

So it is that we hear of the "sea of Fortune,"[1] and even find it described for us:

> Par long temps j'ay nagié en l'onde
> De la cruelle mer parfonde
> De Fortune, qui par son sort
> M'a mené jusques a ung port
> Le plus maudit de tout le monde.
>
> Ung lac y a sans point de bonde,
> Qui d'eaue de pleurs tant fort radonde
> C'on n'y trouve ne fons ne bort:
> Par long temps [j'ay nagié en l'onde
> De la cruelle mer parfonde].[2]

This is only one of the various ways in which Fortune becomes connected with matters of the sea.[3] It is hardly strange, then, that the man of the Middle Ages who purposes a voyage wonders "If that fortuna with him stonde."[4]

makes Fortune's wheel, standing in the middle of the sea, a "caribdis." Cf. Lydgate, *Minor Poems*, ed. MacCracken, I, 69, ll. 293-295:

> From perellys passed with our present passage,
> Future swolwys of fortunys ffloodys,
> Dredfull Caribdys, Syrenes mortal rage.

See Deschamps, *Œuvres*, VI, 71, ll. 19 ff., and notice the phrase "fortune de mer" in the refrain. Cf. Christine de Pisan, *Œuvres*, I, 182 (lxii, 8 ff.); Masuccio, *Il Novellino*, p. 448 ("naufragio che da la invida fortuna lor era apparecchiato").

[1] Charles d'Orléans, *Poésies*, I, 43.
[2] Raynaud, *Rondeaux*, p. 25 (xxviii).
[3] Note also Gerbert of Aurillac, epist. xlv (Migne, vol. CXXXIX, col. 214) "uelut hoc turbulento tempore motum fortunæ refregimus"; Pulci, *Morgante Maggiore*, xx, 45,

> Ma la fortuna ch' è troppo invidiosa,
> Fece che mentre che Morgante mena
> A salvamento il legno ed ogni cosa,
> Subito si scoperse una balena,
> E viene verso la nave furiosa, etc.

[4] Gower, *Confessio Amantis*, ii, 2529.

TorquatoTasso,in his *Gerusalemme Liberata,* describes a

>picciola nave, e in poppa, quella,
>Che guidar gli dovea, fatal donzella.

IV

>Crinita fronte ella dimostra, e ciglia
>Cortesi e favorevoli e tranquille:
>E nel sembiante agli angioli somiglia;
>Tanta luce ivi par ch'arda e sfaville.
>La sua gonna or azzurra, ed or vermiglia
>Diresti; e si colora in guise mille;
>Sì ch' uom sempre diversa a sè la vede,
>Quantunque volte a riguardarla riede

· · · · · · · · · ·

VI

>Entrate, dice, o fortunati, in questa
>Nave, ond' io l'Oceàn secura varco,
>Cui destro è ciascun vento, ogni tempesta
>Tranquilla, e lieve ogni gravoso incarco.
>Per ministra e per duce or mi v' appresta
>Il mio signor, del favor suo non parco.
>Così parlò la donna.[1]

The Christian Fortuna makes a gracious guide on the sea. Thus Fortuna controls affairs of the sea,[2] and it is she

---

[1] *Gerusalemme Liberata,* XV, iii–vi (*Opere,* XXVI, 4 ff.). The omitted stanza is on the change of her colors, like the changing lights in the down of a dove. On page 5 a note to stanza 3 says, "Anche il Tasso in una delle Lettere inedite dichiara esser questa la Fortuna."

[2] For the idea in art, see Fortuna with a sail in the *Mirrour of Maiestie,* pl. 23 (after p. 63; note the inscription); Cousin, *Livre de Fortune,* plates 1 (ship in the background), 63 ("Fortune amenant la Tempête"), and cf. plates 49, 61, 143 (anchor), 157, 161; Fregoso, *Dialogo di Fortuna,* title-page (Fortune walking on the water with sail blown by the wind). Ripa (*Iconologia,* p. 170) thus describes "Fortuna Infelice": "Donna sopra vna naue senza timone, et con l'albero, et la vela rotti dal vento. La naue è la vita nostra mortale, la quale ogn' huomo cerca di condurre à qualche porto tranquillo di riposo; la vela, e l'albero spezzato, et gl'altri arnesi rotti, mostrano la priuatione della quiete, essendo la mala fortuna vn successo infelice, fuor dell' intedimento di colui che opera per elettione." See also Bocchi, *Symbolicae Quaestiones,* symbols xxiii (Fortuna with sail, and rudder?), lxiii (two figures with rudders), xcvii.

who sends the calm or the storm. In none of the passages cited is there a confusion of the goddess with the Italian abstract "fortuna," the literal meaning of which is "storm"; but may it not be possible that that Italian word of special meaning was derived from the abstraction "fortuna" which includes the gifts of our "fortune of the sea"?[1] At any rate, it is quite clear that we are justified in considering the goddess as much concerned with mediaeval ventures on the ocean. She it was whom the sailor thought of at the beginning of his great voyages of traffic and discovery.[2]

(4) The Fortune of Combat

Pico della Mirandola, in his philosophic mood, speaks of "fortuna quae in rebus bellicis plurimum dominatur." [3] To this comment Jean de Meun adds a cynical touch: "Bataille, en coi fortuna seult plus avoir de pooir que vertus." [4] The author of the *Complaynt of Scotlande*, who

[1] Du Cange's earliest reference to the "fortuna" which means storm is in a document of 1242 ("Bartholom. Scribae Annal. Genuenses ad ann. 1242"). There I find the expression ambiguous, as meaning possibly either the goddess or the storm: "Continuo ualida Fortuna maris, et uenti, et pluuiae regnare," etc. Du Cange also cites "Bernhardus *de Breydenbach*, Itiner. Hierosol., pag. 14," as saying, "Nisi forsitan tempestas maris, Fortuna appellata, id faciendum persuaderet." But this document is of the late fifteenth century.

[2] The shifting from a figurative to a literal "sea" and back again in these passages need not cause worry. The figurative could not have arisen without the literal idea. The "sea of life" and its "storms" came, of course, from actual experience of the sea and its dangers. The goddess, guiding the vessel in the sea of life, must have come from the idea of the goddess guiding the real vessel on the sea. At any rate, see the non-figurative uses above, p. 102, n. 1; Masuccio, *Il Novellino*, p. 257; Benoît de Ste. Maure, *Roman de Troie*, IV, 285, ll. 28412 ff.; Gower, *Confessio Amantis*, viii, 1320; Lydgate, *Troy Book*, ii, 3392 f., etc.; Dictys Cretensis, *Belli Troiani*, VI, v (quoted above, p. 101).   [3] *Opera*, I, 350 (*In Astrologiam*, lib. iii, cap. xxvii).

[4] *L'Art de Chevalerie*, p. 131.

elsewhere in his work denies Fortune any reality, tells us that "battellis consistis vndir the gouernance of fortune, ande nocht in the ingyne of men."[1] Thus Fortuna threatens to supplant even Mars and Bellona.[2] She not only wages her own private war with man, but she sits in judgment on the battles of men amongst themselves.

Fortune brings enemies together to provoke a fight.[3] She shows herself completely unfavorable, and sometimes causes the downfall of one particular side;[4] but she is

[1] Page 15, l. 24. With these references cf. Petrarch, *Vite d. Uomini*, II, 645 f. ("fortuna possente . . . in ogni cosa, ma in battaglia potentissima"); Boiardo, *Orlando Innamorato*, I, xvi, 1 ("più si mostra a caso de la guerra"); Guicciardini, *Opere Ined.*, I, 391 ("sottoposte alla potesta della fortuna"), with examples of victims in war.

[2] See Guido Cavalcanti, in *Poeti del Primo Secolo*, II, 320 ("non potrebbe far ch' io Non signoreggi tutto 'l regno mio"); Alberti, *Opere*, I, 202 ("Se cosi s'afferma, la Fortuna molto valere ove Marte s'impacci"). Cf. Gower, *Confessio Amantis*, vii, 892 (Mars stands "upon the fortune of batailes"); Lydgate, *Siege of Thebes*, ll. 4645 ff. (Fortune and Bellona work together), and *Troy Book*, iii, 200 ff. See *Gesta di Federico*, l. 1181 ("Nam Fortuna fauet, gladios Deus ipse ministrat"); contrast Gower, *Vox Clamantis*, iii, 403 ff. ("In cleri bellis scit magis ipse deus").

[3] Petrarch, *Vite d. Uomini*, I[1], 219; Gower, *Confessio Amantis*, ii, 2596 ff.; Lydgate, *Serpent of Division*, p. 51, ll. 16–17 ("þat he of aventure mette with þis manly man Iulius," etc.).

[4] *Gesta di Federico*, ll. 1073 f.; Petrarch, *Vite d. Uomini*, I[1], 211; Boccaccio, *Filocopo*, i (*Opere*, VII, 64), and *De Casibus*, p. 122; Frezzi, *Quadriregio*, I, 284, ll. 29–30 ("contra lei Non è fortezza, o senno, che vi vaglia"); Boiardo, *Orlando Innamorato*, III, i, 48; Medin, *Lamenti*, p. 43, ll. 13 ff.; Machiavelli, *De' Discorsi*, II, xvi (*Opere*, IV, 287); Jean Priorat, *Li Abrejance de l'Ordre de Chevalerie*, p. 53, ll. 1630 ff.; G. de Machaut, *Poésies*, ed. Chichmaref, II, 488, ll. 56 f.; Froissart, *Méliador*, II, 134, ll. 13918 f.; III, 176, ll. 27758 f.; Deschamps, *Œuvres*, V, 371 (mlxxiii); VII, 138, l. 21; *Le Petit Traittiet* (Pierre Michault's *Dance aux Aveugles*, p. 233); Alain Chartier, *Œuvres*, pp. 364 ("puis luy tourna fortune le doz"), 623 ("Fortune a tantost compassé Ung mal tout nouvel"), 641; Chaucer, *Legend of Good Women*, l. 589 ("as Fortune him oghte a shame," — of Mark Antony); Gower, *Mirour de l'Omme*, ll. 22079–22080, and *Confessio Amantis*, ii, 1790–1792; Lydgate, *Troy Book*,

famous for changing sides and may return to us. She is often in doubt herself, but she may again show her smiling face to our hosts;[1] she aids us, and increases our expectations;[2] she bestows victory,[3] and she brings

iii, 2529–2532; iv, 857, 1076 ff., 1088 ff.; v, 417 ff.; also *Siege of Thebes*, l. 4250 ("And thus fortunë hath on Grekys frownyd"), and *Albon and Amphabel*, iii, 494; Barbour, *The Bruce*, vii, 298–299 ("Fortoun has travalit us this day"); *The Complaynt of Scotlande*, p. 15, ll. 15 f. (Fortune adverse to Hannibal).

[1] *Gesta di Federico*, ll. 1699 ("Et rediens Fortuna iuuat uiresque ministrat"), 1703 ("Fortunam transisse uidens"), 2491 f. ("fortuna fauorem Subtraxit"); Dante, *De Monarchia*, II, xi, 45 ("fere Fortunam — ut dicam — incoepti poenituit"); Petrarch, *Vite d. Uomini*, I[1], 319 ("il bollore delle varie cose della fortuna . . . non pare durare in alcuna parte"); II, 357, 643 ("la fortuna parea deliberare"); also *Africa*, vii, 1034 ("Nutabat fortuna die"), cf. v, 211 ff.; Boccaccio, *Donne Famose*, p. 261 (cap. lxxviii, "stando per lungo spazio in dubbio"); also *De Casibus*, pp. 94 ("in decliuum fortunam labentem sentiret"), 109 ("paululum agitare uisa est"), 164 ("seque titubantem monstrauit, quasi dubia"); Pulci, *Morgante Maggiore*, xxiv, 134; Trissino, *Tutte le Opere*, I, 303, col. 2 (*Sofonisba*, "gli arrise la fortuna"); Guicciardini, *Opere Ined.*, I, 391; Gower, *Balades*, xx, 2 (*Works*, I, 354, peace comes after war); also *Cronica Tripertita*, iii, 189 ff. ("Omnes sorte pari dubitant qua parte iuuari. Tunc fortuna rotam diuertit," etc.); Lydgate, *Troy Book*, ii, 6675–6676 ("Fortune can transmewe Hir gery cours"), 8561–8562 ("For as hir whele went aboute rounde, Riȝt so þat day þei wan and lost her grounde"); iii, 2722 ("List Fortune a-wronge hir face wriþe"), 3602 ff.; iv, 1747 ff., 3271 ff. ("sodeyn torn of hir false visage").

[2] Petrarch, *Vite d. Uomini*, I[1], 309 ("suole aumentare le piccole speranze"); II, 645 f.; also *Africa*, vi, 347 ("spem fortuna ferat"); Boccaccio, *Filocopo*, i (*Opere*, VII, 37, 53); *Teseide*, v, 54 (*ibid.*, IX, 168, "Renderò grazie alla fortuna mia"); *Ameto* (*ibid.*, XV, 81); also *Donne Famose*, p. 29 (cap. xi), and *De Casibus*, pp. 80, 140; Jean de Condé, *Dits et Contes*, II, 188, ll. 641–642; Jean Priorat, *Li Abrejance de l'Ordre de Chevalerie*, p. 353, ll. 11230 ff. (cf. Jean de Meun, *L'Art de Chevalerie*, p. 175); Chaucer, *Knight's Tale*, A. 1860 ff.; Lydgate, *Siege of Thebes*, l. 4271; also *Albon and Amphabel*, ii, 809–810; and *Troy Book*, iii, 1312 f., 2651 f., 2832 f., 3185 f.

[3] *Gesta di Federico*, ll. 1206 f. ("palmam Perdere, quam tandem dederat Fortuna secunda"); Petrarch, *Africa*, ii, 188 f.; Ariosto, *Orlando Furioso*, XXIV, xxvi; Chaucer, *Knight's Tale*, A. 915 f.; Gower, *Mirour de l'Omme*, ll. 17092 f., 22024 ff., 22048–22050; Lydgate, *Troy Book*, ii, 1991; Gregory

peace.[1]   In these ways Fortune lives up to her reputation of having particular power in warfare and combat.[2]

(5) THE FORTUNE OF FAME

Since Fortune sends victory in warfare to one side or the other, since her gifts include dignities most conspicuously, and since on her depends success in various kinds of achievements, she is therefore much concerned with the bestowal of fame.   She and Fame are at all times closely associated, but sometimes she appears actually doing the work of Fame.[3]

Smith, *Specimens of Middle Scots*, p. 74 (*The Portous of Nobleness*). See drawing, Scarlattini, *Homo Symbolicus*, II, 54 ("quae dextera sua militem coronet . . . fortunam et uictoriam imperatoris designant"); cf. Ritson, *Ancient English Metrical Romances*, III, 148, ll. 257–258,

> I pray to god and our lady,
> Sende you the whele of vyctory:

Cf. Mead's note on this line in his edition of the *Squyr of Lowe Degre*, Albion Series, Boston, 1904, p. 61, n. 258.

See Ripa, *Iconologia*, p. 171: "Donna che con la destra mano tiene vn cornucopia, et vn ramo d'alloro, con la sinistra mano s'appoggia ad vn timone; significando, ch'ella fa trionfare chiunque vuole, et la dimostratione di ciò si rappresenta con il ramo dell' alloro." See, too, the frontispiece to W. V. Cooper's translation of Boethius (Dent ed.) and his note at p. 169.

[1] Deschamps, *Œuvres*, I, 162 (lxvi); Gower, *Confessio Amantis*, iii, 1840–1841.

[2] See the wheel come full circle, Jean de Condé, *Dits et Contes*, II, 347, ll. 1421 ff. Cf. Gower, *Confessio Amantis*, vii, 3374–3375; also his poem *In Praise of Peace*, ll. 115–116 (*Works*, III, 484); and see the emblem of the Northumbrian in his *Cronica Tripertita*, i, 55 f. (*ibid.*, IV, 315).

[3] See *Poesies Ital. Ined.*, IV, 285; Ariosto, *Orlando Furioso*, XXXIV, lxxiv, and see XXII, xciii ("la vaga Fama"); Chaucer, *Hous of Fame*, iii, 1547 (Fortune is the sister of Fame), 1982 f. (Aventure is the "moder of tydinges"); Gower, *O Deus Immense* (*Works*, IV, 362–364), ll. 66–70,

> Fama ferens uerba que dulcia sunt et acerba.
> Fama cito crescit, subito tamen illa uanescit,
> Saltem fortuna stabilis quia non manet una:

Boccaccio requests Fortuna that his book be not obscure among men: "Et quod obscurum praesentibus nomen meum est, tuo illustratum fulgore clarum apud posteros habeatur."[1] In place of Fortune's handmaids "Wealth" and "Honors," whom Boethius notes,[2] Gower refers to her servants Renomée and Desfame, who fly faster than the swallow, bearing news of her court, to-day fair news, to-morrow ugly; each has a big horn suspended from her neck, and these horns they sometimes exchange.[3] Chaucer, in the *Hous of Fame*, describes his figure of Fame with many of the expressions familiar in the tradition of Fortuna and with much of her apparatus. He gives Fame two trumpets of good and evil rumor respectively. In translating *De Casibus*, Lydgate adds the figure of the two trumpets and the house of Fame, and attributes these to Fortune:

> Principio scire fortunam seu stabilire,
> Non est humanum super hoc quid ponere planum.

Contrast Alex. Montgomerie, *Poems*, 1887, p. 97 (xvi, 5–6):

> In spyt of fortun, I shall flie with fame;
> Sho may my corps, bot not my curage kill.

See Dante, *Inferno*, xv, 70 f.; Petrarch, *Rime*, ed. Albertini, II, 298 (son. xiii); Boiardo, *Orlando Innamorato*, II, xi, 35. In Frezzi's *Quadriregio*, lib. ii, cap. x (I, 134, ll. 1 ff.), "la falsa Opinion" is described with an appearance very much like that of Fortune. See, e. g., in her speech:

> Io fo povero alcun nella ricchezza;
> E fo la povertà allegra tanto,
> Ch' alcun la porta, e nulla n' ha gravezza.

See also Machiavelli, *De'Discorsi*, lib. iii, cap. xxx (*Opere*, V, 128); cf. Gower, *Confessio Amantis*, iv, 1763.

[1] *De Casibus*, VI, i, p. 147.
[2] *Cons. Philos.*, II, pr. ii, 16 ff.
[3] *Mirour de l'Omme*, passage concerning Fortune, beginning at line 22081.

In which processe thou dost gret diligence
as they deserue to yeue them thanke or blame
Settest vp one in royal excellence,
within mine house called the house of fame
the golden trumpet with blastes of good name,
Enhaunceth one to ful hye parties
where Jupiter sitteth among the heuenly skies.

Another trumpet of sownes ful vengeable
which bloweth vp at feastes funerall,
Nothing bright, but of colour sable,
Farre fro my fauour deadly and mortall,
To plonge princes from their estate royal,
whan I am wroth to make them loute lowe
Than of malice I doe that trumpet blowe.[1]

Pierre Michault gives two similar trumpets to Eur and Maleur.[2]

Thus Fortune is never quite free from the charges of those who are discontented with their fame. As her gifts include glory, so we find her pretty much responsible for our reputation, good or bad.

(6) PERSONAL FORTUNA

The idea of having a peculiar cult of one's own Fortuna seems to have been a favorite at all periods. I do not refer merely to what is likely to constitute our idea of one's personal "fortune" in the abstract sense, but to the conception of a tutelary goddess who is particularly interested in one, and who dispenses to one her bounties or withholds them. In the *Morgante Maggiore* we hear the

---

[1] *Fall of Princes*, VI, i, stanzas 16–17 (1554 ed., fol. cxliii[vo] f.; 1558 ed., fol. cxxxiv[vo]).

[2] *La Dance aux Aveugles*, pp. 30 f. Eur stands on a high pillar, with a trumpet of silver; Maleur is "au plus bas du trosne," holding an old worn-out wooden one mended with strings.

PLATE 5

FORTUNE AND SAPIENCE

cry, "O mia fortuna, ove mi guidi o meni?" [1] And in the *Confessio Amantis* we read:

> For whan mi fortune overcasteth
> Hire whiel and is to me so strange,
> And that I se sche wol noght change,
> Than caste I al the world aboute, etc.[2]

The goddess referred to here is certainly personal.[3] Very possibly it was her vogue in this cult which spread the use of the abstract "my fortune," meaning "what my Fortune brings me."

(7) FORTUNA PUBLICA

As the individual believed that a particular Fortune took his case into consideration, that a particular aspect of the goddess had influence over his life, so he held that a special aspect of the goddess held sway over the city and over the state.

The Fortune of the city is certainly uppermost in the laments concerning the destruction of Milan.[4] Florence is

---

[1] Pulci, canto xxvii, st. 188.   [2] Book iii, ll. 1136–1139.

[3] See Lucan, *Pharsalia*, vii, 649; *Poesie Ital. Ined.*, III, 19; Petrarch, *Scritt. Ined.*, p. 312; also *Rime*, ed. Albertini, I, 323 (sest. viii), 341 (son. cc); ed. Mestica, p. 465 (canz. xxvi [xlv], 7–8); also *Vite d. Uomini*, I², 831 ("sua malvagia fortuna"), and *Africa*, i, 280; Boccaccio, *Teseide*, iii, 59–60 (*Opere*, IX, 110); also *De Casibus*, pp. 38, 83 ("mitiorem sibi quam caeteris retrolapsis fortunam existimans"); Masuccio, *Il Novellino*, pp. 280, 359; Sannazaro, *Opere*, p. 428 (*Egloga*); Gareth, *Rime*, II, 307 (*Metamor.*, ii, 30); Alberti, *Opere*, III, 367, 374; Chaucer, *Knight's Tale*, A. 2658 f.

[4] See *Gedicht auf die Zerstörung Mailands* and *Gesta di Federico*. Note in the first of these the lines (22 ff.):

> Nil mireris, homo, quia cuncta sub orbe iubentur
> Ordine fatorum tandem labefacta perire.
> Quicquid Theba fuit, quicquid Troiana iuuentus,
> Quicquid Roma potens, rota mendacissima strauit.
> Experienda fui fortune fraudibus iisdem.

subject to Fortune's sway; [1] so also are Rome [2] and Syracuse.[3] Troy is naturally the most familiar example of the goddess's infidelity:

> E quando la fortuna volse in basso
> L'altezza de' Troian che tutto ardiva,
> Sì che insieme col regno il re fu casso,

says Dante.[4] Thus she caused the greatest of all civic tragedies famous in the Middle Ages.[5]

Not only is Fortune the goddess of the city, but she is also the goddess of the people of the city, and, indeed, of the community.[6] So she becomes the Fortune of the state, and we hear of "l'Italica fortuna" [7] and "la Fortuna degli Spagnuoli." [8]

> Non te pretereat populi fortuna potentis
> Publica, set sapiens talia fata caue,

says Gower.[9]

[1] Fazio d. Uberti, *Liriche*, p. 135 ("Poi che fortuna nel viso ti ride").

[2] Wace, *Roman de Brut*, ll. 3965 f.; Gower, *Mirour de l'Omme*, ll. 22158 ("Rome, a qui fuist mere Fortune et la droite emperere").

[3] Hoccleve, *Regement of Princes*, ll. 3221 f. ("O citee! syn fortune was contrarie To the in o part," etc.).

[4] *Inferno*, xxx, 13–15 (note the mention of "altezza").

[5] See also references to Troy, Rome, Pisa, and many other Italian cities, in Medin's *Ballata della Fortuna* (*Il Propugnatore*, new ser., II[1], 1889, pp. 112 f.; pp. 108 f. show how this poem derives in other ways from Dante). See *Carmina Burana*, p. 45 (lxxv, st. 3); Wright, *Satirical Poets*, I, 21 f.; Boccaccio, *Amorosa Visione*, xxxiv (*Opere*, XIV); Christine de Pisan, *Œuvres*, II, 93, ll. 1482–1483; Alain Chartier, *Œuvres*, p. 474 (Carthage and Troy). Cf. Cousin, pl. 153.

[6] See Chaucer, *Troilus and Criseyde*, i, 138–140 (Fortune controls both Trojans and Greeks); Lydgate, *Troy Book*, iv, 5999 ff.

[7] Gareth, *Rime*, II, 236 (son. cxcix, "L'Italica fortuna ha privilegio Di volger la sua rota," etc.); see also Guicciardini, *Opere Ined.*, I, 275, 288.

[8] Guicciardini, *Opere Ined.*, I, 288.

[9] *Vox Clamantis*, vi, 623–624.

(8) The Fortune of Time

Fortune and Time are frequently named together and are apparently associated.[1] Both give blows, become contrary, raise and ruin.[2] Fortune actually does the work of Time, as we see in such phrases as these: "se la fortuna fa passare il tempo di dieciotto anni";[3] "fortuna . . . Volgendo gli anni nel suo corso lieve";[4] "ella varia i tempi":[5]

> And lat Fortoun wirk furthe hir rage;
> Quhen that no rasoun may assuage,
> Quhill that hir glas be run and past.[6]

Thus Fortuna has a glass, and in one drawing she has, like Father Time, a scythe.[7]

Controlling times and seasons in this way, Fortune may easily come to represent the goddess who is in control of

[1] For Fortune as the goddess of Time, see Fowler, *Roman Festivals*, p. 172. Cf. Cousin's plate 69 ("Fortune, Amor, Tempus, et Locus"; Fortune holds a clock in her hand).

[2] See Boccaccio, *Filostrato*, IV, clxvi (*Opere*, XIII, 168, "tor gli anni"); Pontano, *Carmina*, I, 28 (*Urania*, i, 875–880; Fortune, Tempus, and Locus sit together in the council of the gods); Ariosto, *Orlando Furioso*, I, lvii; XXXIV, lxxiii ("per colpa di tempo o di Fortuna"); G. de Machaut, *Livre du Voir-Dit*, p. 258 ("se Fortune ou li temps me sont contraire"); Laing, *Scottish Worthies*, p. 142 ("Oft Tyme and Fortone ruin'd hes and rais'd"); Pinkerton, *Ancient Scotish Poems*, II, 248, ll. 19–20.

[3] Sercambi, *Novelle*, ed. Renier, p. 303 (no. 86).

[4] Ariosto, *Orlando Furioso*, XLII, lxxxiv.

[5] Machiavelli, *De' Discorsi*, III, ix (*Opere*, V, 60). Cf. Baehrens, *Poetae Latini Minores*, IV, 148, no. 145 ("Iniusto arbitrio tempora dividens").

[6] Dunbar, *Meditatioun in Wyntir*, ll. 23–25 (*Poems*, II, 234). See also Benoît de Ste. Maure, *Roman de Troie*, II, 107, l. 10175; Charles d' Orléans, *Poésies*, II, 84 (xiv).

[7] Cousin, *Livre de Fortune*, pl. 179 ("Fortune tenant un Rasoir"). See a drawing of Time on a wheel, holding a razor and labelled "Occasio," in John Gau's *Richt Vay*, p. 110. As to whether Cousin's "Rasoir" is really a razor, and whether the figure in Gau's book really represents Occasio, see discussion in the text above the drawing. See Cousin, pl. 17.

the opportune moment. Studies of Matzke and others have shown the growth of the confusion between Occasio and Fortuna, from the distichs of Cato according to Élie de Wincestre and Everard down through the works of Politian and Boiardo.[1] This mingling of ideas is represented by the symbolic arrangement of the hair. Fortune, standing for Occasio, has a long forelock, while the back of her head is bald. The forelock one must seize in order to prevail upon the goddess before she slips away:

> Ha! Perceval, fortune est cauve
> Derrière et devant chevelue.
> Maudehait ait ki te salve
> Et ki nul bien te viut ne prie.[2]

So much for the symbolic description.

[1] It would be hard to add to the lists of passages collected by these scholars. See J. E. Matzke, *Source of " To Take Time by the Forelock,"* Mod. Lang. Assoc., *Publ.*, VIII, 303 ff.; G. L. Kittredge on the same subject, *Modern Language Notes*, VIII, 230 ff., and IX, 95; also Karl Pietsch, *ibid.*, VIII, 235 ff. For the confusion with Death, notice Matzke above, p. 331; and see the confusion of Ventura with Occasio in Andrea Calmo's *Lettere*, ed. Rossi, p. 450 ("dietro chalua e-cchol cuffetto inn alto," etc.).

[2] *Perceval le Gallois*, II, 201–202, ll. 6024–6027. See Ariosto, *Orlando Furioso*, XXX, xxv; XLVI, cxxxv. For pictures of this confusion and of Occasio herself with her forelock, see citations referred to in note 1 above; Green, *Shakespeare and the Emblem Writers*, pl. 12, opposite p. 265 (of 1605); Alciati, *Emblems*, Paris, 1534, p. 20 (on a wheel; same in 1536 ed.), Augsburg, 1531, sig. A8 (on a ball); see the *Dream of Poliphilus*, ed. Appell, fig. 5 (at the top of a temple to the sun is a winged female figure, with cornucopia and floating robes, and what seems to be a long forelock. "This figure is made so as to turn with the slightest breeze.") See Cousin, *Livre de Fortune*, pls. 15 ("L'Occasion de la Fortune"), and 17 ("La Fortune ou le Dieu de l'Occasion"); Bocchi, *Symbolicae Quaestiones*, symb. li (a naked figure with a forelock, being lifted from the sea; note the inscription). See reference to these or similar figures in art by Simund de Freine, *Roman de Philosophie*, ll. 291 ff. (and observe Matzke's note, p. lxviii). Also cf. Bocchi's symbol lxxi.

The spirit of this fusion of ideas is found in various passages in which we see Fortune doing the actual duties of Occasio and comporting herself in the manner of the lady of the unique coiffure. Sacchetti puts it thus: "Così fa tutto dì la fortuna, che molte volte si mostra lieta, per vedere chi la sa pigliare; e molte volte chi meglio la sa pigliare, ne rimane in camicia . . . chi non piglia il bene, quando la fortuna e'l tempo gnel concede, il più delle volte, quando si ripensa, il rivorrebbe, e non lo ritruova, se non aspettasse trentasei migliaja d'anni."[1] Thus Fortuna is goddess of time in general and deity of the lucky moment.

(9) THE FORTUNE OF DEATH

Watriquet de Couvin says that Eürs and Fortune are afraid of only one conceivable creature on this earth, and that is Death.[2] But Death and Fortune at an early period are found coöperating quite amicably, with little distinction between their work.[3] Sometimes a trio is formed in

[1] Sacchetti, *Novelle*, III, 269. See also Boccaccio, *De Casibus*, pp. 128 ("seu sic disponente fortuna rerum oportunitatem secutus est"), 225 ("dum expectaret, si forsan fortuna uiam aliquam aperiret ad eam oportunitatum omnium deuenit penuriam, ut," etc.); Machiavelli, *De' Discorsi*, lib. ii (*Opere*, IV, 222); Christine de Pisan, *Œuvres*, III, 34, xlv; Chaucer, *Troilus and Criseyde*, ii, 281 ff.; Lydgate, *Troy Book*, iii, 2001 ff. (l. 2010, "Anoþer tyme he schal hir nat embrace").

[2] *Dits*, p. 398, ll. 47 ff. (Eürs); p. 80, ll. 77 ff. (Fortune). See, too, Lucan's *Pharsalia*, vii, 818. Cf. Boiardo, *Orlando Innamorato*, I, xii, 58; Ariosto, *Orlando Furioso*, III, xvi; Pierre Michault, *Complainte* (*Dance aux Aveugles*, p. 128); Lydgate, *Temple of Glas*, App. I (continuation of MSS.), ll. 362 ff. (Schick's ed., pp. 63 ff.; ll. 389 f., the only remedy against Fortune is death); Dunbar, *Elegy*, ll. 7 f. (*Poems*, II, 63, "Fortun, allace! now may thow weir the sabill").

[3] Dante, canzone x, l. 90; Petrarch, *Rime*, ed. Albertini, II, 155 (canz. viii, "O saldo scudo," etc.); Bernardo Pulci, in Lorenzo de' Medici's *Poesie*

the persons of Love, Death, and Fortune,[1] and in Pierre Michault's *Dance aux Aveugles* these three figures seem to be practically equated.

Before the time of Watriquet de Couvin, indeed, Fortune had actually invaded the territory of Death and taken over his special prerogatives. In one of the minor Latin poets, probably of the period after the Golden Age but before the real opening of the Middle Ages, we read: "Haec [Fortuna] aufert iuuenes ac retinet senes."[2] Antithesis of a similar kind is found in a French *dit* of a much later period, which includes a description of a man who trusts in her, a "*Fols-s'i-fie*":

> Et il cuide miex vivre en granz solempnitez,
> Lendemain est trovez murtris et soubitez.[3]

(1801), II, 90; Ariosto, *Orlando Furioso*, III, xxxviii ("Morte o Fortuna invidíosa e ria"); Alexandre de Bernay, *Li Romans d'Alixandre*, ed. Michelant, pp. 540 f., ll. 33 ff.; Watriquet de Couvin, *Dits*, p. 270, ll. 1245 ff.; Froissart, *Œuvres*, I, 146, ll. 2003 ff.; Lydgate, *Daunce of Machabree*, p. 333, prol., st. 2; also *Troy Book*, iii, 4920 ff., 4971 ff.; and iv, 4271 ff. (all have "Antropos" and Fortune). See *Chaucer's Dream* (or *The Isle of Ladies*), in *Works*, ed. Morris, V, 104, ll. 607 ff. (Death's "subtill double face"); Weinhold, *Glücksrad und Lebensrad*, pp. 21 ff. (the figure of Fortune becomes the figure of Death; on p. 24 see the inscription "nemini parco").

[1] Boccaccio, *Filostrato*, IV, cxx (*Opere*, XIII, 152); Benivieni, *Opere*, p. 126vo; Lorenzo de' Medici, *Poesie* (1801), I, 67; Sannazaro, *Opere*, p. 388, son. lxi; Boiardo, *Orlando Innamorato*, I, xxviii, 36; Christine de Pisan, *Œuvres*, II, 92, ll. 1445 ff. (the figures are not all named, but the ideas are associated). Cf. Chaucer, *Troilus and Criseyde*, iv, 1189 f.; Pulci, *Morgante Maggiore*, vii, 70,

> Tu lasci me come amante fedele
> Perdere insieme e la vita e la dama,
> Che cosi vuol la fortuna crudele.

[2] Baehrens, *Poetae Latini Minores*, IV, 148, no. 145. The author is Asclepiadius, of the fourth century probably, and one of the "twelve sages." For his date, see *ibid.*, p. 42.

[3] Jubinal, *Contes, Dits*, etc., I, 197.

The tradition of Fortune's causing death is widespread and continuous, and takes an important place in all mediaeval elegiac poetry.[1] In art, too, the goddess is closely associated with Death, or she herself by a turn of the

[1] Guido delle Colonne, *Hystoria Troiana*, sig. a 6[vo], col. 2 ("conuertat in cinerem," etc.); sig. i 2, col. 1 ("pendeat mors et ita"); Cino da Pistoia, *Poesie* (1826), p. 140, canz. xv (death of Arrigo VII); Boccaccio, *Filocopo* (*Opere*, VII, 255, VIII, 189); also *Teseide*, v, 94 (*ibid.*, IX, 181), and *Donne Famose*, p. 85 (cap. xxxi); Sercambi, *Novelle*, ed. Renier, p. 304 (no. 86); Masuccio, *Il Novellino*, p. 342; Giov. Fiorentino, *Il Pecorone*, I, 55 (iii, 1); Alberti, *Opere*, III, 380; Boiardo, *Orlando Innamorato*, I, xii, 73, and xxi, 47 ("Per farmi ora morir con crudeltade . . . Di te m'andrò dolendo ne l'Inferno"); II, i, 4; Ariosto, *Orlando Furioso*, VIII, xl–xliv ("what can I give thee more, Fortuna, but my life?"); XX, cxxxii–cxxxiii; XXX, liii; Trissino, *Tutte le Opere*, I, 360 (serv.); Watriquet de Couvin, *Dits*, p. 214, ll. 498 ff. ("A tour de mort sanz redrecier"); *Pierre de la Broche* (Monmerqué and Michel, *Théâtre Français*, pp. 213–214); Philippe de Beaumanoir, *Jehan et Blonde*, ll. 549 ff. (*Œuvres*, II, 20); Jean de Condé, *Dits et Contes*, III, 54, ll. 154 ff.; G. de Machaut, *Poésies*, ed. Chichmaref, II, 371 (*Le Lay Mortel*, ll. 3 ff.), 417 (ll. 62–63, "l'un garist, L'autre mourdrist"), 480 (ll. 195 ff.), 498 (ll. 29 ff.); Froissart, *Œuvres*, II, 21 (ll. 704 f., "jusques à la mort le mainne"), 267 f. (see especially ll. 179 ff.); Deschamps, *Œuvres*, III, 387, ll. 11–15); Christine de Pisan, *Œuvres*, I, 11 (*Cent Balades*, x, "Se Fortune a ma mort jurée"); II, 198 (ll. 1275 ff.), 203 (ll. 1454 ff., "qui a mort me convoye"); III, 304 (lxxxxvi, 15 ff.); also *Livre du Chemin*, p. 5, ll. 110 f.; Alain Chartier, *Œuvres*, pp. 534 (*Complaincte contre la Mort*), 677 ("et fortune sa mort querroit"); Charles d' Orléans, *Poésies*, I, 73 ("elle voulsist hors de ce monde oster"); II, 154; Chaucer, *Troilus and Criseyde*, ii, 335; iv, 260 ff., 274 ff., 1192 ff.; v, 1763–1764 (cf. *Knight's Tale*, A. 925 ff., — the ladies have lost their husbands, — and *Monk's Tale*, B. 3586 ff., 3629 ff., 3644 ff.); Gower, *Vox Clamantis*, i, 1527 f., and *Mirour de l'Omme*, ll. 22061 ff. ("Huy luy fist Roys, et l'endemein L'enpuisonna"); Lydgate, *Troy Book*, ii, 3866 f. (notice "tyme"); iv, 3502 ff., 3601 ff.; the *Pearl*, l. 306 ("þaȝ fortune dyd your flesch to dyȝe"); *Melusine*, ll. 115 f., and the passage 269 ff. (ll. 282–283, thou hast destroyed and damned me); *Chaucer's Dream* (or *The Isle of Ladies*), l. 198 (*Works*, ed. Morris, V, 92); Pinkerton, *Ancient Scotish Poems*, II, 248, ll. 11–12 (*Elegie*), and 250, l. 16, "Quhairin I knaw *Fortoun* hes maid my tomb"). See, in later times, Pischedda, *Canti Popolari*, pp. 36–39.

wheel sends men into the grave.[1] Hence it is not going too far to say that Fortune succeeds in sometimes usurping the place of Death in the thought of the Middle Ages. Some hints as to her methods of causing death are furnished us in the theme of illnesses which she brings, and in the reference to her causing a man to be hanged. Fortune deforms, gives distemper, or brings on a fever;[2] and she may lead one to the gibbet.[3]

(10) Other Cults

The "Fortune of Abundance" in Ancient Rome may be regarded as surviving in the general idea of Fortune the giver, the bestower of riches; but, on the whole, the lavishness of the goddess does not receive so much attention in the Middle Ages as does the naming of her gifts. We know that she gives, but authors spend more of their time in complaining about her reluctance to give. She appears frequently in art with her symbol, the cornu-

[1] See Death turning a wheel, Weinhold, *Glücksrad und Lebensrad*, tafel ii; figure of Death below the wheel, *Fiske's Bibl. Notices*, III, p. 38 (description of the 1637 ed. of Petrarch's *De Remediis*); Death in the background, Fortune and the wheel in the foreground, Du Sommerard, *Album*, vol. II, ser. 4, pl. 40; grave or coffin under the wheel, Boll, *Die Lebensalter*, Abb. 3, 4 (opposite p. 144). See the centrifugal wheel, with a pit or grave under it, noticed on pages 160–163 below; and the wheel of Vita and Mors, discussed by Förster in Herrig's *Archiv*, CXXIX, 45–49 (§ 18).

[2] Boccaccio, *Teseide*, iv, 56 (*Opere*, IX, 138); Burchiello, *Sonetti*, pp. 215–216; Alberti, *Opere*, III, 167 ("febbre"); *Roman de la Rose*, ll. 4916 ff.; Froissart, *Œuvres*, I, 177, ll. 3032 ff.; Dinaux, *Trouvères*, II, 181; Lydgate, *Fabula Duorum Mercatorum*, ll. 197 ff. (one of the merchants falls sick).

[3] Poliziano, *Prose Volgari*, p. 105 (iii), "La Fortuna disse al Salviati: Ecco che io ti appresento il capestro et il cappello verde; piglia quel che tu vuoi." See also Pulci, *Morgante Maggiore*, xi, 101; *Roman de la Rose*, ll. 6545, 6557; Chaucer, *Monk's Tale*, B. 3924; Lindsay, *Satyre of the thrie Estaits*, l. 4022 (Dissait, about to be hanged, says, "I trow wan-fortune brocht me heir").

copia,[1] but such drawings perhaps derive straight from classical art rather than from contemporary popular thought.[2]

Bona and Mala Fortuna survive clearly enough in favorable and unfavorable Fortune.[3] Perhaps in Gower's line, "Tho was the fortune of prouesse," [4] we have the idea of Fortuna Virilis! In the Fortune who limes or snares we have possibly a reawakening of the idea of Fortuna Viscata.[5]

Such are the principal divisions of the great cult of Fortuna during mediaeval times. To all intents and purposes Fortune has become the goddess of love, of the sea, of combat, and of fame, the deity of the individual, of the city and of the state, of time and of death. She is the bestower, and she is sometimes kind and sometimes unkind. Let us turn back for a moment to the cults in the period of the Empire in Rome.[6] There we find the following classification sufficient to cover practically all the

[1] See Ripa, *Iconologia*, p. 170 ("*Fortuna Buona* . . . *Donna* . . . che . . . con la sinistra mano tiene un cornucopia"; and see four other cases on pp. 169–171, two with the cornucopia in the right hand); Barbier de Montault, *Traité*, I, 163, § 5; Bocchi, *Symbolicae Quaestiones*, symbols xxiii, lxiii, xcvii; Cousin, pls. 5, 11, 101, 113, 145; Reinach, *Répertoire*, II, 247 ff.

[2] See Arnobius, *Adversus Gentes*, vi, 25 (Migne, vol. V, col. 1214). Cf. Boethius, *Cons. Philos.*, II, met. ii, 5–6; William of Malmesbury, *Gesta Regum*, I, 230, § 189; Gower, *Confessio Amantis*, prol., ll. 137–140,

> For every climat hath his diel
> After the tornynge of the whiel,
> Which blinde fortune overthroweth;
> Whereof the certain noman knoweth.

[3] Cf. pp. 40 ff., above.
[4] *Confessio Amantis*, prol., l. 98.
[5] See p. 82, above. Cf. Cousin, pl. 3.
[6] See *Smith College Studies in Modern Languages*, III, 153–156.

specialized cults of the worship of Fortune during her most flourishing period: Fortuna Bona and Mala; Fortune of the city; Fortune of love; Fortuna Dux, Fortune of the sea (the goddess behind the storm, or the deity who guides the vessel if we include Fortuna Dux); Fortune of the individual, of war, and of fame. The parallel of the cults is striking enough in itself without further comment.

It may be objected, however, that in the Middle Ages we find merely the evidence of Fortune at work, whereas in Rome we have the established cults themselves; and that the comparison of Fortune's functions with her cults is arbitrary and misleading. In answer to such an objection I may say that I have compared her duties and activities in Rome, as inferred from her cults and from the passages in which her work is described, with her similar duties and activities in later times, and I have suggested that, although these duties were not formally prescribed or labelled during the Middle Ages in the manner of officially accepted worship, yet they themselves suggest the survival of the older cults in spite of public disapproval. The worship was stamped out, the temples were in ruins; but the force of the old cults remained alive, and, like a spirit among the ruins, Fortune continued to guide on land and on sea, to arbitrate in the clash of warfare, to bestow the laurel wreath, to bring lovers into each other's arms, and to lead her devotee with particular attention through hours and days, until she saw fit to borrow the shears from Atropos and snip his thin-spun thread of life.

CHAPTER IV

THE DWELLING-PLACE OF FORTUNE

IN the literature of ancient Rome there are few, if any, hints for the description of Fortune's dwelling-place. She dwelt naturally with the other gods, and this home did not take the form of an actual house. Her temples might have offered some suggestions, but apparently they were not conceived under any symbolism which would carry out the allegory of the goddess. Of course, mediaeval writers always tried to be allegorical in depicting her. Some material concerning palaces fit to be the residence of Fortune may be found in the study of the palace of Venus in the Court of Love,[1] but the passages containing such details seem to have had little influence on the conceptions of Fortune's castle.

There is one description of the abode of Venus, however, which has possibly contributed some ideas. Claudian (fl. A.D. 400) tells us in his poem *De Nuptiis Honorii et Mariae* that the home of Venus is in a flat plain, on the top of a mountain which man cannot climb. The place is enclosed by a golden wall. It is not subject to storms of wind or snow; but perpetual spring reigns, flowers bloom, and birds sing continually. Two fountains are there, one sweet and one bitter, in which the arrows of Cupid are tempered. The palace where Venus is enthroned is a

[1] Neilson, *Origins and Sources of the Court of Love*, pp. 11 ff.

scene of splendor, built of precious stones and other rich materials. In it dwell various divinities besides Venus and her son — Licentia, Irae, Excubiae, Lacrymae, Pallor, etc.[1] In this summary of Claudian's description the important elements to note are (1) the inaccessible mountain; (2) the garden, here not exposed to storms of any kind; (3) the fountains of sweet and bitter liquid; (4) the sumptuous and brilliant palace; (5) the court.

These details are strikingly similar to some of those assigned to the dwelling-place of Fortune in mediaeval times as we shall see it later depicted; but without some further construction the symbolic meaning of the picture is not satisfactory for the cult of Fortune. Boethius gives us an account of a house that suits the inconstant character of the fickle goddess, when he offers us advice about the kind of figurative abode which we who seek security should avoid:

> Quiquis uolet perennem
>   Cautus ponere sedem
> Stabilisque nec sonori
>   Sterni flatibus euri
> Et fluctibus minantem
>   Curat spernere pontum,
> Montis cacumen alti,
>   Bibulas uitet harenas.
> Illud proteruus auster
>   Totis uiribus urget,
> Hae pendulum solutae
>   Pondus ferre recusant.
> Fugiens periculosam
>   Sortem sedis amoenae
> Humili domum memento
>   Certus figere saxo.

---

[1] See Claudian, *De Nuptiis*, ll. 49 ff. A summary of the description appears in Neilson's *Court of Love*, pp. 15 f.

Quamuis tonet ruinis
    Miscens aequora uentus,
Tu conditus quieti
    Felix robore ualli,
Duces serenus aeuum
    Ridens aetheris iras.[1]

Here the lofty mountain becomes an exposed and particularly dangerous site for a dwelling,[2] and all the more so if it is surrounded by the sea. The hill is swept by a gale, and, perhaps because of its pride in comparison with the modesty of the "humili saxo," it all the more tempts the gods to smite it. One might object that this is a peculiarly risky location for even the goddess of chance to select for her permanent home; but, as I have shown elsewhere,[3] the Fortune who first chooses this scene for her activities is the abstraction personified and not the goddess, the type and not the symbol. In other words, worldly possessions rest on a shaky foundation and are exposed to the winds of adversity, which naturally the real goddess could not suffer.

[1] *Cons. Philos.*, II, met. iv: "He that would build on a lasting resting-place; who would be firm to resist the blasts of the storming wind; who seeks, too, safety where he may contemn the surge and threatening of the sea; must leave the lofty mountain's top, and leave the thirsting sands. The hill is swept by all the might of the headstrong gale; the sands dissolve, and will not bear the load upon them. Let him fly the danger in a lot which is pleasant rest unto the eye; let him be mindful to set his house surely upon the lowly rock. Then let the wind bellow, confounding wreckage in the sea, and thou wilt still be founded upon unmoving peace, wilt be blessed in the strength of thy defence; thy life will be spent in calmness, and thou mayest mock the raging passions of the air" (trans. W. V. Cooper, Dent ed.). For the suggestion of this passage, see Galpin, Mod. Lang. Assoc., *Publ.*, XXIV, 337 f.

[2] Note, too, the emphasis on the danger of the "bibulas harenas," with obvious Scriptural reference.

[3] *Smith College Studies in Modern Languages*, III, 189.

I

The first actual account of the house of Fortune was given in the twelfth century by Alanus de Insulis, in his poem the *Anticlaudianus*. His description runs as follows:

In the midst of the sea there is a cliff, which the water lashes continually and with which the wave disputes and has strife. This cliff, beaten in various wise and smitten by continual movement, is now fully buried in the waves; again, rising from the sea, it breathes the upper air. It does not retain its shape. Each moment various changes transform it. Now it is covered with flowers and Zephyr breathes upon it; again, Boreas cruelly destroys all the flowers. There are trees of diverse nature. One remains barren, the other brings forth fruit. One rejoices in new leaves, the other "reft of leaves doth weep." One is green, more are sere. One blooms, the others are flowerless. One rises high, the others sink to earth. One has increase, the others waste away. The laurel wanes, the myrtle gives fruit. The olive is dry, the willow bears. Here thorn-thickets, armed with their darts, threaten wounds, and the shaggy yew hurts the hands as it leaps up. Seldom sings the nightingale. The owl, messenger of adversity, prophesies dire events.

Here two streams flow, different in source, in appearance, and in taste. One has a very sweet liquid. With its honey it seduces many, and they that drink the waters thirst for more. Numberless drinkers it afflicts with the dropsy. With gentle murmur it sports along and flows past the cliff. Men desiring more of it plunge in, to bathe all their limbs in its tide. Submerged as they are, the stream carries them along until the fickle wave bears them again to land. The other stream is dark and sulphurous. Its color confounds the sight, its savor the taste, its rush the ear, and the nostril wearies of its insipid odor. On the banks rivers of tears drown many who fear to plunge into the torrent. The stream carries along a great throng, to bury them in its floods. Now it sucks some down, and now it spues them forth. This stream joins the sweet one and compels it to become cloudy and bitter.

The house of Fortune is suspended on the steep cliff and threatens to fall. It suffers all the tempest of the winds. Part of the building swells upon the hill, the other part slopes down to the bottom of the valley as if ready to sink there. One part gleams with silver and sparkles with gems, the other part is squalid with cheap material. One part stands proud with a lofty roof, the other part gapes with an opening. "Here Fortune hath a dwelling-place, if ever yet any unstable thing abideth anywhere, if any moving thing doth cease to move."¹

Here we have the full description of the house, and we may note the following details: (1) the scene is apparently laid on an island; (2) the house is situated on a lofty cliff, an elevation of land; (3) it suffers the winds of both Zephyr and Boreas; (4) the garden has both fruitful and barren trees; (5) it has two streams, one sweet, one bitter; (6) the house is constructed partly of rich material and partly of cheap. We may see the similarity of this abode to that of Venus in Claudian's poem, and yet the contrast is striking. In Claudian everything is pleasant, peaceful, and enduringly comfortable; in Alanus half of Fortune's house is forbidding and perilous.

As I have elsewhere observed,² Jean de Meun took over this entire description from Alanus and put it into the *Roman de la Rose*.³ Petrarch refers to the account of Alanus when he says:

> Fuor tutt'i nostri lidi
> Ne l'isole famose di Fortuna,
> Due fonti à: chi de l'una
> Bee, mor ridendo; e chi de l'altra, scampa.⁴

The details are reproduced again in Taillevent's *Régime de Fortune*:

> Sur lac de dueil, sur riuiere ennuieuse,
> Plaine de cris, de regretz, et de clains,
> Sur pesant sourse et melencolieuse,

---

¹ *Anticlaudianus*, VII, viii–ix, and VIII, i (Migne, vol. CCX, cols. 557–560).

² See *Smith College Studies in Modern Languages*, IV, 7.

³ Lines 5944 ff.   ⁴ *Le Rime*, ed. Mestica, p. 208 (canz. xviii, 77 ff.).

Plaine de plours, de souspirs, et de plains:
Sur grans estangz d'amertume tous plains,
Et de douleur sur abisme parfonde,
Fortune là sa maison tousiours fonde
A l'vng des lez de roche espouentable,
Et en pendant, affin que plustost fonde,
En demonstrant qu'elle n'est pas estable.

The house is partly rich, partly poor; on one side are barren fields, on the other grain and fruit. There sits Fortune surrounded with abundance; and so on.[1]

The French tradition, which begins with the *Roman de la Rose* and continues in the *Régime de Fortune*, appears again in Lydgate's *Disguising at London*, where, with an acknowledgment of indebtedness to the *Roman*, the author speaks of Fortune's dwelling. He says it is on a barren rock. On one side is a little mountain "lyke an yle," on which grow fresh flowers, trees, and fruit; birds sing there and "Zepherus" makes the weather clear. But suddenly comes a wave that causes everything to fade. Fortune's hall is located there: one side is rich with precious stones; the other, in ruins, is daubed with clay. As Fortune's house is "unstable," so she is "deceyvable." [2]

The descriptions thus far owe most of their material ultimately to Alanus, who in turn found some hints in his predecessors: (1) literal detail of scenery in the Court of Love, and most of all in Claudian (with, however, the symbolic fountains); (2) symbolic suggestion and symbolic detail in Boethius. The points to note in the tradition from Alanus are chiefly these: (1) the island, (2) the mountain, (3) the garden, (4) the palace, (5) the court.

---

[1] Alain Chartier, *Œuvres*, p. 713 (bal. iv).

[2] Brotanek, *Englischen Maskenspiele*, pp. 309 ff. Note also Fortune's house in tapestry in Mâle's *L'Art Religieux*, p. 368; and see plate 7 below.

The court grows out of the conception of the goddess as queen of the household, and so is added here.

II

THE ISLAND

The symbolic idea of the island in the accounts of Fortune's home is clearly that of the remoteness and inaccessibility of the desired fortune. It is covered with the glamour that always plays about the mental picture of a distant and particularly delightful region. In Roman and mediaeval times, travellers on sea often came home with tales of some island recently discovered, where the climate was wonderfully pleasant, where the sun shone more gently than anywhere else, where strange and delicious fruits grew, and where life was as sweet as the waters of a certain fountain which bubbled there. Such discoveries are rarer nowadays, when the world is entirely charted and when school geographies can tell the "products" of any far-off point of land; but that this was not always the case is the happy fact to which we owe such ideas as the "Isles of the Blessed" and the "Beautiful Isle of our Dreams."

Whether island or not, however, the desirable country has nearly always been bounded in some way by water. The suggestion may come as I have described; or some such conception as that of the "river Jordan" may spring from a certain physiological fact which is often noted — that at the approach of death the sufferer hears "the sound of many waters" in his ears and tells the people about him of the queer noise. Perhaps this sensation is caused by the circulation of the blood pulsating against the sensitive nerves of the ears. However this may be, in death and at other times the barrier of water generally seems to separate us from the desired country; and so we hear of Atlantis, Avalon, the Isles of the Hesperides, the Isles of the Blessed, the Isle of Joy, the Isle of Ladies, the Happy Isles, and so on. The idea is familiar in the folk-lore of many parts of the world.[1]

More obviously related to our topic are the so-called Fortunate Isles, famous in classical and mediaeval times.[2] Whether they were islands of real or of imaginative experience is of no importance for us here. Perhaps some sea-rover actually happened on the Canary Islands (or others), and found them enjoyable enough to call "Fortunate." At any rate, the Fortunate Isles became a classic example of the longed-for realm. Plutarch describes them;[3] Dante refers to Orosius's account of them;[4] Vincent of Beauvais gives some space to his comment on them, and says, "Propter soli fecunditatem easdem paradisum uocauerunt."[5] These islands have by reputation a delightful climate, abundant fruits, and indeed everything a person could wish. As Aeneas Sylvius puts it:

[1] See Nutt, *The Happy Otherworld*, in *The Voyage of Bran* (ed. Meyer and Nutt), I, 148, 271 ff. So, too, in *Pilgrim's Progress* a river encircles the Celestial City. Milton speaks of enchanted islands (*Comus*, i, 50, 517), refers to Eden as "the happy isle" (*P. L.*, ii, 410, and cf. iii, 567, 570), and says the world itself was "built on circumfluous waters calm" (*P. L.*, vii, 269–270). The mediaeval castle was surrounded by a moat filled with water as a safeguard against intruders; but the idea of the happy island is far older than the Middle Ages. Further material is afforded in my article in the Mod. Lang. Assoc., *Publ.*, XXXIII, 627 ff., and in the notes appended thereto.

[2] See *Voyage of Bran*, I, 284.

[3] In his life of Sertorius (*Lives*, ed. Langhorne, 1819, IV, 11–12). See Dieterich, *Nekyia*, p. 32. They appear on various ancient maps.

[4] *De Monarchia*, II, iii, 87 ff.   [5] *Speculum Historiale*, I, lxxix.

PLATE 6

CHARYBDIS

PLATE 7

THE DWELLING–PLACE

Eae insulae cum saluberrimum aërem haberent, et frugibus abundarent: loca uero incontinenti opposita, propter diluuii humiditatem, pestilentia et frugum sterilitate laborarent, Fortunatae sunt cognominatae.[1]

Islands like these, existing in the popular idea of the world and clearly very well known, would surely have had some influence on an author's description of Fortune's residing-place. She is, I think, described as living on an island because (1) the mythical idea of the country of abundance and riches, or the desired region of whatever kind, usually took the form of an island, and because (2) there was a belief in some actual islands that bore as their name a derivative from the name of the goddess.

The idea of an island is elsewhere associated with Fortuna. De Guilleville puts Fortune and her wheel out in the sea like a floating rock or a Charybdis.[2] As the pilgrim is swimming along, he sees in the water ahead a great tree standing upright:

> Et cuiday quen vne ysle fust
> Du que tout oultre la mer fust.

This tree proves later, as we shall see, to be a property of the goddess.

The house of Boiardo's Fata Morgana is on territory

---

[1] *Historia de Asia Minori*, cap. lxxviiii (a mistake for lxxiv), in his *Opera Omnia*, p. 355.

[2] *Rommant des Trois Pelerinaiges*, fols. lxvj^vo-lxvij^vo. There is a colored drawing of this idea (marked F), in Nathaniel Hill's *De Guileville*, opp. p. xlii; also a woodcut, xvii, opp. p. xlv. See the wheel half-submerged in water in Van Staveren's *Auctores Mythographi*, 1742, frontispiece. Here the symbolic significance of the water is slightly different from that of the sea surrounding the island: it means here simply adversity, and does not particularly bar the approach of any one. Alberti (*Il Teog.*, ii, *Opere*, III, 204), in discussing Fortune's inconstancy, refers to a moving island described by Pliny.

surrounded by water. In the *Orlando Innamorato* Orlando says:

> E vo' ch' intendi, se le cose strane
> Son date ad altri ancor da la Fortuna.
> Mio padre è Re de l'Isole lontane,
> Dove il tesor del mondo si raduna.[1]

This realm is not Fortune's, however; it belongs to the "Fata del Tesoro," Morgana.[2] In it are all the riches in the world to make one happy. In Boiardo's description of the Fata and her dwelling-place, this is but one of many points of resemblance to Fortune and her house.

The idea of an island, then, is a natural development, springing probably from the mythical idea of the happy but unattainable isle of the Otherworld, and appearing in some form in nearly all the accounts of Fortune's home. As a symbolic attribute, it is merely one more of the many spontaneous growths that mark the vitality of the worship of the goddess.

III

The Mountain

The conception of a mountain as a figure of inaccessibility and adversity is common enough. One speaks of "scaling" one's difficulties or "surmounting" an obstacle; and it is the mountain of Purgatory, we remember, which one has to climb on the way to Paradise. The mountain obviously can also symbolize degrees of exaltation and humiliation in worldly dignity. In *Li Romanz de la Poire*, Fortune attributes to herself certain powers:

[1] I, xxi, 49.   [2] See I, xxii, 36; xxv, 5.

Reïne sui del mont,[1] ci le poez veoir.
L'un met del val el mont et puis le faz cheoir.[2]

Watriquet de Couvin places a whole city (of which Fortune is porter) on a mountain-top:

Moult i sont riche li citains,
Se touz jors leur durast si tains,
Mais il leur faut, combien qu' il tarde,
Quant le mains s'en donnent de garde;
Quar cil qui au plus haut demeure
Trebusche et chiet en petit d'eure
En mains c'on ne tourne sa main
Reversoient, et soit et main,
Tout bas ou fons de la valée.

King, duke, prince, and lord are cast down,

Car cilz qui plus haut se seoit,
Plus griément cheü se veoit.

In the horrible valley below Death receives the victims.[3]
The figure is doubled in Nicole de Margival's *Panthère d'Amours*. The lover travels to the house of Fortune:

Tant alames par nos jornees,
Par montaignes et par valees,
Qu'en assez petite saison
Venismes droit a la maison
De Fortune l'aventureuse.
Moult est la maison perilleuse,
Car elle siet toute sus glace,
Qui dure quel temps que il face.[4]

Here the road to the house lies partly across mountainous country, and the foundation of the house itself is a rock

<hr/>

[1] I. e., "world."

[2] Lines 45–46. For the mountain in such descriptions and in folk-lore, see Mod. Lang. Assoc., *Publ.*, XXXIII, 606 ff.

[3] *Dis de l'Escharbote*, ll. 101 ff. (*Dits*, pp. 400 ff.). Cf. the wheel on the mountain ("le plus haute kil ueist onques") in the *Mort Artu*, p. 220.

[4] *Panthère*, ll. 1958–1965.

of ice, which includes the idea of brittleness or lack of durability, and perhaps the idea of slipperiness in climbing.[1]

Thomas, Marquis of Saluzzo, in his *Chevalier Errant* (a document of the fourteenth or early fifteenth century), develops the figure of the mountain still further. The dwelling of Fortune is on the highest rock that the eye has ever seen. It dominates the whole country. At the top are two fearful precipices, near which the goddess is seated on a throne upheld by three lions. She rises in wrath and causes kings and emperors to be thrown from the height. On the side of the rock is a more terrible scene, for there traitors of all kinds are drawn and quartered.[2]

Similarly, in Fregoso's *Dialogo di Fortuna* we read of the approach, over a hard and thorny road,[3] to a beautiful palace on a mountain-top, where Fortune dispenses

[1] On Chaucer's rock of ice, see Sypherd's *Studies in Chaucer's Hous of Fame*, pp. 117 f. Sir William Jones borrows Chaucer's rock of ice for his "Palace of Fortune" (*Works*, 1807, X, 214). Cf. also Fame's house in Dekker's *Troia-Nova Triumphans* (*Mod. Lang. Notes*, XXXIII, 178 f.). See the mention of a house of glass in *La Folie Tristan* (ed. J. Bédier, Paris, 1907), ll. 295–310 of the Oxford text. The house seems to be situated in the air. For the whole matter the references in Mod. Lang. Assoc., *Publ.*, XXXIII, p. 610, n. 30, should be consulted.

[2] See the summary of § vi, in Gorra's *Studi*, pp. 45 ff. Cf. G. de Machaut, *Poésies*, ed. Chichmaref, II, 415, ll. 15–18:

> Et Fortune m'a dou vent
> D'un tourbillon
> Tumé jus de sa maison
> En fondement.

[3] Cf. the difficult approach in Frezzi's *Quadriregio*, I, 147 (lib. ii, cap. xiii, 1 ff.), and in Nicole de Margival's *Panthère*, ll. 1958 ff. The barrier to Fortune's abode is like that to the approach of the Otherworld or the Earthly Paradise, and is probably related to it. For material with regard to the latter, see my article in *Mod. Lang. Notes*, XXXIV, 321 ff., especially p. 322 and note 3. Cf. the lofty mountain forest in Spanish literature, *ibid.*, p. 324, n. 9.

gifts. One must have a guide to go up the mountain, because it is so slippery:

> Et quando piu felice, e piu giocondo,
> Di questi alcun nel colmo esser si crede
> Spesso se troua in un momento al fondo.

The guides waiting for travellers are Iuista, Audacia, Fraude, Lealta, Valore, Prudentia, Fortezza, and so on. Whoever ascends to the top lives there secure, without fear of Fortune.[1]

The idea of the mountain is referred to by Jean de Condé:

> Cil haus mons le te fait savoir
> Que tés lieve haitiez au main
> Qu'en mains c'om ne tourne sa main,
> Trebuche et muert en petit d'eure.[2]

Ariosto interprets the figure of the mountain in the following manner:

> Questo monte è la ruota di Fortuna,
> Nella cui cima il volgo ignaro, pensa
> Ch' ogni quiete sia, nè ve n'è alcuna.[3]

Thus he, too, lays chief emphasis on the idea of exaltation and humiliation.

The mountain, then, according to Alanus, meant the difficulty of reaching Fortune's gifts and the perishable foundation on which they rest. Nicole de Margival stressed the second of these ideas. In Thomas of Saluzzo, Fregoso, Jean de Condé, and Ariosto we have a new interpretation: the mountain appears to mean degrees of

---

[1] *Dialogo*, caps. xiii ff. The lines quoted, and the names of the guides, are in cap. xv, sig. C8.

[2] Baudouin and Jean de Condé, *Dits et Contes*, iii, 54, ll. 160–163.

[3] *Rime e Satire*, p. 207 (sat. iii).

honor and exaltation bestowed by Fortune. But, whatever the meaning ascribed to the figure, it seems to persist in pictures of Fortune's house,[1] and perhaps the most enduring idea connected with it is that of the inaccessibility of the top and the slipperiness of the sides.[2]

IV

The Garden

The beautiful garden on the mountain-top in Claudian's poem does not change; but Fortune's garden, ac-

---

[1] Cf. Trissino, *Italia Liberata*, II, 78 f. (lib. xi):

> Qui presso è la penisula di Circe,
> C'hà sopra il monte un' odorata selva
> Di cedri, e di verdissimi cipressi;
> Ove è una Fata di valore immenso,
> Nominata Plutina, che nel volto
> Par giovinetta, & è matura d'anni;
> Tal che di età non cede a la Sibilla.
> Gran tempo fà, ch'ella divenne cieca;
> Ma se potesse racquistar la vista,
> Faria veder di se cose mirande;
> Poi sù quel monte una spelunca giace,
> Circondata dal mar verso Ponente, etc.

With this, compare the description of the plateau of Venus given by Claudian, referred to above, pp. 123 f. See *Melusine* (ll. 4621–4634), where Palestine dwells on a high mountain to guard her father's treasure there:

> Till som approche and come, of linage our,
> To that hy mountain by fors and strenght he
> To ascende an-hye Aboue the hill to see,
> The tresour caste oute, and after shall conquere
> The lande of promission by hys powere.

In the *Contention between Liberality and Prodigality* (1602, Malone Soc. reprint, 1913, act iv, scene iv), Prodigalitie, assisted by Dicke Dicer and Tom Tosse, scales the wall of Fortune's dwelling.

[2] For the slipperiness of one's stand in Fortune's house, cf. *Carmina Burana*, p. 45, lxxv, st. 1 ("O varium fortune lubricum"); G. de Machaut,

cording to Alanus, suffers continual variation. The hint for this symbolism, like that of the rock and the sea, was also, perhaps, found in Boethius:

> Licet caelo proferre lucidos dies eosdemque tenebrosis noctibus condere, licet anno terrae uultum nunc floribus frugibusque redimire nunc nimbis frigoribusque confundere.[1]

Somewhat different from the tradition of the changing garden is the scene of Fortune's home in the dream of Aeneas Sylvius:

> Iam noctis decurso spatio, syderibus dubiis postquam pigri Boetae frigida farrata circumegerant, uisionem hanc habui. In locos laetos et amena uireta deueni, gramineus campus in medio fortunati nemoris erat, riuo cinctus et muro, duae illic portae. . . . Illic florea prata, riui tum lacte tum uino currentes, frigidi fontes, lacus piscibus pleni, balnea suauissima, densi luci, uineta semper uuis onusta, arbores perpetui autumni, quales hortus Hesperidum, uel Pheates habuisse creduntur. Poma quorum sola pascaris odore per syluas, ferae mansuetae captu faciles: Volucres et aesui, et cantui natae, unicus est apud Aethiopes locus Heliotrapezam nuncupatus, opiparis

---

Remede de Fortune, l. 1030 ("Et ses richesses glace en four"); Hoccleve, *Regement of Princes*, ll. 1352 ff.; James I, *Kingis Quhair*, stanzas 9, 163 (the slippery footing on the wheel); John Stewart, *Roland Furious*, xi, 125–126 (the "slipprie solas" of Fortune "als schortlie slyd As yse dissolues vith flam of feruent fyre"). See Shakespeare's *Troilus and Cressida*, III, iii, 84–88:

> Which when they fall, as being slippery standers,
> The love that lean'd on them as slippery too,
> Do one pluck down another and together
> Die in the fall. But 'tis not so with me:
> Fortune and I are friends.

[1] *Cons. Philos.*, II, pr. ii, 21 ff. "The heavens may grant bright sunlit days, and hide the same beneath the shade of night. The year may deck the earth's countenance with flowers and fruits, and again wrap it with chilling clouds" (Cooper's trans.). Cf. Henricus Septimellensis, *Trattato*, 1730, p. 10:

> Sic solet arboreas Boreas euoluere frondes,
> Sic rota mortales, sic aqua saeua rotam.

epulis semper refertus quibus indiscretim omnes uescuntur: apud quem lacus tenuis laticis haustu saluberrimus. Hic plurima sunt huiusmodi loca, mensae sub arboribus paratae gemmatis uasculis paterisque aureis oneratae. Nullum ualernum comparari uino potest, quod ex uiuo saxo illic manat. Mella passim fluunt, arundineta saccharo plena. Omne genus aromatum ex arbore cadit. Auri et argenti inexhaustae minerae. Lapilli praeciosi tanquam cerusa in nemoribus pendent, uenustae puellae, elegantesque iuuenes perpetuas ducunt choreas. Quicquid musicum est, illic resonat. Nan tam uoluptuosam suis sequacibus paradisum Mahometus repromisit, quam hic uidisses. Dispensatores huc et illuc discurrebant, Bachus Ceres et Venus.[1]

There is little left to add to this picture. We must note that the scene is not subject to change: the abundance does not decrease, the stream flows with untainted honey, the splendor is not diminished.

Fregoso's *Dialogo di Fortuna* gives us the picture of a great tree on the top of his mountain, on which ripen wondrous apples which Fortuna gives away to those who ascend.[2] In Boiardo's *Orlando Innamorato*, Roland enters a wonderful garden, where he sees a fountain made of precious stones, beside which lies the beautiful Fata Morgana.[3]

De Guilleville's pilgrim, it will be remembered, sees a tree standing in the middle of the ocean. As he approaches he discovers that the tree is full of nests, some high, some low, some large, some small:

[1] *Pontif. Epist.*, I, cviii (*Opera Omnia*, pp. 611–612).

[2] *Dialogo*, cap. xiii. See also the tree bearing golden apples "as large as the human head", in *Orlando Innamorato*, II, v, stanzas 7–8; and, at I, xxv, st. 11, cf. the antlers of the white stag, their branches laden with treasures. A fruit-tree of some kind is always found in the Otherworld garden, from which these accounts, of course, derive in various ways. Cf. Mod. Lang. Assoc., *Publ.*, XXXIII, 624 ff., with references.

[3] *Orlando*, II, viii, 40 ff.

Et en diuerses branches mis
Par semblant larbre creux estoit
Enhault dedens vng trou auoit
Par lequel vne main aux nidȝ
Tendait vng croq a mon aduis
Pour les oyseaulx ius trebucher
A son pouoir et desnicher.

Below are several persons thrusting their heads out to look up at the top and often stretching out their hands to get hold of the higher branches; the goddess Fortune has a forked stick to pull them down. The tree is the world, with men of different rank in it; Fortune with her forked stick pulls some of them down, but she uses the crook to help others up.[1]

Here the significance of the tree is changed. It has become the symbol of varying degrees of dignity, and its fruit does not represent the gifts of Fortune. Perhaps Deschamps had a tree like this in mind, when he wrote:

Car par orgueil vient tribulacion.
Fortune a tost getté feur,
De l'arbre hault les fueilles et la fleur;
Mais pou grieve l'arbre d'umilité.[2]

Another picture in a manuscript shows us a large tree, with Fortune standing on the top and armed men in the branches. This is obviously the tree of warfare and success in war.[3] It is hard to tell whether there is any idea of exaltation or humiliation intended in the relative height of the branches, but apparently there is no such meaning.

[1] *Rommant des Trois Pelerinaiges*, fols. lxvj v⁰ f. See the lines (fol.lx vij),

Sur lespaule vng baston portant
Crochu et fourchu par deuant.

[2] *Œuvres*, III, 134, ll. 40–43. Fortune turns the leaves *of her book: ibid.*, X, p. lxxxv (lxxvi, 13–15).

[3] For a description of the picture, see Sir Gilbert Hay's *Manuscript*, I, pp. lxxiii ff.; the picture itself is in a folder at the back of the volume. The MS. is of the year 1456 or later (see introd., p. xix). See also *L'Arbre des Battailles*, by Honoré Bonet, British Museum MS., Royal 20 C viii, f. 2v⁰.

The garden, the flowers, and the tree, then, are all elements in the descriptions of Fortune's abode. Of Fortune herself we read in one place:

> Her right syde full of somer flours,
> The tother oppressed with winters stormy showres.[1]

Flowers, therefore, and the tree with its fruit mean prosperous Fortune. Sometimes, however, as in De Guilleville and Deschamps, the tree represents the idea of varying degrees of dignity, and once at least it relates to success in war.

V

THE PALACE

According to Alanus's view, the palace in which Fortune lives is partly rich and sumptuous and partly squalid and perilous; but there are other ideas about her dwelling which do not carry on this tradition. Watriquet de Couvin's city on the mountain, for example, is

> une cité cretelée
> De marbre, à bretesche et à tour,
> Faite de riche noble atour,
> Car n'est hom qui onques veïst
> Plus bele ne tant haut seïst. . . .
> Car plus y ot de melodie
> .C. mile tans que ne vous die;
> Ce sembloit paradis terrestre. . . .
> Or doi de la cité conter,
> De quoi Fortune les clés porte,
> Et est portière de la porte,

---

[1] Lydgate, *Fall of Princes*, VI, i, st. 3 (fol. cxliii of 1554 ed., cxxxiv of 1558 ed.) Cf. Boethius, *Cons. Philos.*, II, met. v, 6–9; and see Galpin, Mod. Lang. Assoc., *Publ.*, XXIV, 339. For an account of the Vatican drawing of Fortune crowned with flowers and holding a bunch of them, see Barbier de Montault, *Traité*, I, 163, § 5.

Car sanz li n'i puet estre entrée
Personne ne passer l'entrée.[1]

Of this description two points are worth noting: (1) the city is beautiful, being constructed of marble; (2) there is a gate through which can pass only such persons as its keeper (in this case Fortune herself) permits.

Nicole de Margival, in his account of the castle of Fortune, keeps true to the idea of Alanus:

Mais moult belle est d'une partie,
Et noble et de tous biens garnie;
De l'autre partie est si gaste
Que nul n'i a ne pain ne paste,
Et est ruïneuse et deserte,
Si despeciee, si desperte,
Que s'il espartist, pleut ou vente,
Nulz ne mest la qui ne s'en sente;
Car la pluie, vens et espars
Se fierent ens de toutes pars.[2]

The gates of Fortune's house are described by Aeneas Sylvius:

Duae illic portae, et altera cornea, altera candenti nitens elephante. Muri altissimi ex adamante constructi. . . . Nulli accessus ad portas nisi per pontes, qui tamen cathenis eleuati paucis aduenientibus dimittebantur. . . . Veni ad coream portam, in cuius summo haec uerba literis antiquis inscripta, conspexi: paucos admitto, seruo pauciores.[3]

---

[1] *Dis de l'Escharbote*, ll. 74 ff. (*Dits*, pp. 399 f.). In the *Roman de Fauvel*, Fortune's home is in "Macrocosme,"

Une cité de grant fantosme,
Qui fu jadis faite pour l'omme
Que Raison Microcosme nomme

(Längfors's ed., ll. 1852–1854).

[2] *Panthère*, ll. 1966–1975.

[3] *Pontif. Epist.*, I, cviii (*Opera Omnia*, p. 611).

Here we must note the two gates, the bridges crossing the
river which has been already referred to,[1] and the inscription. To this account of Fortune's estate the description
of the home of the Fata Morgana is again strikingly
similar. The Fata's realm is surrounded by a river over
which is a bridge with two armed figures standing guard
beside it. When Orlando attempts to go across, the bridge
is demolished, and, though a new one rises in place of
the one that disappears, the same thing always happens
again; but he finally leaps the river.[2] He is told of a horn,
which, if blown, will destroy the whole world.[3] He comes
to a cavern, where, in the cornice of black rock, are cut
the words:

> Tu che sei giunto, o Dama, o Cavaliero,
> Sappi, che quivi facile è l'entrata,
> Ma il risalir da poi non è leggero,
> A cui non prende quella buona Fata, etc.[4]

The palace of Fortune in Fregoso's *Dialogo* is beautiful
with the kind of beauty that deceives the eye. It is surrounded by a great wall, which apparently guards the
structure of precious stones. Four large portals, with a
triumphal arch and a tower on each, face the four points
of the compass, to show that people may enter from all
climes and at all seasons. At the top of the palace is a
colossus of gold.[5]

[1] Above, pp. 129 f. Cf. Mod. Lang. Assoc., *Publ.*, XXXII, 627 f. and notes.

[2] *Orlando Innamorato*, II, viii, 19–23. For such bridges across the river-
barrier, see Mod. Lang. Assoc., *Publ.*, XXXIII, 635 f. and notes; for the
armed figures, see *Mod. Philol.*, X, 511 f.

[3] *Orlando Innamorato*, II, vii, 42. Perhaps this comes from the same story
which is told in the original ballad of "Childe Roland to the dark tower
came." The "slughorn" is here to be set to the lips, and the dark tower
practically belongs to Fortune.   [4] *Ibid.*, II, viii, 39.

[5] *Dialogo di Fortuna*, caps. xiii–xv. Cf. the description of Frau Saelde's
house in Heinrich von dem Türlin's *Diu Crône*, ll. 15649 ff.; note the detail of

The chief elements in the palace of Fortune, then, are (1) the bridges over the encircling river, (2) the precious materials out of which the city is built, (3) the portals. The descriptions vary considerably, but the important and persistent idea is the richness of the castle and the difficulty in entering it.

VI

THE COURT

Within the palace Fortune is naturally queen, and, as we have observed,[1] this conception of her royalty is frequent enough. In the *Roman de la Rose* she is dressed "cum une roïne";[2] in Watriquet de Couvin she controls the inhabitants of the city — kings, dukes, princes, lords, and the rest.[3]

As for the actual palaces of Fortune, in that of Nicole de Margival's *Panthère* the goddess stands at the entrance to receive travellers, assigning them to one of the two parts of the house, which are designated Prosperity and Adversity.[4] Here she clearly exercises the power of a monarch; and in the *Chevalier Errant* of Thomas of Saluzzo she has a similar dignity, for in her palace are found all the great personages of all time — Penthesilea, Pope Gregory, Agamemnon, Caesar and Hector (two of

precious stones and the towers. See, too, the palace in Machiavelli's *Capitolo di Fortuna* (*Opere*, VII, 367):

Sopra un palazzo da ogni parte aperto
Regnar si vede, ed a verun non toglie
L'entrar in quel, ma è l'uscire incerto.

[1] Above, p. 60.   [2] Line 6146.
[3] *Dis de l'Escharbote*, ll. 115 ff., and see 169 ff. (*Dits*, pp. 400 ff.).
[4] *Panthère*, ll. 1976 ff. For another use of the names Prosperity and Adversity, see below, p. 164, n. 2.

the Nine Worthies), Nebuchadnezzar, Pharoah, Nero, Attila, and so on.[1] Christine de Pisan puts guards at the various doors of her palace of Fortune: Dame Richece at the first, surrounded by princes, dukes, counts, cardinals, and bishops; Esperance at the second; and Poverty at the third, with Atropos. Famous men inhabit the castle — Richard the Second, Pierre de Lusignan, and so on,[2] all of them presumably Fortune's subjects or attendants, who dwell with her.

Aeneas Sylvius gives the most luxurious account of the court scene:

Tentoria illic purpurea erant, margaritis ornata, quae centum iugera cooperiebant. In medio solium erat peraltum, lucens claris Smaragdis, miri praeterea lapides, ebur, solium uestiebant. . . . Incredibile est gemmarum, quae illic perlucent, si quis referat multitudinem. Ipsa fortuna grandis matrona, duplicis aspectus, blando uultu, nunc terrifico: Vestibus auratis gemmatisque altiorem chorum tenebat, oculis grandioribus. Sed plerunque clausis in auribus caeras uidi illa de naui petitas, quae Siculos cautus effugit remige surdo. Cadeceum in manu tenebat. In dextera eius dominatus sedebat honor, fauor, splendor, gaudium, officium, festus, risus, amor coniugum, uigor, rubor, decus, cantus, potus. Nec minori loco, fama, gloria, uictoria, nobilitas, reuerentia, pax, laetitia, potentia, forma, laus, gratia, suauitas, iocunditas [etc.] . . . Ad pedes eius quasi ancillae siue pedistequae, diuitiae, pecuniae, delitiae, blanditiae, uoluptatesque stabant arrectis auribus, si quid iussisset hera auditurae facturaeque. In gramine uero locoque decliui sellae plurimae

---

[1] Gorra, *Studi*, pp. 47 ff.

[2] Koch, *Christine de Pizan*, pp. 68–69 (summary of *La Mutacion de Fortune*, pts. ii–iii). There is a hall attached, where paintings depict philosophy, the sciences, the history of the Jews, etc. See also Machiavelli, *Capitolo di Fortuna* (*Opere*, VII, 367):

> Tutto il mondo d'intorno vi si accoglie
> Desideroso veder cose nuove,
> E pien d'ambizion, e pien di voglie.

Chance and Lot sit over the doors (p. 368).

cernebantur orchestra tectae, ubi plurimas umbras sedere conspexi [the throng below her include all the famous names in history]. . . . Post hae ad sinistram me uerti.   Ibi paupertas sedebat, ignominia, derisus, iniuriae, morbi, senectus, tormenta, carceres, fames, dolor, stridor, timor, pudor, odium [etc., etc.] . . . et mille malorum nomina, campi sitientes nudi ac lapidibus tecti.[1]

VII

SUMMARY

The dwelling-place of Fortune is, then, first described in a long account by Alanus de Insulis. From this account two traditions of the site develop: (1) that of the island, (2) that of the mountain. The mountain receives special attention in Nicole de Margival, Thomas of Saluzzo, and in Fregoso, with whom it becomes a symbol not only of inaccessibility and danger, but of degrees of dignity accorded by Fortuna. Essential points in the description of the site are the garden, the flowers, and the trees; the tree, like the mountain, also becomes a special symbol of degree of exaltation. The castle sometimes leaves the direct line of tradition from Alanus and appears merely as a sumptuous palace which is not divided into good and wretched sections. Later, perhaps through influence from the Court of Love, it becomes the scene of a splendid court, with numerous courtiers taken from history.[2]

To sum up the meanings implied in all of these symbols, the permanent ideas seem to be: (1) the inaccessi-

[1] *Pontif. Epist.*, I, cviii (*Opera Omnia*, pp. 613 ff.).

[2] See the borrowed details of all these points in Chaucer's *Hous of Fame* (cf. Sypherd's *Studies*, pp. 112 ff.). Sir William Jones, in the eighteenth century, restores the house to Fortune by borrowing features from Chaucer's poem: see his *Palace of Fortune (Works*, 1807, X, 211–229), and E. Koeppel's article on it in *Englische Studien*, XXVIII, 43–53.

bility of the house of Fortune, (2) its richness, and (3) the varying rewards received on getting there. In other words, the benefits of Fortune are hard to achieve, they are precious from a worldly point of view, they are bestowed in different measure. A celestial atmosphere clings about the place.[1] The island, and possibly the mountain, have an ancestry in folk-lore with which the idea of "the happy Otherworld" is connected. Perhaps the conception is not entirely unrelated to our present figure of a "Castle in Spain." At any rate, the whole image is not so much a poetic creation as an automatic growth developing according to its own laws, and the same elements persist in nearly all the descriptions, in whatever way these may be interpreted.

[1] See the word "paradis" on p. 140, above; and cf. the islands on pp. 130 f. Cf. the paradise on the mountain of purgatory (Dante, *Purgatorio*, xxviii), with its double river, its flowers, and its gentle breeze; cf., too, the islands in the *Voyage of Bran* (see p. 130 above). The *Roman de la Rose*, l. 5941, has "Qu'ele ait en paradis maison."

CHAPTER V

FORTUNE'S WHEEL

NO symbolic attribute is so familiar in accounts and pictures of Fortune as the wheel. It so often appears in the portrayals of her, either as turned by her fickle hand or as standing near her with the possibility of suddenly beginning to revolve, that even when we find it alone, without the goddess, we are strongly tempted to call it Fortune's wheel anyway. But the wheel is a symbol with an almost limitless significance. At one time or another the circular form has been used to typify speed,[1] travel, guidance,[2] the endless round of monotonous existence, changeableness, the sun,[3] the earth, God, and eternity.[4] Definition is therefore necessary to determine what the peculiar meaning of Fortune's wheel is, and to discover what particular wheel rightly belongs to her.

In order to suit the character of Fortune most appropriately, the wheel must in some way represent the idea of variation and change. It must do so even in the case of

---

[1] The wheel with a wing upon it. Cf. Cousin's *Livre de Fortune*, pl. 115. See p. 45, notes 3, 4, above.

[2] The steering-wheel. Cf. the windlass figure in Horace, *Carmina*, III, x, 10.

[3] See Gaidoz, *Le Dieu Gaulois*, § xvi, pp. 56 ff.

[4] In fact, some scholars believe that in Roman times the wheel was not associated particularly with Fortuna. See Roscher, who notes (cols. 1506–1507) that in art the wheel is not commonly related to Fortune, but cites examples from literature to show that the use must have been known. See also Matzke on the source of "To take Time by the Forelock," Mod. Lang. Assoc., *Publ.*, VIII, 328.

the Christian figure, for she too is outwardly a variable creature. This idea the wheel can present in at least two ways: (1) it would seem untrustworthy enough merely in its function of turning, and (2) it would form an insecure footing for the goddess.

How did such symbolism become associated with Fortuna? The stages of development might have been as follows: In its earliest use the wheel seems to have meant instability rather than variation.[1] Just as the castle of Fortune stands on a shaky foundation, so Fortune herself may be thought of as standing on some changing, roving pedestal; and what better pedestal for her than a sphere or a ball?[2] The figure of Fortune standing on a sphere was known in the art of ancient Rome,[3] and is preserved in drawings of the middle ages.[4] Art in the flat, in bas-reliefs, reproduced the ball by means of a circular line, and so the wheel came into use as a symbol of instability. The figure of Fortune standing on a wheel persisted in mediaeval art, which in these drawings copied the old Roman figures.[5]

[1] For the development in Rome, see Weinhold's *Glücksrad und Lebensrad;* for some suggestion of this order of development, see Roscher, col. 1506.

[2] I leave out of account the question whether this ball was originally the sun or the moon. By the time Fortune became fickle, the idea of sun or moon was certainly lost, and so the process of interpretation becomes the same.

[3] See Roscher, col. 1504; Gaidoz, *Le Dieu Gaulois,* p. 56. J. A. Hild, in Daremberg-Saglio's *Dictionnaire,* p. 1277, says that the sphere is of purely Roman origin and that the cornucopia is the Greek symbol. The development of the wheel as here described is suggested by Kirby Smith, *The Elegies of Albius Tibullus* (N. Y., 1913), pp. 306 ff., n. 70.

[4] See above, p. 45, n. 4.

[5] According to Barbier de Montault (*Traité,* I, 163, § 5), in the episcopal chair at St. Bertrand de Comminges Fortune stands on a broken wheel and thus fails in her footing. In Cousin's figure 193 she stands on a globe

But Fortune who totters about on a wheel in art or in literature is not so much the goddess as the type. Not until the wheel itself becomes a symbol of variation, turned possibly by the hand of the goddess, have we a really good allegory for the divine figure. This is the figure, it is significant to note, out of which the Middle Ages made so much, and it is the complexities of this representation that the following study will attempt to make at least a little clearer. The method of study will be to consider, first, the possible origins or beginnings of the idea in Rome, and, secondly, the later developments in mediaeval literature and art.

I

The Classical Figure

The wheel of Fortune in Roman art apparently does not represent the conception of a wheel directly controlling man's affairs.[1] The idea in art is merely, as I have

with her wheel broken on the ground beside her. See also Scarlattini's descriptions, *Homo Symbolicus* (1695), II, 70; and, much earlier, Alciati's emblem of "In Occasionem" in the 1536 edition of his emblems (ed. Green, *Fontes Quatuor*, 1870, wheel upright), and in the Lyons, 1551, edition (ed. Green, *Flumen Abundans*, 1871, p. 133, wheel flat). Schoonhoven's second emblem shows Fortune, or "Sors," prostrate on her flat wheel. Fortune shared the symbol of the wheel with the Fates and with Nemesis: see Roscher, col. 1506; Alciati's "Nec Verbo nec Facto quenquam Laudendum" (1531 ed. of emblems, Green's *Fontes Quatuor*, 1870, sig. A 7); and cf. Cousin's plates 127, 129. The idea of Fortune standing on a wheel is introduced by Lydgate into his translation of De Guilleville's *Pelerinaige de l'Homme* (see Lydgate's *Pilgrimage of the Life of Man*, ll. 19470 ff.) For the wheel in Greek, Professor Yeames of Hobart College has given me references to Herodotus, i, 207, and to Sophocles, fragment 809 (cf. Jebb's note on the *Antigone*, 1156 f.).

[1] Galpin (Mod. Lang. Assoc., *Publ.*, XXIV, 332) makes this observation. See S. L. Wolff, *Greek Romances in Elizabethan Prose Fiction*, p. 387, n. 31.

already suggested, that Fortune is on a moving foundation. In literature, however, we see a closer connection between the wheel and the fortunes of men. A few examples are enough to illustrate this idea.

Ammianus Marcellinus has,

> Fortunae uolucris rota, aduersa prosperis semper alternans; [1]

and in another place,

> Ea uictoria ultra homines Procopius sese efferens, et ignorans quod quiuis beatus uersa rota Fortunae ante uesperum potest esse miserrimus.[2]

Seneca makes one of his choruses sing:

> Ut praecipites regum casus
> Fortuna rotat! [3]

Here we see a vital relation between the wheel and human fortune. In the first two examples there does not seem to be any implication that Fortune herself revolves with the wheel, or shows that instability which had been symbolized in the figure of her standing on such a foundation; in the last one (which, by the way, is fully three centuries earlier) Fortune appears to rotate human affairs by her own power. It seems ridiculous to suppose that — at least after the wheel received any conscious attention — there was any conception of its having arbitrary power to turn human life without the superior control of the goddess.[4]

---

[1] *Res Gestae*, XXXI, i, § 1.   [2] *Ibid.*, XXVI, viii, § 13.

[3] *Agamemnon*, ll. 71–72. See, too, Cicero's oration against Piso, cap. x, "Fortunae rotam pertimescebat." Cf. *Aeneid*, vi, 748–749; Tibullus, I, v, 69–70, and cf. the notes in Kirby F. Smith's edition, 1913, p. 306.

[4] In the confused figure described below (pp. 152 ff.), where Fortune herself is turned on the wheel, she has really become a type, as the discussion shows.

By the fifth or sixth century, at any rate, the wheel was no longer thought of as independent. Boethius uses the figure of Fortune's controlling it as if the idea were perfectly familiar. He makes Fortune say:

Rotam uolubili orbe uersamus, infima summis summa infimis mutare gaudemus. Ascende si placet, sed ea lege, ne uti cum ludicri mei ratio poscet, descendere iniuriam putes.[1]

Here the goddess herself professes to turn the wheel; low becomes high and high becomes low; one may voluntarily ascend to the top, and therefore human figures are conceivably attached to the wheel. There is not the slightest hint that Fortune revolves with it; on the contrary, she is in charge of affairs and does not suffer the reversals.

Unfortunately we have no smooth succession of references to the wheel from the time of Boethius to that of Dante. We must leap a gulf of several centuries and pass on to the twelfth before we can tell what tradition has been established; but there in many works we find Fortune responsible for the turns of the wheel. For instance, we read:

Sic fortuna uices uariat, sic infima summis
Summaque commutat, sua cum rota uoluitur, ymis.[2]

Again, Fortune herself revolves the wheel in the description by Henricus Septimellensis;[3] and the theme of "high and low" is found, together with Fortune's control of the wheel, in *Floire et Blanceflor*,[4] in *Le Donnei des*

---

[1] *Cons. Philos.*, II, pr. ii, 28–31.

[2] *Gesta di Federico*, ll. 441–442; see discussion of date, pref., pp. xiv ff.

[3] *Trattato*, 1730, pp. 14 f.

[4] Page 92, ll. 2243 ff., which are almost literally taken over from Boethius; notice l. 2244, "fait sa roe torner."

Amants,[1] and in Marie de France's "lai" of *Guigemar.*[2]
These allusions might seem to settle the tradition from
the classics, for at first glance the train of development
seems to be as follows: classical literature connects the
wheel intimately with the turns of human affairs; Boethius puts man himself on the wheel and seems to suggest
that Fortune herself turns it, probably by hand; writers
in the twelfth century use this conception as if it were
quite established and thoroughly familiar.

But there is another tradition which may cause us a
little difficulty. Sometimes a passage remains ambiguous
as to whether the wheel is actually turned by the goddess,[3] but in the first quarter of the twelfth century Honorius of Autun describes a figure which he apparently owes
to tradition and in which Fortune herself clearly suffers
the revolutions of the great symbol:

> Scribunt itaque philosophi quod mulier rota innexa iugiter cir-
> cumferatur; cuius caput nunc in alta erigatur, nunc in ima demerga-
> tur. Rota haec quae uoluitur est gloria huius mundi quae iugiter
> circumfertur. Mulier rotae innexa est fortuna gloriae intexta.
> Huius caput aliquando sursum, aliquando fertur deorsum, quia
> plerique multocies potentia et diuitiis exaltantur, saepe egestate et
> miseriis exalliantur.[4]

Now, it seems clear that the philosophers to whom Honorius refers did not include Boethius, for the latter's description is certainly not specific enough for any such

---

[1] Edited by G. Paris, in *Romania*, XXV, 505, ll. 277 ff.

[2] Lines 538 ff. See, too, Alanus de Insulis (twelfth century), *Anticlaudianus*, VIII, i (Migne, vol. CCX, col. 560).

[3] See Orderic Vital, in Bouquet's *Recueil*, XII, 723, C ("Fortune ceu rota
uergibilis est," etc.); Wright, *Satirical Poets*, II, 215 ("Quem rota Fortunae
transuexit ad astra repente"), but cf. I, 307 ("Contrahat illa manum," etc.);
Carmina Burana, p. 47, lxxvii, stanzas 2, 3.

[4] *Speculum Ecclesiae* (Migne, vol. CLXXII, col. 1057, C).

elaborate interpretation as this, even granted that Honorius could have understood him in this way. Moreover, there is nothing to show that Honorius conceives Fortune as turning the wheel in the way definitely described by Boethius and as commonly accepted by tradition. Yet the conception of Honorius is not without some followers. Wace writes:

> Fortune trop par es muable,
> Tu ne pues estre un jor estable,
> Nus ne se doit en toi fier:
> Tant fais ta roe fort torner,
> Mult as tost ta color muée
> Tost es chaoite, tost levée. . . .
>
> Tost as un vilain halt levé
> Et un roi em plus bas torné.[1]

In the *Roman de la Rose* Fortune "siet où milieu comme avugle";[2] in Chaucer and Lydgate she "turneth as a bal."[3]

What are we to do in this quandary? Apparently we must consider that after the time of Boethius two traditions were established, one in which Fortune turns the wheel, and one in which she herself is turned thereon. In the second figure she logically should have no control over the turns.

In just this inconsistency, perhaps, lies the solution. In Honorius Fortune has no power over the wheel; in Wace she apparently has a borrowed control. The tradition is not direct, the ideas are not precisely the same. In Honorius Fortune revolves and her head goes where her feet should be; in Wace she simply rises and falls; in the *Ro-*

---

[1] *Roman de Brut*, ll. 1965 ff.
[2] Line 5926.
[3] Chaucer, *Truth*, l. 9; Lydgate, *Troy Book*, i, 1506; ii, 2027.

man de la Rose she is stationary; in Chaucer and Lydgate she revolves like a ball — the wheel-figure itself is not even presented. In other words, I do not think these passages have enough points of contact to establish a tradition. Wherever Honorius found his ideas, then, I do not think he got them from Boethius, nor do I think he passed them on to his successors. The writers following him chronologically seem to have original touches, introducing only a similar confusion of type and symbol. Lydgate is indebted to Chaucer, and Chaucer's line certainly appears to take nothing from any of the other passages.

The point, then, is this: that the main tradition from classical literature is the figure of Fortune turning her wheel, on which mankind and the estate of man depend, and that this idea has some actual beginnings in early Roman times.

II

The Mediaeval Figure

Whatever meaning was originally attached to the wheel, or whichever of the gods was chiefly associated with it in ancient Rome, by the time of the Middle Ages it primarily belonged to Fortuna, as the preceding section of this chapter implies. We find it in portraits of her again and again.[1] The *Awntyrs of Arthure* refers to her as

[1] See reference to a poem, "de rota Fortunae," in *Notices et Extraits*, XXVIII,[2] 407, no. xii. See *Gedicht auf die Zerstörung Mailands*, ll. 24 ff.; Bourdillon, *Early Editions of the Roman de la Rose*, p. 110, § 40; Piaget, *Martin le Franc*, p. 178, n. 2; Nathaniel Hill, *De Guileville*, woodcut xvii (opposite p. xlv of Appendix), also colored drawing F (opposite p. xlii); Dan Michel, *Ayenbite*, p. 76; Durrieu, *Boccace de Munich*, plates ii, ix, xviii; *Bocace des Nobles Maleureux*, fol. xlvj^{vo} (same as Hill's woodcut xvii). See also notes on pp. 148 f., above.

"that wondirfull whele-wryghte." [1] Even the wheel itself takes over descriptive epithets and themes which commonly belong to the goddess. [2] In literature, from the time of Boethius apparently, mankind was thought of as revolving on the wheel itself; and, although such an idea was foreign to Roman art, mediaeval drawings show actual men on the rim of the wheel turning at the will of the goddess. [3]

The wheel itself we may now consider as a special topic, and we shall study its treatment and the various ways in which it works. It may have two different meanings. First, there may be a vague, indefinite connection between it and the objects bestowed by Fortune, — wealth, accident, and the like, — which it controls. As it turns, so man's fortune changes; [4] just how the change is brought about we are not informed, — merely, Fortune turns her wheel. Secondly, we learn that men are them-

[1] Madden's ed., st. xxi, 258; Wright, *Reliquiae Antiquae* (1843), II, 8.

[2] See Faral, *Recherches*, p. 48, l. 227 ("Fortuna, crudelior *asside surda*"); Ariosto, *Orlando Furioso*, XXXIV, lxxiv ("la ruota instabile"); Philippe de Beaumanoir, *La Manekine*, ll. 4639 ff. (*Œuvres*, I, 144; notice the themes); Gower, *Confessio Amantis*, v, 7445 ("blinde whiel"), and *Mirour de l'Omme*, l. 22100 ("roe ades muable"); Chaucer, *Knight's Tale*, A. 925, and *Monk's Tale*, B. 3636 ("false wheel"); Lydgate, *Temple of Glas*, App. I (continuation of MSS., Schick's ed., p. 63), l. 363 ("double whel").

[3] This point in mediaeval art is observed by Galpin (Mod. Lang. Assoc., *Publ.*, XXIV, 333), and by Wolff (*Greek Romances in Elizabethan Prose Fiction*, p. 387).

[4] See Saviozzo, *Alcune Poesie Inedite*, p. 30; Fazio d. Uberti, *Liriche*, p. 253, ll. 47–48; Poliziano, *Le Stanze*, etc., ed. Carducci, 1863, pp. 86 (*La Giostra*, ii, st. 36), 361 (l. 133, "De' ben che la fortuna attorno gira"); Giov. Fiorentino, *Il Pecorone*, II, 135 (xxii, 2); Pulci, *Morgante Maggiore*, xvii, 2; *Roman de la Rose*, ll. 6878–6880; *Girart de Rossillon*, ll. 447–448; Chaucer, *Monk's Tale*, B. 3587–3588; Gower, *Mirour de l'Omme*, ll. 10942 ff., and *Confessio Amantis*, prol., 560 ff.; Lydgate, *Troy Book*, ii, 8561–8562; v, 2636. See the wheel of divination described by Förster in Herrig's *Archiv*, CXXIX, 45–49 (§ 18, "Sphaera Apulei," etc.).

selves attached to the wheel; they are revolved with it, and so their estates change.[1]

A man may be on the highest point of Fortune's wheel,[2] and may yearn to stay there.[3] Or he may feel that nobody else has ever suffered quite so much from the goddess and reached so low a stage on her wheel — an idea founded on a widespread conviction, common particularly to romantic temperaments, that one's own torture is unique in being greater than anybody else's. Henricus

[1] *Poeti del Primo Secolo*, I, 515, and II, 329; Medin, *Ballata della Fortuna*, in *Il Propugnatore*, new ser., II[1] (1889), 112 f.; Lorenzo de' Medici, *Poesie* (1801), I, 169 ("Ventura," etc.); Aeneas Sylvius, *Opera Omnia*, p. 761, B ("Hac conditione ascendimus"); Ariosto, *Orlando Furioso*, X, xiv; Adam de la Halle, *Jeu de la Feuillée*, ll. 788 ff.; *Roman de Fauvel*, ll. 78 ff.; Philippe de Beaumanoir, *La Manekine*, l. 4641 (*Œuvres*, I, 144, "Tout le mont a sa roe tient"); Gorra, *Studi* (Thomas of Saluzzo, § vii), p. 76, "assis en haut de sa roe"; De Guilleville, *Rommant des Trois Pelerinaiges*, fol. lxvij; G. de Machaut, *Poésies*, ed. Chichmaref, II, 312, ll. 104–106; Taillevent, *Regime de Fortune*, bal. iii (Alain Chartier's *Œuvres*, p. 712, "Et puis les fiert de se paulme en la ioe"); Charles d'Orléans, *Poésies*, I, 77 ("tourner à rebours"); Gower, *Confessio Amantis*, vi, 292–293; viii, 1736–1737; and *Mirour de l'Omme*, ll. 21985 ff.; Lydgate, *Siege of Thebes*, ll. 1131–1134, 1148–1149; and *Troy Book*, ii, 2020 ff.; Sibbald, *Chronicle*, III, 477,

> That old blind Dame, delytes to let the joy
> Of all, such is her use, which dois convoy
> Her quheill by gess: not looking to the right,
> Bot still turnis up that pairt quhilk is too light.

Cf. with this Boccaccio's *Amorosa Visione*, cap. xxxi (*Opere*, XIV, 127, "Gravandomi di si noioso pondo"). See drawings in Lydgate's *Falls of Princes*, ed. 1554: at the end of the prologue one with five figures on the wheel; at fol. cxliii, one with seven figures on it. See plate 10, below.

[2] Boccaccio, *Lettere* (*Opere*, XVII), p. 118; Benivieni, *Opere*, p. 261vo (really 201vo; the climber cannot get higher); Pulci, *Morgante Maggiore*, xxv, 275; Barbazan, *Fabliaux*, I, 139, l. 130 ("ëu la roe haus"); Jean de Condé, *Dits et Contes*, II, 347 ("Or le fera plus haut aler Que il ne fust onques d'assés"); Lydgate, *Troy Book*, iv, 1751 ("hiʒest prikke of Fortunys whele"); also *Serpent of Division*, p. 56, l. 2 ("enhansed a man hieste upon hir whele"), p. 65, l. 23 ("þe hiest prikke of hir unstable whele"), and cf. p. 64, ll. 2–4.

[3] Boccaccio, *Filocopo*, ii (*Opere*, VII, 158–159).

Septimellensis felt that he had suffered more than the rest of humanity, and the "Manekine" likewise conceived her trials to be particularly great.[1] Sometimes Fortune turns one so exceedingly far down on the wheel that it will never be possible to rise again.[2] In fact, in one case we read:

La miserabil fortuna che abbassato per li vostri inganni mi vede assai mi nuoce, e niuno aiuto mi porge, anzi s'ingegna con sollecitudine continua di mandarmi più giù che la più infima parte della sua ruota, se far lo potesse, e quivi col calcio sopra la gola mi tiene, nè possibile m'è lasciare il doloroso luogo.[3]

Both these conceptions involve the idea that the wheel can stop. Boethius and those who take his doctrine have assured us that it is useless to attempt to stop it — that it revolves ceaselessly;[4] and yet we do find certain passages where it seems to have paused or where there is an implication that it may pause on occasion.[5]

[1] See *Smith College Studies in Modern Languages*, III, 195; IV, 10.

[2] See Boccaccio, *Filocopo*, iii (*Opere*, VII, 254-256), ii (*ibid.*, 131-132, "più infima parte della sua ruota"), iv (*ibid.*, VIII, 202); Gower, *Balades*, xx, 2 (*Works*, I, 354, "mon estat ne voi changer jammes"); Watriquet de Couvin, *Dits*, p. 214, ll. 498 ff. (*Mireoirs aus Princes*).

[3] Boccaccio, *Filocopo*, iii (*Opere*, VII, 299). Cf. Boethius, *Cons. Philos.*, II, met. i, 3 ff.; see the same idea in Benoît de Ste. Maure's *Roman de Troie*, IV, ll. 25215 ff.; and cf. Froissart, *Œuvres*, III, 213 (*Trésor Amoureux*, bal. iv, 5 ff.).

[4] Boethius, *Cons. Philos.*, II, pr. i, 56-58; Wright, *Satirical Poets*, I, 364 ("fortuna lubrica nescit Mobilitas fixisse rotam"); *Roman de Fauvel*, ll. 79-80 ("qui de tournier ne se terme"); Poliziano, *Le Stanze*, etc., ed. Carducci, 1863, p. 384 (implies that the wheel will never become stable); Masuccio, *Il Novellino*, p. 439 ("chi è colui che possa la . . . rota fermare?"); *Roman de la Rose*, ll. 6432 ff., 6646 ff.; Lydgate, *Assembly of Gods*, l. 319 ("redy to turne without let"); also his *Beware of Doubleness*, in Skeat's *Chaucerian and other Pieces*, p. 292, ll. 41-42 ("goth round aboute A thousand tymes, day and night"); and his *Serpent of Division*, p. 66, l. 26 ("so ofte turnith up and downe").

[5] Hildebert de Lavardin, *De Infidelitate Fortunae* (Migne, vol. CLXXI, col. 1424, A), "Stante rota fortuna fauet"; Sannazaro, *Opere*, p. 351 (son. xxvii, "Che le Rote stan ferme in suo vigore"; cf. Boccaccio, *Filocopo*, iv,

But apparently the malign object of the goddess is accomplished in other ways than by sinking her victim on the wheel; at least the expression describing her work is different. Thus, she may turn her wheel *the wrong way*, a phrase which seems to explain the passages in which she is said to turn the wheel "against us," "contrairement," and so on.[1]

Man himself also plays a part in the game. In Boethius, as we have seen, he is invited to ascend with the wheel; that is, he voluntarily submits to endure the turns of Fortune, hoping, it is implied, that he may somehow struggle to the top, or, arrived there, may manage to maintain his position. The *Kingis Quair*, for example, tells us:

> For sothe it is, that, on hir tolter quhele,
> Euery wight cleuerith into his stage,
> And failyng foting oft, quhen hir lest, rele
> Sum vp, sum doune.[2]

Opere, VIII, 110, "se la sua ruota stesse ferma"); *Renart le Nouvel* (*Roman du Renart*, ed. Méon, IV, 457), ll. 8010 ff. (once mounted this king cannot be put down; the passage is quoted in *Smith College Studies in Modern Languages*, IV, 5); *Awntyrs of Arthure*, st. xxi, 253 ("whills þe whele standis").

[1] Of course, from one point of view any way except upward is the wrong way, and therefore the wheel may not be thought of as choosing a new path. See, however, Chrestien de Troyes, *Roman du Chevalier de la Charrette*, p. 174 ("m'as bistornée"; also in Philippe de Beaumanoir's *Manekine*, l. 1085); *Girart de Rossillon*, l. 1308 ("contrairement"); G. de Machaut, *Poésies*, ed. Chichmaref, I, 176, l. 19 ("Sa roe vuet encontre moy tourner"; cf. also II, 312, ll. 104–106); Gower, *Confessio Amantis*, i, 2624 ("the whiel is al miswent"). In Cousin's plate 117 the wheel is turning from right to left, instead of the usual way. Cf. plates 4 and 10 in this volume; also the wheel at Beauvais.

[2] Stanza 9; cf. st. 163. See, too, Boccaccio, *Filocopo*, ii (*Opere*, VII, 158–159, "quanto potrò in alto mantenermi mi manterrò"); Pucci, *Poesia Popolare*, ed. Ferri, p. 125, st. vii (let him who sits on the wheel beware lest he fall); Simund de Freine, *Roman de Philosophie*, ll. 303 ff. Cf. Furnivall, *Political*,

PLATE 8

SEVERAL WHEELS

Plate 9

"Et m'as si geté en la boe."

Pierre de la Broche, stanza 12, l. 6.

The wheel, then, in the Middle Ages means relative exaltation or humiliation in worldly dignity. It is turned by Fortune, and man is often actually attached to the rim, where he suffers the consequent changes of position. It may or may not stop, according to your own idea of the matter; it probably goes amiss somehow. But there seems to be a notion that it is your own fault if you suffer, because you have a certain control over the question whether you will get on the wheel at all.

III

Themes in the Description of the Wheel

Several themes in the description of the wheel have already been suggested in the matters studied in the preceding sections of this chapter: sometimes Fortune stands on the wheel; sometimes she is attached to it and revolves with it; the wheel puts man's affairs into good or bad condition; Fortune revolves man's estate on the rim; the wheel may cease to move (or it expressly may not!); man may climb on it and may struggle to the top. But there are further developments of some of these ideas, which may now be briefly described.

Clearly the most impressive trick of the wheel is to whirl a man from the top to the bottom. Man "falleth ofte unsofte," [1] and he is not likely to forget it. Concerning this act a particular riming formula which obtained some popularity came into vogue:

Religious, and Love Poems, pp. 265 ("Ware the Wheel!"), 266 ("ȝif þou be cointë, þou ssalt liue"); Lydgate, *Troy Book*, i, 784 ("who clymbeth hyȝe may not falle softe"); *Awntyrs of Arthure*, st. xxi, 253 ("Maye no man stere hy of strengthe, whills þe whele standis").

[1] Lydgate, *The Churl and the Bird*, st. 30.

Sire, mains gentius hom seoit ier sor la roe,
qui por le votre mort est ceus en le boe.[1]

A man is now on top of the wheel and then below in the mud. Since the wheel is regarded as standing upright, generally with the lower part of the rim near the ground, this figure need not include the idea of one's being cast off by centrifugal force. Even in such a line as the following,

Et m'as si geté en la boe,[2]

the idea of one's being entirely thrown off from the rim of the wheel is not stated definitely; [3] the meaning seems to be merely that one is in about as disagreeable a position as the device can offer. It may be regarded, however, as a step in the direction of the centrifugal idea.

The figure of the wheel's casting a man into the mud is carried even farther in *Athis and Prophilias*, where we

[1] Alexandre de Bernay, *Li Romans d'Alixandre*, ed. Michelant, p. 522, ll. 2–3. This is the earliest instance of the use of this formula that I can find. Galpin (Mod. Lang. Assoc., *Publ.*, XXIV, 334) gives the history of the *roe-boe* rime. See also Rutebeuf, *Œuvres* (1874), I, 105, ll. 33–37; *Romanz de la Poire*, ll. 37–40; *Roman de la Rose*, ll. 3998–3999, 4910–4911, and (*ibid.*, IV, 33–34) Jean de Meun's *Testament*, ll. 652–655; Sieper, *Les Échecs Amoureux*, p. 85; Galpin, in *Mod. Lang. Notes*, XXIX, 62–63; *Pierre de la Broche* (Monmerqué and Michel, *Théâtre Français*, p. 211, st. 3). A variant of the rime *roe-boe* is the rime *roe-moe*: see Philippe de Beaumanoir, *Jehan et Blonde*, ll. 2509–2510 (*Œuvres*, II, 79); *Pierre de la Broche*, as above; *Girart de Rossillon*, ll. 447–448; Froissart, *Œuvres*, III, 213 (*Trésor Amoureux*, bal. iv, 5 ff.); Jubinal, *Contes, Dits,* etc., I, 917; *Li Romanz de la Poire*, ll. 9–52; Montaiglon's *Recueil de Poésies Françoises*, p. 84; *Le Petit Traittiet du Malheur de France* (appended to Pierre Michault's *Dance aux Aveugles*), p. 233; and cf. Chaucer *Troilus and Criseyde*, iv, 6–7.

[2] *Pierre de la Broche*, as above. See also *Le Dit de l'Empereur Coustant*, ed. Wesselofsky, in *Romania*, VI, 162, ll. 23 ff.; and cf. the Italian *ruota-mota*, in Benivieni's *Dela Vanita Inganni* (*Opere*, p. 154 ᵛᵒ).

[3] See, however, Henryson, *The Paddok and the Mous*, l. 171, "Now on the quheill, now wrappit to the ground."

read that the man is plunged very deep — "Tost le re-
trebuche an l'abisme." [1] Baudouin de Condé gives us a
vivid picture of a similar scene rather more developed:

> In the tower of Love's prison stands Fortune, turning a wheel of
> four spokes. The spokes on high uphold the lords of the world, the
> lower part of the wheel supports those who are worth nothing at all
> Those on high have success in love:

> > Li autres rais si aval baisse,
> > Ke jusk'en la cartre s'abaisse,
> > Là ù cil sunt qui n'ont d'amours
> > Fors les travaus et les dolors.

> The wheel turns about, putting some on high and others low:

> > Les autres torne contreval
> > En la prison, ù li traval
> > Et les grans paines sunt d'amours.

> The prison below is a gloomy place, dark for want of the light
> which love spreads. Serpents, whose bite is desire, breed there. [2]

In this account the wheel sends its victims down into the
prison; at least, they are turned there on the surface of the
wheel, although they seem to have a chance of getting out
again. [3] Baudouin tells us that one comes to Fortune and
voluntarily climbs on the wheel, [4] whereupon the individual is in danger of the prison.

A description of remarkable similarity, close enough
indeed to suggest actual influence, is found in the *Kingis
Quair* of James I of Scotland, whose narrative runs as
follows:

> The author went to Fortune and found her waiting beside her
> big wheel, to which a multitude of folk were clinging.

---

[1] Line 1979. Cf. Jubinal, *Contes, Dits*, etc., I, 196, "Demain sera getez en
la terre parfonde."

[2] *Li Prisons d'Amours*, ll. 839 ff. (*Dits et Contes*, I, 297–308).

[3] Lines 1065 ff.   [4] See ll. 1027 ff.

And vnderneth the quhelë sawe I there
An vgly pit, as depe as ony helle,
That to behald thereon I quoke for fere;
Bot o thing herd I, that quho there-in fell
Come no more vp agane, tidingis to telle.

The wheel was slippery: many failed in their footing and were rolled to the ground. Some were too sore to climb again, others Fortune picked up safe and sound. A new swarm filled the empty places. Fortune called the author by name, bidding him climb on the wheel; and he must be quick about it, for time was passing.[1]

Here the author seeks Fortune concerning affairs of love, as the chief figure does in Baudouin's poem; the wheel is practically a wheel of love, and the author succeeds in his suit, "thankit be Fortunys exiltree." Some do not rise again after their fall, but others Fortune is prevailed upon to assist; all voluntarily climb on the wheel; and, most important of all, beneath the wheel is a pit.

Other suggestions for the picture of Fortune as given in the *Quair* and the *Prisons d'Amours* are to be found in some versions of the *Mort d'Arthur*, and perhaps in these lines of the twelfth-century *Cursor Mundi* :

Dame fortune turnes þan hir quele
And castes vs dun vntil a wele.[2]

---

[1] See the *Quair*, stanzas 159 ff. For discussion of the sources of this idea, see Lawson's introduction, pp. lx ff., and for its influence see p. lxxiv; but his suggestions do not account for the most important element, the pit.

[2] Lines 23719–23720. Cf. the descriptions in the stanzaic *Morte Arthur*, ll. 3168 ff., and Malory's *Morte Darthur*, book xxi, ch. iii. The French *Mort Artu* (ed. J. D. Bruce, Halle, 1910) p. 220, has a different account; also the alliterative *Morte Arthure*, ll. 3250 ff. See Bruce's note, *Mort Artu*, p. 291. The wheel in the Alexandrian fragment of *Cassamus*, or *Les Voeux du Paon* (ed. Rosskopf, p. 69, l. 405), is connected with lovers, but there is no pit; nor is there any in Skeat's edition of Alexander's *Wars* (Early English Text Soc., Extra Series, No. 47, p. 104), although here there are flood-gates and drenching. The idea of the pit appears again, however, in Painter's trans-

Here, to be sure, there is a chance of recovery for a time, till Death claims one. In art, however, there is a familiar representation of a wheel with a grave or a coffin beneath it,[1] and perhaps this idea alone, often found in pictures of Fortune, was enough to suggest the figure of the pit.

The idea of the centrifugal action might easily have been suggested by the roulette or by other actual uses of the wheel in real life. But the truth is that this conception does not play a large part in literature,[2] and herein the *Quair* shows about the closest approach to a use of the figure. How successful and moving the scene is in King James's poem may be gathered from the inspiration the lines offered to Dante Gabriel Rossetti, who took over the theme and plan for his *King's Tragedy*. Rossetti's most powerful passages are those recounting Fortune's work. The poem leads to a sublime climax of emotion, and strikes its final note in the lines,

lation of Boaistuau's French paraphrase of *Romeo e Giulietta* (New Shakspere Soc., Series 3, I, 111):

"And thus a month or twayne, they continued their joyful mindes, to their incredible satisfaction, until Lady fortune enuious of their prosperity, turned hir Wheele to tumble them into sutch a bottomlesse pit, as they payed hir vsury for their pleasures past, by a certayne most cruell and pitifull death."

On the pit, see Post's *Sources of Juan de Mena*, in *Romanic Review*, III, 243–245.

[1] See Boll, *Die Lebensalter*, cut opposite p. 144 (Abb. 4), date *circa* 1461; Weinhold, *Glücksrad und Lebensrad*, tafel ii; Heider, *Mitteilungen*, p. 117; and p. 173, below. Note the wheel with the inscription "Omnia mors tollit," Heider, *op. cit.*, p. 114. Cf. E. G. Millar, *English Illuminated Manuscripts*, Paris and Brussels, 1926, pl. 54.

[2] The use of the wheel in *Les Échecs Amoureux* does not involve the centrifugal figure. For discussion of this point, see *Mod. Lang. Notes*, XXIX, 197. For centrifugal force, see Chaucer's *Troilus and Criseyde*, iv, 6, "whan a wight is from hir wheel y-throwe"; Lydgate's *Daunce of Machabree*, prol., st. 2, "Fortune hath them from her whele ytrow; and his *Siege of Thebes*, l. 890, "From her wheel she plongëd hym a-doun."

Through the dusk where the white face lay
In the Pit of Fortune's Wheel.[1]

So much may be said for the motion of Fortune's wheel; now for the figures attached to it. The most common conception, perhaps because it seems the simplest and most natural, and perhaps because it may therefore be the oldest, is that of the wheel with four human figures on the rim. This theme is so definitely marked that it deserves special study.

Since it seems likely that the idea originated in art from its peculiarly visual quality, I shall give a typical example taken from a mediaeval drawing. On the top of the wheel is a crowned youth sitting on a throne and holding a sceptre; at the right is a figure falling, his crown dropping from his head; at the bottom is a figure prostrate; on the left is a man climbing, extending his hands toward the youth at the top. The figures are inscribed respectively, Regno, Regnavi, Sum sine Regno, and Regnabo. This picture is exceedingly familiar in mediaeval art.[2] In one of Boccaccio's descriptions of

[1] *Works*, 1888, I, 172.

[2] See *Carmina Burana*, p. 1; Du Sommerard, *Les Arts au Moyen Age*, Album, vol. II, ser. 8, pl. 30 (also in Molinier's *Manuscrits et Miniatures*, p. 291), and ser. 4, plates 38, 39; *Bibliotheca Casinensis*, IV, 83, nos. 145, 146 (at the middle of the circle is inscribed "Prosperitas Adversitas"; cf. the use of these names above, p. 143); Durrieu, *Boccace de Munich*, planches ii, ix, xviii; Didron, *Annales Archéol.*, XVI, 338, plate; Gregor Reisch, *Margarita Philosophica*, lib. viii, cap. xvi, plate (inscribed Glorior Elatus, Descendo Mortificatus, Axi Rotor, — figure supine, — Ad Alta Vehor; and cf. similar inscriptions on the title-page of the 1539 German translation of *De Remediis*, noted in Fiske's *Bibliographical Notices*, III, p. 34, § 69); Barbier de Montault, *Traité*, I, pl. x (opp. p. 160), no. 102; Bourdillon, *Early Editions of the Roman de la Rose*, p. 110, § 40 (see *Liber Fortunae* described by Längfors in *Romania*, XLV, 265 ff.). For discussion and many references, see Weinhold, *Glücksrad und Lebensrad*, pp. 10 ff. Wackernagel ("*Glücksrad und die Kugel*

PLATE 10

BOCCACCIO AND FORTUNE

Fortune we read: "I saw men climbing the wheel by their wits, and arrived at the top they said, 'I reign.' Others, failing, seemed to say, 'I am without reign.'"[1] In another place the "formula of four," as we may call this theme, gives the topics and titles to a series of poems, beginning with a speech by Fortune and then proceeding with a monologue by each of the four figures:

FORTUNA. — I am that Fortuna who has made and unmade kings and emperors. It is of no avail to worship me. Let him beware who sits at the top of the wheel. Let each hold fast to his treasure.

REGNO. — I reign at the top of the wheel, as Fortune has destined me. But if the wheel turns I may be deprived of power. Be moderate, ye who are in power, lest you fall to earth. Behold the honor I am paid because I sit at the top of the wheel.

REGNAVI. — I reigned for a while, then Fortune put me down and deprived me of everything good. Her friendship avails not. No friend remains when a man falls. Do not be confident when you are rising; Fortune makes you fall with deadly blows. Hearken to my case, how I gained and lost this honor.

REGNABO. — I shall reign if Fortune pleases and the wheel turns to the fourth place. I shall be above and rule all the world. How great is my pleasure then! Virtue moves me to speak such words, because I plan to do justice and punish those who have maliciously robbed the men of good estate. What joy I shall have to be able to punish them!

SUM SINE REGNO. — I am, as you see, without reign, down low in wretchedness. Fortune has disclaimed me. If I should mount

---

des Glücks," in his *Kleinere Schriften*, I, 251 f.) relates the four-formula to the four quarters of the moon; with this idea cf. Novati's *Carmina Medii Aevi*, p. 44, st. vi. See the peculiar variation, with a crowned ass on top of the wheel, in *Catalogue des Livres de Rothschild*, I, 255 (title-page of the 1506 ed. of Martin le Franc's *Lestrif de Fortune et de Vertu*). Cf. Brant's *Narrenschiff*, ed. Simrock, pp. 85, 129 (figure at the left with human head, falling); and see Bergner, *Handbuch der Kirchlichren Kunstaltertümer in Deutschland*, p. 584. Note the frontispiece and plates 5 and 11 in the present volume.

[1] *Amorosa Visione*, cap. xxxi (*Opere*, XIV, 126).

on this wheel, every man would be friendly to me. Let each take warning who considers me:

> Appresso de Iesu ella è unita
> Questa cattiva che nel foco arda,
>   E sta tanto sentita,
>
> Dando et tollendo ove più li pare
> Tal gratia li ha voluto dio donare.[1]

The formula is adapted to a dramatic use in the *Mystère de Bien-Advisé et Mal-Advisé,* where we see the figures acting parts:

Bien-Advisé and Mal-Advisé, after meeting and consulting with Franche-Volonté, and after visiting the house of Raison and calling on Foy, become separated. Mal-Advisé travels with Folie, Hoquélerie, and so on. Presently, however, the two men meet at the house of Fortune. Mal-Advisé wishes to try the wheel, but Fortune makes him retire in favor of four men in whom she is interested — Regnabo, Regno, Regnavi, Sum sine Regno. These figures climb on the wheel, and after successive turns Fortune takes Regnavi and Sine-Regno and "les precipite de sa Roüe"; whereupon "ces deux personages se voyans sans espoir d'y remonter, vomissent mille injures contre cette inconstante." Nothing abashed, Fortune takes Regnabo and Regno under her protection, while Bien-Advisé advises the two left despairing to go to Confession. Meanwhile Fortune, after some diversion in revolving Regno and Regnabo on the wheel, makes them fall also. The Vices take them to Malle-Fin, from whom they are conducted to the torments of demons. The two good disciples who have confessed go to Bonne-Fin and are turned over to Penitence, who, after beating them with rods, leads them to Paradise and the awaiting angels.[2]

Such is the dramatic and literary use of the formula of four. Besides these treatments, we have occasional brief allusions to the theme elsewhere in literature.[3]

---

[1] *Alcune Poesie Inedite del Saviozzo et di altri autori,* ed. G. Ferraro, pp. 51 ff.

[2] Frères Parfaict, *Théâtre François,* II, 113 ff.

[3] See Gorra, *Studi,* pp. 57–59 (MS. fr. 12460, Bibl. Nat., year 1345); Furnivall, *Political, Religious, and Love Poems,* p. 251; Frezzi, *Quadriregio,* I, 149, ll. 4 ff.; Gower, *Vox Clamantis,* ii, 155.

PLATE 11

THE FOUR FIGURES

There is a peculiar variation of the wheel with human beings attached to it, in which we find a human figure not lying on the periphery but stretched across the face. Fortune takes over Ixion's wheel and Ixion along with it.[1] Honorius of Autun, after describing the wheel on which, according to the report of the philosophers, Fortune is tied, continues:

Dicunt etiam quod quidam apud inferos damnatus per radios rotae sit diuaricatus; quae rota sine intermissione ab alto montis in ima uallis feratur et iterum alta repetens denuo relabatur.[2]

This is in close relation to his discussion of Fortune's wheel. Walter Map goes still farther:

Ixion ibi uoluitur in rota. Nec hic desunt Ixiones, quos uolubilitas torquet fortunae. Ascendunt ad gloriam, ruunt in miseriam.

. . .

Habemus et nos Ixiones, quos sorte sua uolubilis fortune torquet.[3]

In Frezzi's *Quadriregio* Ixion suffers on one of the seven wheels of Fortune there conceived:

Colui, che su e giù ha tante doglie,
E'Ission', ed ha tal penitenza,
Che volle a Giove già toglier la moglie.[4]

It is not strange, then, that in Henryson's *Orpheus and Eurydice* Ixion's wheel takes over many of the characteristics of the symbol of Fortune.[5]

[1] See Gaidoz, *Le Dieu Gaulois*, pp. 44 ff.
[2] *Speculum Ecclesiae* (Migne, vol. CLXXII, col. 1057, C).
[3] *De Nugis Curialium*, ed. Wright, pp. 6, 239 (written before 1189). These references were given to me by Professor James Hinton of Emery College.
[4] I, 149–150. Noted by Post, "Sources of Juan de Mena," in *Romanic Review*, III, 229 and n. 22.
[5] See ll. 261 ff.; notice 475 ff., and cf. 485–488,

That warldly men sumtyme ar castin hie
Apon the quhele, in grete prosperitee,

IV

OTHER MEDIAEVAL CONCEPTIONS OF FORTUNE'S WHEEL

We have thus far observed some of the more common themes, all of which depend on the idea that Fortune's wheel revolves mankind either on its circumference or on its face; but there are conceptions which give it other activities or possibilities. The wheel, to be sure, may still revolve the fortunes of mankind or may turn man himself from top to bottom, but it accomplishes such changes in a slightly different way and generally with added symbolism.

> And wyth a quhirl, unwarly or thai witte,
> Ar thrawin doun to pure and law estate,

with Walter Map's "Ascendunt ad gloriam, ruunt in miseriam," quoted above. See, too, Brant's *Narrenschiff*, ed. Zarncke, p. 57, § 56, ll. 48–52 (cf. Simrock's ed., p. 129 ff.):

> Ixion blibt syn rad nit stan
> Dann es loufft vmb, von wynden kleyn
> Sellig, wer hofft jnn gott alleyn,
> Er fellt, vnd blibt nit jn der höh
> Der steyn.

The idea of men tied to the wheel or broken on it is suggested in Boccaccio's *Amorosa Visione*, cap. xxv (*Opere*, XIV, 102), and in Sannazaro's *Opere*, p. 387. Cf. Cousin's plate (No. 17), where an old man with wings is lying on the rim of the wheel. For figures attached to a wheel (not Fortune's) in the Inferno, see late references in Marie de France's *Espurgatoire Saint Patriz*, ll. 1121 ff.; De Guilleville's *Pelerinage de l'Ame*, Roxburghe Club, ll. 4873 ff. (a devil turns this "wheel of torment," the figure at the top is whirled down and his head is dashed at the bottom), 5309 ff. ("two strong Satans" turn this wheel); A. van Staveren's *Auctores Mythographi*, 1742, frontispiece (cf. above, p. 131, n. 2); Petit de Julleville's *Histoire de la Littérature Française, Moyen Age*, II, 416–417, plate representing the stage-setting for the Passion play at Valenciennes, 1547 (MS. fr. 12536, Bibl. Nat.).

For example, the wheel is sometimes figured as having a course on which it turns. Perhaps this means only that it goes "round and round"; but when we read of its changing this course we must understand either that it goes backwards or that it travels on a special road and selects a new path.[1] We do find an apparent reference to the road:

> Perchè mentre girato sei dal dorso
> Di ruota per allor felice e buona,
> La qual cangia le volte a mezzo il corso.
> E non potendo tu cangiar persona,
> Nè lasciar l'ordin, di che il ciel ti dota,
> Nel mezzo del cammin la t'abbandona.
> Però, se questo si comprende e nota,
> Sarebbe un sempre felice e beato,
> Che potesse saltar di ruota in ruota.[2]

Here the wheel becomes for all practical purposes a wheel of travel, a vehicle.[3] Moreover, — and this leads to our next topic, — several wheels of Fortune are sometimes mentioned.

[1] See Lydgate, *Beware of Doubleness*, in Skeat's *Chaucerian and other Pieces*, p. 292, ll. 43–44 ("Whos cours standeth ever in doute For to transmew"); Chaucer, *Troilus and Criseyde*, i, 138 ff. Cf. p. 158 above.

[2] Machiavelli, *Capitolo di Fortuna* (*Opere*, VII, 369; and see 368, "con tante ruote").

[3] For the wheel as a vehicle, see *Roman de la Rose*, ll. 6168–6171; Galpin, *Roman de la Rose*, pp. 340 f. See also Sannazaro, *Opere*, p. 379,

> Rota par che vi affide;
> E vi spiani dinanzi e fossi, e monti;

Gower, *In Praise of Peace* (*Works*, III, 481 ff.), ll. 115–116,

> The werre hath set his cart on thilke whieles
> Wher that fortune mai noght be believed.

See Gaidoz, *Le Dieu Gaulois*, p. 58, the wheel of Fortuna Redux. Cf. *Perceval le Gallois*, I, 80 (prose, twelfth century): "Li chevaliers qu'ele moine aprés lui sénéfie la roe de fortune; car, tout autresint conme li chars vet sor les roueles, demoinne ele le siècle aus II damoiseles qui la suivent."

In the *Roman de Fauvel* good and bad Fortune are symbolized, with the usual mediaeval concreteness and complexity, by two wheels, one fast and the other slow, within each of which is another small wheel that has a contrary movement. All four "font l'estat du monde tourner." [1] Frezzi introduces a further complication by conceiving seven great wheels, "come spere in questo Mondo." The fourth is taller than the rest and reaches up to Jove; those on each side are decreasingly smaller. On the wheels are various characters, those aloft rejoicing in happiness, those below suffering disaster. [2]

So much for the mechanism of the wheel, with the usual symbolism of its control over the casual affairs of life or over the figures of men themselves. But the wheel was held to have power, not only over man's worldly affairs, but also over his spiritual condition. Thus, a figure might

---

[1] See Längfors's ed., ll. 1931–1940; and the summary in Gorra's *Studi*, pp. 55–56. For two wheels see pl. 9 in the present volume. Cf. the three wheels in Juan de Mena: Post, "Sources of Juan de Mena," *Romanic Review*, III, 225. Perhaps the suggestion for several wheels comes from a natural comparison of the wheel of Fortune to the earth (see, e. g., Wright, *Satirical Poets*, II, 39, "ut rota mundus; Quippe uolubilis, et uariabilis, ac ruibundus") and then to the spheres. See Pulci's *Morgante Maggiore*, ii, 49, and xxii, 38, where it is hard to tell what "le volubil rote" means.

[2] *Quadriregio*, I, 148 (lib. ii, cap. xiii, 13 ff.). Ixion (cf. p. 167 above) is on the fastest wheel; Rienzo Tribuno on the second; Bernabò of Milan is on the third, and his nephew on another. See also, in Guillaume de Machaut's *Livre du Voir-Dit*, pp. 333–334 and note, the four little circles within a great one, round which is written, "Affluo, discedo, talis ludus cui me do." The poem gives the inscriptions on all the other circles, and says of the fifth or surrounding one, which "met tout à destruccion,"

> Et vescy la droite escripture
> Que Tytus Livius figure:
>   Pense & regarde qui je sui,
>   Quant tu le saras hé-m' & fui.

This wheel is reproduced in plate 8 above.

be filled with pride at the top of the wheel, but later at the bottom feel correspondingly humble, the two estates of pride and humiliation being caused by the frame on which he is turning.[1] Buti gives us an interesting wheel, which is worth reproducing here to show one elaboration of this idea:[2]

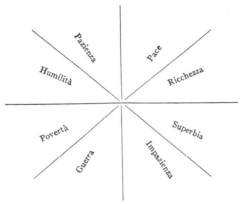

Apparently the qualities on the right side of this wheel would be at the highest part according to most conceptions, since pride comes at the supreme moment of achievement;[3] but in Buti's figure the highest point seems to be actually between Pazienza and Pace,[4] and, falling, one drops first into that dangerous kind of peace

[1] See *Le Roman du Renart*, ed. Méon, I, p. x (Orgueil and Guille near the top of the wheel, apparently representing the estate of Renard while he sits in power).

[2] *Commento sopra la Divina Commedia*, I, 214. See also Vernon, *Readings on the Inferno of Dante*, I, 246.

[3] Cf. Cousin, *Livre de Fortune*, pl. 119, in which the inscriptions, marking six appropriate figures, run round the wheel thus, beginning at the top: "Ex Divitiis Superbia, Ex Superbia Bellum, Ex Bello Paupertas, Ex Paupertate Humilitas, Ex Humilitate Pax, Ex Pace Divitiae."

[4] Cf. *ibid.*, pl. 93, "Fortunae Patiæntia Victrix."

or composure which may go farther — into an excess of luxury. This is a distinctly original touch. The wheel, as usual, revolves clock-wise, and here the idea of unlimited revolutions is perfectly conceivable. One might regard it as a wheel analyzing the range of experience in a certain kind of human life. The moral question is not introduced.

In other wheels, however, we do find a reference to the moral question. People rise to their proud positions by fraud, but they always fall again.[1] Virtue is necessary to keep one's position:

Tout adès fermement s'i tient
Ki aime Diu et carité,
Et a de son proisme pité;
Car qui sagement s'i avise,
Cele roe que on devise,
N'est sans plus que cis morteus mondes.[2]

Or sometimes the wheel, like the similar figure in the Orphic mysteries, is a wheel of monotonous, whirling durance, submission to which is caused by too much concern in worldly interests and from which one would fain escape:

Puisqu' homme est a sa dure rouhe
Englué par concupiscence,
Il peut aussytost choir en bouhe,
Qu'estre eslevé en audience:
Et ny a point de difference
Du bas au hault; car ille est ronde,
Et tourne sur ung gond le monde.[3]

---

[1] *Renart le Nouvel,* in Méon's edition of *Le Roman du Renart,* IV, 459, note, ll. 13 ff. ("C'est roe de dampnation"). See *Smith College Studies in Modern Languages,* IV, 5, where the whole passage is quoted. Cf. the *Petit Traittiet du Malheur de France,* appended to Pierre Michault's *Dance aux Aveugles,* pp. 233 f.   [2] *Renart le Nouvel,* ll. 26–31.

[3] Pierre Michault, *La Dance aux Aveugles,* p. 100. For the relation of Avarice to Fortune, see Baudouin de Condé, *Dits et Contes,* I, 34. Cf. the

Wheels of worldly "concupiscence" are perhaps represented by any of the wheels on which the worldly estate of man changes.[1] The logical end of immorality, following its lowest estate, is death; and so we come to the wheels which show us a grave or a coffin below, and indeed we find some turned by Death himself.[2] This kind no longer belongs to Fortune, though it is a possible development from hers, as she rules Death. It is, however, concerned not with the idea of morality or immorality, — there is usually no succession of moral stages through which man passes, — but with the typical periods or "ages" of his life. In art there are several wheels with the seven ages definitely marked; [3] perhaps it was such a

idea in *Les Échecs Amoureux* discussed in *Modern Language Notes*, XXIX (1914), 197; and cf. the wheel of Sensual Desire in De Guilleville's *Rommant des Trois Pelerinaiges*, fol. xlij vo f.

[1] See the "formula of four" above, pp. 164 ff.; also Weinhold, *Glücksrad und Lebensrad*, p. 15 (Honor, Prosperitas, Paupertas, Adversitas). Barbier de Montault (*Traité*, I, 163, § 3) describes the wheel of human life at Beauvais with twelve persons on it, one at the top, five climbing, five falling, and a prone figure at the bottom. The one at the top offers one hand to help those who are ascending and pushes with his sceptre those who are falling. See three figures on the wheel: Didron, *Annales Archaeol.*, I, 433 f. (Bibl. Amiens, MS. 216); also *ibid.*, plate opposite p. 422.

[2] See Fiske's *Bibliographical Notices*, III, 38, § 77 (German translation of *De Remediis*, 1637); Weinhold, *Glücksrad und Lebensrad*, p. 24, and tafel ii (here Death turns the wheel); Tommaso Pischedda, *Canti Popolari*, p. 37 ("E ti spalanca — Un negro avel"); also see the wheel of the seven ages, just below. Cousin's plate of "Ultima Fortuna" (*Livre de Fortune*, pl. 199) represents Fortune and Death hurrying on together with a wheel between them; Death's hand is on the wheel and Fortune's is on his arm. See also *Du Sommerard's* plate 40, described on page 120, n. 1, above; and cf. pp. 117 ff.

[3] See Heider, *Mitteilungen*, p. 117. On the relation of the ages to the planets and the seven deadly sins, see Boll's *Lebensalter* (and, incidentally, see the seven circles of the seven planets on Fortune's three wheels in Juan de Mena, Post's " Sources," p. 225). See Green, *Shakespeare and the Emblem Writers*, pl. 15 (same as Boll's pl. 3, opposite p. 144), and pp. 406–409; cf.

picture that Jacques had in mind in his famous speech. If we were expected to imagine that the wheel of the seven ages turned more than once, we might see in it a resemblance to the Buddhistic "wheel of life," with its succeeding revolutions standing for successive lives of mankind in just such a wheel of durance as we find in the Orphic mysteries.[1] But we are not justified, I think, in believing that the Middle Ages imagined a turn beyond the final state of death.

These, then, are the various new interpretations and constructions of the wheel. I believe it is always Fortune's symbol, whether borrowed for the time being or not. Now it apparently serves as a vehicle whirling on a course of its own; again, it is attached to a more elaborate mechanism; or it becomes doubled or tripled, and perhaps even generates a sevenfold engine on which humanity turns. It revolves man's feelings as well as his social status; and either this wheel or one like it turns man from the cradle to the grave — a conception of the "wheel of

Weinhold, *Glücksrad und Lebensrad,* tafel ii (nine figures on the wheel). On the entire subject, see, besides Boll and Green, Weinhold's *Glücksrad,* pp. 21 ff., and Barbier de Montault's *Traité,* I, 163, § 4.

[1] See L. Austine Waddell, *The Buddhism of Tibet,* pp. 102 ff., where the twelfth stage of the wheel (see p. 110) is "Decay and Death." It is interesting to compare the other stages with the wheel of "Pazienza" and "Pace" (p. 171 above): (1) Unconscious Will; (2) Conformations; (3) Consciousness; (4) Self-consciousness; (5) Sense-surfaces and Understanding; (6) Contact; (7) Feeling; (8) Desire; (9) Indulgence; (10) Fuller Life; (11) Birth of Heir; (12) Decay and Death; then back to (1) Unconscious Will. In the centre of the wheel are often figured a serpent, a cock, and a pig in pursuit of each other round the wheel, symbolizing ill-will, lust, and stupidity. For the relation of the wheel to the Orphic cycle, see Waddell, p. 109, n. 2. For Orphism and the wheel, see Jane E. Harrison, *Prolegomena to the Study of Greek Religion* (Cambridge, 1908), pp. 588 ff., with the inscription (pp. 588, 669), "I have flown out of the sorrowful weary Wheel."

life" which seems more likely to come from the symbol of Fortune[1] than from any external source like the Buddhistic figure. Thus Fortune's wheel assumes no small importance in the thought of man's existence.[2]

V

SUMMARY

In a review of the development of Fortune's wheel in the mediaeval period, six important points are made

[1] Boll derives this wheel from Fortune's: his two plates both show the goddess.

[2] A few references to other wheels, which I have collected by chance in my study, may be of use to some other investigator of the subject:

For the wheel of God, with the rim controlled by Fate, see Boethius, *Cons. Philos.*, IV, pr. vi (with the rim transferred to Fortune in *Les Échecs Amoureux*, see *Mod. Lang. Notes*, XXIX, 197; see the wheel of Fate in Petrarch's *Bucolicum Carmen*, p. 141, ecl. x, l. 15, and in his *Africa*, ii, 293). Cf. the wheel with Christ on it, Gaidoz, *Le Dieu Gaulois*, pp. 83–84. For the wheel of God in general, see Elizabeth of Schönau's description (Migne, vol. CXCV, col. 136; and cf. Ezekiel i, 15–17; x, 9–10):

Vidi non procul ab eis duos arietes, grandes, et praeclaros, ante signum crucis, et sustinentes in humeris suis rotam nimiae claritatis, et mirae magnitudinis. His omnibus ita perspectis, in haec uerba prorupi dicens: "Leuate oculos cordis uestri ad deificum lumen; attendite et uidete gloriam, et maiestatem Domini."

One recalls the three rings of three colors symbolizing the Trinity in Dante's *Paradiso*. A wheel of fire is described by Friedrich Vogt in Weinhold's *Zeitschrift des Vereins für Volkskunde* (Berlin, 1893), III, 349 ff.; for its relation to the wheel of Fortune, see pp. 368–369.

For the wheel of the sun among the Gauls, see Alexandre Bertrand, *Nos Origines: La Religion des Gaulois, les Druides et le Druidisme* (Paris, 1897), pp. 185 ff., and see pl. xxii. For the wheel of Saint Katherine, see Lydgate's *Minor Poems*, ed. MacCracken, I, 122 (l. 59), 134 (l. 19), and, for an Easter wheel, 377. The wheel of Desire moderated by the wheel of Temperance is described by Froissart, *L'Orloge Amoureus* (*Œuvres*, I, 59); the wheel of Victory in the *Squyr of Lowe Degre*, ed. E. W. Mead, l. 258; the wheel of the law, with a thousand spokes symbolizing the symmetry and completeness of the law, by Waddell, *The Buddhism of Tibet*, p. 389 (for pictures of it, see pp. 134, 337).

clear: (1) In classical literature the wheel is intimately
connected with the changes of man's estate.   (2) In
Boethius we have practically a beginning of the two
great conceptions, (*a*) Fortune turning the wheel, (*b*)
mankind actually on the rim.   (3) The tradition after
Boethius, starting in the twelfth century, gives us chiefly
the figure we find in his portrayal.   (4) Throughout the
Middle Ages the general idea is that Fortune turns the
wheel, on which mankind clings; in the line of this development occurs the "formula of four."   (5) There is
another tradition showing various figures attached to the
face of the wheel, among them Fortune herself and Ixion.
(6) A perversion of the wheel-figure culminates in the
"wheel of life" or the "wheel of the seven ages," apparently because Fortune's wheel seemed to dominate in
every phase of human life.

The wheel as a symbol should be dwelt upon particularly because it is so mediaeval in its conception.   The
mediaeval imagination was primarily concrete: it necessarily visualized the symbol as an actual image with the
real figures of men turning upon it.   Nor was this the fig-
ment of one mind alone.   The representation delighted
many, and writers enjoyed alluding to it and elaborating
it, perhaps adding a wheel or two more in order to en-
hance the effect.   In its final forms the figure is the creation, not of one poet alone, but of hundreds.

One point more is worth remarking — that the picture
of Fortune standing on the wheel satisfied Roman art.
But in its last analysis that figure is, as I have said, poor
allegory, for the Fortune depicted with such an unsteady
footing is not the goddess but the type.   Obviously, however, the Roman artist did not analyze the idea in that

way. He could hardly have meant us to think of Fortune as revolving with the wheel; probably he used the wheel as a symbol of instability, as something to identify the goddess with that quality. But neither the picture in Roman art nor that in Roman literature was satisfactory to the mediaeval artist. He represented Fortune as strictly the goddess turning the wheel with her own hand; and only in a few cases did he leave room for confusion with her less dignified offspring "fortune" — that is, with her gifts to humanity.

CONCLUSION

Any attempt to bring together the various threads of thought in the preceding chapters is not merely impossible, it is really futile. For this study as a whole, instead of being an extensive analysis of the problem of Fortune, is in itself only a summary. Some observations, however, follow inevitably from the material which we have reviewed. In the first place, our chief question in this investigation, at the end of the study as at the beginning, must be that of the actual survival of the goddess.[1] We can have no complete proof of her existence, but are there no marks by which we may fairly decide in her favor — by which, that is, we may feel justified in believing that an actual faith in her persisted? What, after all, are the peculiar marks of a religious growth that distinguish it from a poetic fiction?

As I should judge, they are somewhat as follows: (1) continued vitality, which keeps the personified figure from becoming outworn; (2) the independence of any historical period, to show that the cult is something more than a part of some artistic creed or aesthetic fad; (3) an automatic development of external media in which we

[1] Cf. F. von Bezold, *Das Fortleben der antiken Götter im mittelalterlichen Humanismus*, p. 76: "Natürlich handelt es sich dabei nirgends um eine offene Rückkehr zu den göttlichen Personen der heidnischen Mythologie. Aber es kommt immerhin zu einer so leibhaftigen Veranschaulichung einzelner antik-philosophischer Begriffe, dass sie fast den Charakter von Gottheiten erhalten oder mindestens als nicht wegzudenkende Faktoren der Weltregierung erscheinen. Dies gilt vor allem von der Natur, dem Schicksal und der rätselhaften Gestalt der Fortuna."

Plate 12

THE COURT OF FORTUNE

find the figure embodied — a growth of symbolism, in other words; (4) the use of ritual for purposes of devotion or for an indication of faith.

Of these marks, Fortuna shows all, except possibly the fourth. And even there, the prevalence of games of chance, throwing up a coin to decide an issue, and various other minor superstitions which somehow fail to go out of usage, seem to give the visible sign of some sort of credulity, however flippantly concealed or humorously defended. The vitality of the cult in all its aspects is perhaps its most salient quality, and the power of the goddess to gather to herself the apparatus of half-for-gotten folk-lore and to give it life and meaning must have some significance. Thus the trappings of old religions, in the material taken from accounts of the Earthly Paradise or the realm of the Otherworld, and the wheel itself, no matter what its source, are charged with new power in the literature of the period. Moreover, the goddess still continues in our own day to ride prosperously and reign: I have found about sixteen references in *Roderick Random*, with the old formulae still going strong; Meredith glances at the problem in the *Egoist*; a "Business Man's Calendar" prays briefly that "Good Fortune spin her wheel right merrily for you"; and wherever one searches an allusion is sure to turn up. The skeptic denies her existence, but in the next moment shows his belief in mere chance; the rationalist is likely to continue something like the Aristotelian solution; the imaginative writer may give her proper space in the skies. But in one way or another she goes on, "of chaunges newe lady and princesse," a favorite of the romanticist, and a phantom of delight to pique the intellect of everybody. Only a few, and they stand out by contrast, have seen in Fortune the servant of God performing the Divine Will, and thus disposing of chance in the only way in which it may be adequately dealt with and disposed of at the same time. These have been, it is true, crass idealists. Some of them were also great poets.

BIBLIOGRAPHY

BIBLIOGRAPHY

Adam le Bossu (*i. e.*, Adam de la Halle); *Le Jeu de la Feuillée*, ed. Ernest Langlois, Paris, 1911.

Adenes le Roi; *Li Romans de Berte aus Grans Piés*, ed. A. P. Paris, Paris, 1836.

Alberti, Leon Battista; *Opere Volgari*, ed. Anicio Bonucci, 5 vols., Firenze, 1843–49.

Albertus Magnus; *Opera*, Lugduni, 1651: vol. II, *Physicorum;* vol. IV, *Ethicorum*.

Alciati, Andrea; [*Emblemata*, 1531–1546], ed. Henry Green, *Emblematum Fontes Quatuor* (Holbein Soc.), London, 1870; [1551, etc.l, ed. Green, *Emblematum Flumen Abundans* (Holbein Soc.), 1871.

Alexandre de Bernay; *Li Romans d'Alixandre*, par Lambert li Tors [*i. e.*, Lambert le Court] et Alexandre de Bernay, ed. H. Michelant, Stuttgart, 1846.

Appell, J. W., editor; *The Dream of Poliphilus* (Venice, 1499), reproduced for the Department of Science and Art in Photo-Lithography, [London], 1893. (Woodcuts.)

Aquinas, St. Thomas; ed. Pope Leo XIII, *Opera*, II, Roma, 1884.

Arber, E., editor; *The Dunbar Anthology*, 1401–1508 A.D., London, 1901.

Ariosto, Lodovico; *I Cinque Canti* (Opere, VII), Firenze, 1824.

Ariosto, Lodovico; *L'Orlando Furioso*, 6 vols., Firenze, 1823–24.

Ariosto, Lodovico; *Rime e Satire* (Opere, VIII), Firenze, 1824.

Arpe, P. F.; *Theatrum Fati, siue notitia scriptorum de Providentia, Fortuna, et Fato*, Rotterdam, 1712.

Athis und Prophilias, ed. A. Weber, Staefa, 1881.

Aubry, Pierre; *Le Roman de Fauvel*, reproduction photographique du manuscrit français 146 de la Bibliothèque Nationale, Paris, 1907.

Awntyrs of Arthure at the Terne Wathelyne, The, ed. Sir F. Madden in his Syr Gawayne, etc. (Bannatyne Club, Publ. 61), pp. 93–128, London, 1839.

Baehrens, Aemilius, editor; *Poetae Latini Minores*, 5 vols. (in two), Lipsiae, 1879–83.

Bannatyne Manuscript, The, ed. George Bannatyne (Hunterian Club), Vol. III, [Glasgow], 1896.

Barbazan, Étienne de; *Fabliaux et Contes*, new ed., 3 vols., Paris, 1808.

Barbeu du Rocher, A.; *Ambassade de Pétrarque auprès du Roi Jean le Bon*, Académie des Inscriptions et Belles-Lettres, Mémoires présentés par Divers Savants, Deuxième Série, III, 172–228, Paris, 1854.

Barbier de Montault, X.; *Traité d'Iconographie Chrétienne*, Vol. I, Paris, 1890.

Barbour, John; *The Bruce*, ed. W. W. Skeat (Scottish Text Society), 2 vols., Edin. and London, 1894.

Baudouin de Condé and Jean de Condé; *Dits et Contes*, ed. Auguste Scheler, 3 vols., Bruxelles, 1866–67.

Bembo, Pietro; *Opere*, ed. A. F. Seghezzi, Vol. I, Milano, 1808.

Bembo, Pietro; *Rime*, ed. P. A. Serassi, Bergamo, 1745.

Benivieni, Girolamo; *Opere*, col commento dello Giovanni-Pico Mirandolano, etc., stampato in Venetia per Nicolo Zopino e Vincentio compagno, 1522.

Benoît de Sainte-Maure; *Le Roman de Troie*, ed. Léopold Constans (Société des Anciens Textes Français), 6 vols., Paris, 1904–12.

Bergner, H.; *Handbuch der Kirchlichen Kunstaltertümer in Deutschland*, Leipzig, 1905.

Bertrand, A.; *Nos Origines: la Religion des Gaulois, les Druides, et le Druidisme*, Paris, 1897.

Bezold, F. von; *Das Fortleben der antiken Götter im mittelalterlichen Humanismus*, Bonn and Leipzig, 1922.

Bibliotheca Casinensis, seu Codicum Manuscriptorum qui in tabulario Casinensi asseruantur series, Vol. IV, Ex typog. Casinensi, 1880.

Bocace des Nobles Maleureux; printed at Paris by Nicolas Couteau, 1538.

Boccaccio, G.; *De Casibus Virorum Illustrium*, ed. Hieronymus Ziegler, Augustae Vindelicorum, 1544. (See also Lydgate's translation below, two editions, 1554, 1558; and Bergen's edition, 1923.)

Boccaccio, G.; [*De Claris Mulieribus*] "Delle Donne Famose," trans. M. Donato degli Albanzani di Casentino, 3d ed., Bologna, 1881.

Boccaccio, G.; *Della Geneologia de Gli Dei*, trans. Gioseppe Betussi, Venetia, 1588.

Boccaccio, G.; *Lettere Volgari*, Firenze, 1834. (Appended, with separate pagination, to his Opere, vol. XVII, 1834.)

Boccaccio, G.; *Opere*, ed. I. Moutier, 17 vols., Firenze, 1827–34.

Boccace de Munich, Le, by Paul Durrieu, Munich, 1909. (Plates of the Munich manuscript, with explanatory text.)

Bocchi, Achille; *Symbolicarum Quaestionum de Universo Genere . . . libri quinque,* Bononiae, 1574.

Boethius, A. M. S.; *Philosophiae Consolatio,* ed. R. Peiper, Lipsiae, 1871.

Boethius; *The Consolation of Philosophy,* translated by W. V. Cooper (Dent ed., Temple Classics), London, 1902.

Boiardo, M. M.; *Orlando Innamorato,* ed. Antonio Panizzi, 5 vols., London, 1830–31.

Boll, Franz; *Die Lebensalter,* in Neue Jahrbücher für das Klassiche Altertum, XXXI, 89-145, Berlin, 1913.

Bouquet's *Recueil;* see Orderic Vital.

Bourdillon, F. W.; *The Early Editions of the Roman de la Rose,* London (Bibl. Soc.), 1906.

Bracci; *Canti Carnascialeschi Trionfi, Carri, e Mascherate,* 2d ed., by O. Guerrini, Milano, 1883.

Bran, The Voyage of, ed. Meyer and Nutt, Vol. I, London, 1895.

Brant, Sebastian; *Narrenschiff,* ed. Karl Simrock, Berlin, 1872.

Brant, Sebastian; *Narrenschiff,* ed. F. Zarncke, Leipzig, 1854.

Brendan, Saint; see *Bran, The Voyage of.*

Brotanek, R.; *Die Englischen Maskenspiele,* Wien and Leipzig, 1902.

Bruce, The; see Barbour.

Burchiello; *Sonetti,* Londra, 1757.

Buti, Francesco da; *Comento sopra la Divina Comedia,* Vol. I, Pisa, 1858.

Calmo, Andrea; *Lettere,* ed. Vittorio Rossi, Torino, 1888.

Canter, H. V.; *"Fortuna" in Latin Poetry,* in [North Carolina] Studies in Philology, XIX, 64 ff.

Capella, Martianus; [*De Nuptiis Philologiae et Mercurii*], ed. F. Eyssenhardt, Lipsiae, 1866.

Carducci, Giosuè, editor; *Cantilene e Ballate,* Pisa, 1871.

Carmina Burana; see Schmeller.

Carter, J. B.; *The Religion of Numa and other Essays on the Religion of Ancient Rome,* London, 1906.

Cavalcanti, Guido; poems in Poeti del Primo Secolo, II, 276–369, Firenze, 1816.

Chambers, E. K., and Sidgwick, F.; *Early English Lyrics,* London, 1907.

Chartier, Alain; *Œuvres,* ed. André Duchesne, Paris, 1617.

186 BIBLIOGRAPHY

Chaucer, Geoffrey; *Complete Works*, ed. W. W. Skeat, 6 vols., Oxford, 1894.
Chaucer, Geoffrey; *Poetical Works*, ed. R. Morris, Vol. V, London, 1891.
Chaucer, Geoffrey; *Poetical Works*, ed. Thomas Tyrwhitt, London, 1843.
Chaucerian and other Pieces, ed. W. W. Skeat, Oxford, 1897. (Supplementary to his edition of the Works, with which it is classed as vol. VII.)
Child, F. J., editor; *The English and Scottish Popular Ballads*, Vol. III, Boston, 1888.
Chrestien de Troyes, ed. Wendelin Foerster, Halle: *Erec und Enide*, 1896; *Cligés*, 2d ed., 1901; *Yvain*, 2d ed., 1902; *Wilhelm von England*, 1911.
Chrestien de Troyes; *Perceval le Gallois;* see *Perceval.*
Chrestien de Troyes and Godefroy de Laigny; *Le Roman du Chevalier de la Charrette* [ed. P. Tarbé], Reims, 1849.
Christine de Pisan; *Leben und Werke*, ed. Friedrich Koch, Goslar a. Harz, 1885.
Christine de Pisan; *Le Livre du Chemin de Long Estude*, ed. Robert Püschel, Berlin and Paris, 1881.
Christine de Pisan; *Œuvres Poétiques*, ed. Maurice Roy (Société des Anciens Textes Français), 3 vols., Paris, 1886–96.
Cino da Pistoia; *Poesie*, ed. S. Ciampi, Pistoia, 1826.
Colonne, Guido delle; see Guido.
Complaynt of Scotlande, The, ed. J. A. H. Murray (Early English Text Society, Extra Series, Vol. XVII), 1872.
Contention between Liberality and Prodigality, The (1602), reprinted, Malone Soc., London, 1913.
Conti, Giusto de'; *La Bella Mano*, in Lirici Antichi, pp. 1–192, Venezia, 1784.
Cousin, Jean; *Le Livre de Fortune*, pub. Ludovic Lalanne, Paris and London, 1883.
Couteau, N.; see *Bocace des Nobles Maleureux.*
Cranstoun, James, editor; *Satirical Poems of the Time of the Reformation* (Scottish Text Society), 2 vols., Edinburgh, 1891–93.
Cumont, Franz; *The Oriental Religions in Roman Paganism*, Chicago, 1911.
Dante Alighieri;*De Monarchia*, in Tutte le Opere, ed. E. Moore, pp. 339–376.
Dante Alighieri; *La Divina Commedia*, ed. C. H. Grandgent, 3 vols., Boston, 1909–13.

Dante Alighieri; *Tutte le Opere*, ed. E. Moore, 3d ed., Oxford, 1904.
Daremberg, Charles, and Saglio, Edmund; *Dictionnaire des Antiquités Grecques et Romaines*, Vol. II (ii), Paris, 1896.
Débat de Lomme Mondain et du Religieux; appended to Pierre Michault's Dance aux Aveugles, pp. 299–332, Lille, 1748.
Deschamps, Eustache; *Œuvres Complètes*, ed. Le Marquis de Queux de Saint-Hilaire and Gaston Raynaud (Société des Anciens Textes Français), 11 vols., Paris, 1878–1903.
Dictys Cretensis Ephemeridos Belli Troiani libri sex, ed. F. Meister, Lipsiae, 1872.
Didron, A. N.; *Annales Archéologiques*, Vols. I, XVI, Paris, 1844, 1856.
Didron, A. N.; *Iconographie Chrétienne, Histoire de Dieu*, Paris, 1843.
Dieterich, Albrecht; *Nekyia*, Leipzig, 1893.
Dinaux, Arthur; *Les Trouvères, Jongleurs, et Ménestrels du Nord de la France*, etc., 4 vols., Paris, 1837–65. (Vol. I, *Les Trouvères Cambrésiens*, is 3d edition.)
Dit de l'Empereur Coustant, Le, ed. A. Wesselofsky, in Romania, VI, 161–198, Paris, 1877.
Donnei des Amants, Le, ed. G. Paris, in Romania, XXV, 497–541, Paris, 1896.
Doren, A.; *Fortuna im Mittelalter und in der Renaissance*, in Vorträge der Bibliothek Warburg, II, 1 Teil, pp. 71–144, Berlin, 1924.
Douglas, Gavin; *Poetical Works*, ed. John Small, 4 vols., Edinburgh, 1874.
Dream of Poliphilus, The; see Appell.
Dreves, Guido Maria; *Analecta Hymnica Medii Aevi*, Vol. XXI, Leipzig, 1895.
Du Cange, C. D.; *Glossarium Mediae et Infimae Latinitatis*, III, 575, Niort, 1884.
Dunbar, William; *Poems*, ed. John Small (Scottish Text Society), 3 vols., Edin. and London, 1893.
Dunbar Anthology; see Arber.
Durrieu, Paul; see *Boccace de Munich*.
Du Sommerard, Alexandre; *Les Arts au Moyen Âge*, Album of plates, Vol. II, Paris, 1838.
Duyse, Florimond van; *Het Oude Nederlandsche Lied*, Vol. II, Antwerp, 1905.
Échecs Amoureux, Les; see Sieper.

Eger and Grine; in Bishop Percy's Folio Manuscript, ed. Hales and Furnivall, I, 341-400, London, 1867.

Eilers, F. W.; *Dissertation on "The Parson's Tale,"* etc., in Essays on Chaucer, ed. Chaucer Soc., Part V, No. xvi (pp. 501-610), London, 1882, "Englisht," 1884.

Escoufle, L', roman d'aventure, ed. H. Michelant and P. Meyer (Société des Anciens Textes Français), Paris, 1894.

Extrait du Mystère de Bien-Advisé et Mal-Advisé, in Histoire du Théâtre François (see Parfaict), II, 113-144.

Faral, Edmond; *Recherches sur les Sources Latines des Contes et Romans Courtois du Moyen Âge,* Paris, 1913.

Federico; see *Gesta.*

Ferrario, Giulio, compiler; *Poesie Pastorali e Rusticali,* Milano, 1808.

Ferri, Ferruchio; *La Poesia Popolare in Antonio Pucci,* Bologna, 1909.

Fiske, Daniel Willard; *Bibliographical Notices,* III: Petrarch's *De Remediis Utriusque Fortunae,* Florence, 1888.

Floire et Blanceflor, ed. E. Du Méril, Paris, 1856.

Förster, Max; *Sphaera Apulei und Glücksrad,* in Herrig's Archiv für das Studium der Neueren Sprachen, CXXIX, 45-49, Braunschweig, 1912.

Folie Tristan, Les Deux Poèmes de; pub. Joseph Bédier (Société des Anciens Textes Français), Paris, 1907.

Fowler, W. Warde; *The Roman Festivals of the Period of the Republic,* London, 1899.

Fregoso, Antonio Phileremo; *Dialogo di Fortuna,* novamente stampato per Nicolo d'Aristotile detto Zoppino, Venetia, 1531.

Frezzi, Federigo; *Il Quadriregio* [Vol. I], Accad. Rinvig. di Foligno, Foligno, 1725.

Froissart, Jean; *Méliador,* ed. Longnon (Société des Anciens Textes Français), 3 vols., Paris, 1895-99.

Froissart, Jean; *Œuvres, Poésies,* ed. Scheler, 3 vols., Bruxelles, 1870-72.

Furnivall, F. J., and others, editors; *Originals and Analogues of Chaucer's Canterbury Tales* (Chaucer Society), London, 1872-87.

Furnivall, F. J., and others, editors; *Political, Religious, and Love Poems* (Early English Text Society), London, 1866, reëdited 1903.

Gaidoz, Henri; *Études de Mythologie Gauloise:* I, *Le Dieu Gaulois du Soleil et le Symbolisme de la Roue,* Paris, 1886.

Galpin, S. L.; *Centrifugal Force applied to Fortune's Wheel,* Mod. Lang. Notes, XXIX, 62-63, Baltimore, 1914.

Galpin, S. L.; *Fortune's Wheel in the Roman de la Rose*, Mod. Lang. Assoc., Publ., XXIV, 332–342, Baltimore, 1909.

Garden, Alexander; *A Theatre of Scottish Worthies*, etc., ed. David Laing (Hunterian Club, No. 41), [Glasgow], 1878.

Garencières, Jean de; see Piaget.

Gareth, Benedetto (Il Chariteo); *Rime*, ed. E. Pèrcopo, Part II, Napoli, 1892.

Gau, John; *The Richt Vay to the Kingdom of Heuine*, ed. A. F. Mitchell (Scottish Text Society), Edin. and London, 1888.

Gautier de Coincy; *Les Miracles de la Sainte Vièrge*, ed. A. E. Poquet, Paris, 1857.

Gedicht auf die Zerstörung Mailands, ed. Dümmler, Neues Archiv der Gesellschaft, etc., XI, 466–474, Hannover, 1886.

Gesta di Federico I in Italia, ed. Ernesto Monaci, Roma, 1887.

Ghirardacci, Cherubino; *Historia de Bologna*, Vol. III (MS.), 1657.

Giornale Storico della Letteratura Italiana, Vol. XIV, Torino, etc., 1889.

Giovanni Fiorentino, Ser; *Il Pecorone*, 2 vols., Milano (Soc. Tipogr.), 1804.

Girart de Rossillon, Le Roman en Vers de, ed. Mignard, Paris and Dijon, 1858.

Gorra, E.; *Studi di Critica Letteraria*, Bologna, 1892.

Gower, John; *Complete Works*, ed. G. C. Macaulay, 4 vols., Oxford, 1899–1902: I, French works; II–III, English; IV, Latin.

Graf, Arturo; *Miti, Leggende e Superstizioni del Medio Evo*, E. Loescher, 1892.

Grant Mal fist Adam; see Suchier.

Green, Henry; *Shakespeare and the Emblem Writers*, London, 1870.

Green, Henry; see Alciati, and *Mirrour of Maiestie*.

Grimm, Jacob; *Deutsche Mythologie*, 4th ed., by E. H. Meyer, Vol. III, Berlin, 1878.

Gude and Godly Ballatis; see Mitchell.

Guicciardini, Francesco; *Opere Inedite*, ed. P. and L. Guicciardini, Vol. I, Firenze, 1857.

Guido delle Colonne; *Hystoria Troiana Guidonis*, [Strassburg, 1489].

Guillaume de Guilleville; *Le Pelerinage de l'Âme*, ed. J. J. Stürzinger (Roxburghe Club), London, 1895.

Guillaume de Guilleville; [*Le Rommant des Trois Pelerinaiges*, c. 1500, perhaps 1484?]. The first of the three poems is "Le Pelerinaige de l'Homme" (cf. Lydgate's translation below).

Guillaume de Machaut; *Le Livre du Voir-Dit* (Société des Bibliophiles Français), Paris, 1875.

Guillaume de Machaut; *Œuvres*, ed. E. Hoepffner (Société des Anciens Textes Français), 2 vols., Paris, 1908–11. (The *Remede de Fortune* is in vol. II.)

Guillaume de Machaut; *Poésies Lyriques*, ed. V. Chichmaref, 2 vols., Paris, 1909.

Hammond, E. P.; *The Departing of Chaucer*, Modern Philology, I, 331–336, Chicago, 1903.

Hanford, J. H.; *The Debate Element in the Elizabethan Drama*, Kittredge Anniversary Papers, pp. 445–456, Boston and London, 1913.

Harrison, Jane E.; *Prolegomena to the Study of Greek Religion*, 2d ed., Cambridge, 1908.

Hastings, J.; *Encylopædia of Religion and Ethics*, Vol. VI, New York, 1914.

Hay, Sir Gilbert; *Gilbert of the Haye's Prose Manuscript* (1456): Vol. I, *The Buke of the Law of Armys, or Buke of Bataillis*, ed. J. H. Stevenson (Scottish Text Society), Edin. and London, 1901.

Heider, G.; *Das Glücksrad und seine Anwendung in der christliche Kunst*, in Mitteilungen d. Kaiserl. Königl. Central Commission, etc., IV Bd., 1859, pp. 113 ff.

Heinrich von dem Türlin; *Diu Crône*, ed. G. H. F. Scholl (Bibliothek des Litt. Vereins, XXVII), Stuttgart, 1852.

Henry the Minstrel; *The Actis and Deidis of the Illustere and Vailȝeand Campioun Schir William Wallace, Knicht of Ellerslie*, ed. James Moir (Scottish Text Society), Edin. and London, 1889.

Henryson, Robert; *Poems and Fables*, ed. David Laing, Edinburgh, 1865.

Herzhoff, Richard; *Personificationen lebloser Dinge in der altfranzösischen Litteratur des 10. bis 12. Jahrhunderts*, Berlin, 1904.

Hill, Nathaniel; *The Ancient Poem of Guillaume de Guileville, entitled Le Pelerinage de l'Homme, compared with the Pilgrim's Progress*, London, 1858.

Hoccleve, Thomas; *Works*, ed. F. J. Furnivall (Early English Text Society), 3 vols., London, 1892–97. (Part III, *The Regement of Princes*.)

Holkot, Robertus; [*Opus . . . super sapientiam Salomonis*, 1483.] Hain-Copinger,* 8757; Proctor, 2352.

James I of Scotland; *The Kingis Quair*, ed. A. Lawson, London, 1910; ed. W. W. Skeat (Scottish Text Society), Edin. and London, 1884, 2d ed., 1911.

Jean de Meun; *L'Art de Chevalerie*, ed. U. Robert (Société des Anciens Textes Français), Paris, 1897.

Jean de Meun; *Le Plaisant Jeu du Dodechedron*, Lyons, 1581.

Jean de Meun; *Testament*, in Le Roman de la Rose, ed. Méon, IV, 1–116, Paris, 1814.

Jean de Meun and Guillaume de Lorris; *Le Roman de la Rose*, ed. D. M. Méon, 4 vols., Paris, 1814.

Jean le Seneschal; *Les Cent Ballades*, ed. Gaston Raynaud (Société des Anciens Textes Français), Paris, 1905.

Jebb, R., editor; Sophocles, *The Antigone*, 3d ed., p. 206, Cambridge, 1900.

Jennaro, Pietro Jacopo de; *Li Canzonière*, ed. G. Barone, Napoli, 1883.

Jones, Sir William; *Works*, Vol. X, London, 1799.

Jubinal, Achille; *Jongleurs et Trouvères*, Paris, 1835.

Jubinal, Achille; *Nouveau Recueil de Contes, Dits, Fabliaux . . . des XIIIᵉ, XIVᵉ, et XVᵉ Siècles*, 2 vols., Paris, 1839–42.

Kingis Quair; see James I.

Kittredge, G. L.; *Anniversary Papers* (Harvard University), Boston and London, 1913.

Kittredge, G. L.; *To Take Time by the Forelock*, Mod. Lang. Notes, VIII, 230–235 (cols. 459–469), Baltimore, 1893.

Koch, Friedrich; see Christine de Pisan.

Koeppel, Emil; *Shelley's "Queen Mab" und Sir William Jones's "Palace of Fortune,"* Englische Studien, XXVIII, 43–53, Leipzig, 1900.

Längfors, Arthur; *Une Énigme dans le Liber Fortunae*, Romania, XLV, 265–268, Paris, 1919.

Längfors, Arthur; see *Roman de Fauvel*.

Laing, David, editor; see Garden.

Latini, Brunetto; *Il Tesoretto e il Favoletto*, ed. Gio. Batista Zanoni, Firenze, 1824.

Leyser, Polycarp; *Historia Poetarum et Poematum Medii Aeui*, Halae Magdeb., 1721.

Lindsay (or Lyndsay), Sir David; *Ane Satyre of the thrie Estaits* (1602), ed. Fitzedward Hall (Early English Text Society), London, 1869.

Lindsay (or Lyndsay), Sir David; *Poetical Works*, ed. David Laing, 3 vols., Edinburgh, 1879.

Lindsay, Robert, of Pitscottie; *The Historie and Cronicles of Scotland*, ed. J. G. Mackay (Scottish Text Society), 2 vols., Edin. and London, 1899.

Lounsbury, T. R.; *Studies in Chaucer*, 3 vols., New York, 1892.
Lydgate, John; *S. Albon und Amphabel, ein Legendenepos*, ed. C. Horstmann, [Berlin, 1882].
Lydgate, John; *The Assembly of Gods*, ed. O. L. Triggs (Early English Text Society), London, 1896.
Lydgate, John; *A Balade for a Momyng*, in Rudolf Brotanek's Englischen Maskenspiele, pp. 306–308, Wien and Leipzig, 1902.
Lydgate, John; *A Balade made at the Departyng of Thomas Chaucyer on Ambassade in to Fraunce*, Modern Philology, I, 333–336, Chicago, 1903.
Lydgate, John; *Beware of Doubleness*, in W. W. Skeat's Chaucerian and other Pieces, pp. 291–294, Oxford, 1897. (Vol. VII of his edition of Chaucer.)
Lydgate, John; *The Flour of Curtesye*, ibid., 266–274.
Lydgate, John; *The Churl and the Bird*, translated from the French. Facsimile reprint of Caxton's edition (c. 1478), Cambridge, 1906.
Lydgate, John; *The Daunce of Machabree*, in Monasticon Anglicanum, pp. 333–339, London, 1718.
Lydgate, John; *A Desguysing at London*, in Rudolf Brotanek's Englischen Maskenspiele, pp. 309–317, Wien and Leipzig, 1902.
Lydgate, John; *Fabula Duorum Mercatorum*, ed. Gustav Schleich (Quellen und Forschungen zur Sprach- und Culturgeschichte der Germanischen Völker, ed. Brandl and others, No. 83), Strassburg, 1897.
Lydgate, John, translator; *A Treatise . . . shewing . . . the Falles of sondry most notable Princes* [from Boccaccio; London, 1554], Richard Tottel.
Lydgate, John; *Minor Poems*, ed. H. N. MacCracken (Early English Text Society), Pt. I, London, 1911.
Lydgate, John, translator; *The Pilgrimage of the Life of Man*, from Guillaume de Guilleville (Early English Text Society), 3 pts., London, 1899–1904; also 1 vol., Roxburghe Club, 1905.
Lydgate's *Reson and Sensuallyte*, ed. Ernst Sieper (Early English Text Society), 2 vols. (in one), London, 1901–03.
Lydgate, John; *The Serpent of Division*, ed. H. N. MacCracken, London and New Haven, 1911.
Lydgate, John; *The Siege of Thebes*, ed. Axel Erdmann (Chaucer Society), London, 1911.
Lydgate, John; *The Temple of Glas*, ed. J. Schick (Early English Text Society), London, 1891.

Lydgate, John, translator; *The Tragedies, gathered by John Bochas, of all such Princes*, etc. [*The Falls of Princes*, from Boccaccio], London, John Wayland, [1558].

Lydgate, John; *Troy Book*, ed. Henry Bergen (Early English Text Society), 3 vols., London, 1906–10.

Lydgate and Burgh's *Secrees of the old Philisoffres*, ed. Robert Steele, London, 1894.

Maccio, Paulo; *Emblemata*, Bononiae, 1628.

Machaut; see Guillaume de Machaut.

Machiavelli, Niccolò; *Opere*, 10 vols., Italia, 1826.

Mailands, Gedicht auf die Zerstörung, ed. Ernst Dümmler, Neues Archiv, XI, 466–474, Hannover, 1886.

Mâle, Émile; *L'Art Religieux de la Fin du Moyen Âge en France*, Paris, 1908.

Malmesbury, William of; *De Gestis Regum Anglorum* (Rolls Series), Vol. I, London, 1887.

Map, Walter; *De Nugis Curialium*, ed. Thomas Wright (Camden Society), London, 1850.

Margarita Philosophica, by Gregor Reisch, [2d ed., Argentinae, 1504].

Marie de France; *The Espurgatoire Saint Patriz*, with original Latin text, ed. T. A. Jenkins, Chicago, 1903.

Marie de France; *Die Lais*, ed. Karl Warnke, Halle, 1885; 3d ed., 1925.

Martin le Franc; *L'Estrif de Fortune et de Vertu*. See A. Piaget's Martin le Franc, pp. 175–188, Lausanne, 1888; also Catalogue des Livres de Rothschild, I, 253–256, Paris, 1884.

Masuccio Salernitano; *Il Novellino*, ed. Luigi Settembrini, Napoli, 1874.

Matzke, J. E.; *On the Source of the Italian and English Idioms meaning "To take Time by the Forelock,"* Mod. Lang. Assoc., Publ., VIII, 303–334, Baltimore, 1893.

Medici, Lorenzo de'; *Opere*, ed. Grand Duke Leopold II, Vols. I, III, Firenze, 1825.

Medici, Lorenzo de'; *Poemi*, ed. R. Carabba, Lanciano, 1911.

Medici, Lorenzo de'; *Poesie*, 2 pts. (in one), Londra, L. Nardini, 1801.

Medin, A.; *Ballata della Fortuna*, in Il Propugnatore, New Series, II (i), 101–144, Bologna, 1889.

Medin, A.; *Lamenti de' Secoli XIV e XV* (Operette Inedite o Rare, VI), Libr. Dante in Firenze, 1883.

Melusine; *The Romans of Partenay or of Lusignen, otherwise known as The Tale of Melusine*, trans. from La Coudrette, ed. W. W. Skeat (Early English Text Society), London, 1866, reprinted 1899.

Metcalfe, W. M., editor; *Legends of the Saints* (Scottish Text Society), 3 vols., Edin. and London, 1896.

Michault, Pierre; *La Dance aux Aveugles*, ed. Lambert Douxfils, Lille, 1748.

Michel, Dan; *Ayenbite;* see Morris.

Migne, J. P.; *Patrologiae Cursus Completus*, Latin series, Vols. V, VI, XXIII, XXXIII, CXXXIX, CLXXI, CLXXII, CLXXVIII, CXCV, CCX, CCXVII, Paris, 1844–55.

Mirrour of Maiestie, The, or the Badges of Honour, ed. Henry Green and James Croston (Holbein Soc.), Manchester and London, 1870.

Mitchell, A. F., editor; *A Compendious Book of . . . the Gude and Godlie Ballatis* (Scottish Text Society), Edin. and London, 1897.

Molinier, Auguste; *Les Manuscrits et les Miniatures*, Paris, 1892.

Molinier, H. J.; *Essai Biographique et Littéraire sur Octavien de Saint-Gelays*, Paris, 1910.

Monmerqué, L. J. N., and Michel, F.; *Théâtre Français au Moyen Âge*, Paris, 1842.

Montgomerie, Alexander; *Poems*, ed. James Cranstoun (Scottish Text Society), Edin. and London, 1887.

Montgomerie, Alexander; *Poems*, supplementary volume, ed. George Stevenson (Scottish Text Society), Edin. and London, 1910.

Morris, Richard, editor; *Dan Michel's Ayenbite of Inwyt* (Early English Text Society), London, 1866.

Mort Artu, ed. J. D. Bruce, Halle, 1910.

Mure, Sir William, of Rowallan; *Works*, ed. William Tough (Scottish Text Society), 2 vols., Edin. and London, 1898.

Neilson, W. A.; *The Origins and Sources of the Court of Love* (Studies and Notes in Philology and Literature, VI), Boston, 1899.

Nicole de Margival; *Le Dit de la Panthère d'Amours*, ed. H. A. Todd (Société des Anciens Textes Français), Paris, 1883.

Notices et Extraits des MSS. de la Bibliothèque Nationale, Vol. XXVIII, pt. ii, Paris, 1878.

Novati, Francesco; *Carmina Medii Aeui* (Operette Inedite o Rare, IV), Libr. Dante in Firenze, 1883.

Nutt, Alfred; *The Happy Otherworld, in the Mythico-Romantic Literature of the Irish*, in The Voyage of Bran, ed. Meyer and Nutt, I, 101–331, London, 1895.

Occleve; see Hoccleve.

Orderic Vital; *Historia Ecclesiastica*, in Martin Bouquet's Recueil des Historiens, XII, 585–770, Paris, 1877.

Orléans, Charles d'; *Poésies Complètes*, ed. Charles d'Héricault, 2 vols., Paris, 1896.

Ortiz, Ramiro; *Fortuna Labilis*, Bucharest, 1927,

[Parfaict, François et Claude, frères]; *Histoire du Théâtre François*, Vol. II, Paris, 1745.

Paris, Gaston; *Chansons du XVe Siècle* (Société des Anciens Textes Français), Paris, 1875.

Patch, H. R.; *Fortuna in Old French Literature* (Smith College Studies in Modern Languages, IV, No. 4), Northampton, Mass., July, 1923.

Patch, H. R.; *Fortune's Wheel and Boethius*, Mod. Lang. Notes, XXIX, 197, Baltimore, 1914.

Patch, H. R.; *The Goddess Fortuna in the Divine Comedy*, Thirty-third Annual Report of the Dante Soc. [Cambridge, Mass.], pp. 13–28, Boston, 1916.

Patch, H. R.; *The Tradition of the Goddess Fortuna* (Smith College Studies in Modern Languages, III, 131–235), Northampton, Mass., 1922.

Pearl, The, ed. C. G. Osgood (Belles-Lettres series), Boston and London, 1906.

Perceval le Gallois, ou le Conte du Graal, ed. Charles Potvin (Soc. des Bibliophiles Belges), 6 vols., Mons, 1866–71.

Petersen, K. O.; *The Sources of the Parson's Tale* (Radcliffe Monographs, No. 12), Boston, 1901.

Petit de Julleville, Louis; *Histoire de la Langue et de la Littérature Française*, Moyen Âge, Vol. II, Paris, 1896.

Petit Traittiet du Malheur de France; appended to Pierre Michault's Dance aux Aveugles, pp. 209–244, Lille, 1748.

Petrarch, F.; *Address to John of France*; see Barbeu du Rocher.

Petrarch, F.; *Africa*, ed. F. Corradini, in Padova a Francesco Petrarca, etc., pp. 77–474, [Padova, 1874].

Petrarch, F.; *De' Rimedii dell' Una e dell' Altra Fortuna*, volg. D. Giovanni Dassanimiato, pub. C. Stolfi (Collezione di Opere Inedite o Rare), 2 vols., Bologna, 1867.

Petrarch, F.; *Il Bucolicum Carmen*, ed. A. Avena, Padova, 1906.

Petrarch, F.; *Lettere [Famigliari]*, ed. G. Fracassetti, IV, Firenze, 1866.

Petrarch, F.; *Lettere Senili*, volg. da Fracassetti, Firenze, 1869.

Petrarch, F.; *Le Rime*, ed. Carlo Albertini, 2 vols., Firenze, 1832.

Petrarch, F.; *Le Rime*, ed. G. Mestica, Firenze, 1896.

Petrarch, F.; *Le Vite degli Uomini Illustri*, trans. Donato d. Albanzani da Pratovecchio, ed. L. Razzolini, 2 vols. (vol. I in two parts, paged continuously), Bologna, 1874–79.

Petrarch, F.; *Scritti Inediti*, pub. Attilio Hortis, Trieste, 1874.
Philippe de Remi, Sire de Beaumanoir; *Œuvres Poétiques*, ed. H. Suchier (Société des Anciens Textes Français), 2 vols., Paris, 1884-85.
Piaget, Arthur; *Jean de Garencières*, Romania, XXII, 422-481, Paris, 1893.
Piaget, Arthur; *Martin le Franc, Prévot de Lausanne*, Lausanne, 1888.
Picinelli, Filippo; *Mundus Symbolicus*, trans. Augustino Erath, 2 vols. (in one), Coloniae Agrippinae, 1681.
Pico della Mirandola, G. F.; *Opera*, 2 vols. (in one), Basileae, [1601].
Pierre de la Broche; see Monmerqué and Michel, pp. 208-215.
Piers the Plowman, The Vision of William concerning, ed. W. W. Skeat, 2 vols., Oxford (Clarendon Press), 1886.
Pietsch, Karl; *On the Source of "To Take Time by the Forelock,"* Mod. Lang. Notes, VIII, 235-338 (cols. 469-475), Baltimore, 1893.
Pinkerton, John, editor; *Ancient Scotish Poems*, 2 vols., London, 1786.
Pischedda, Tommaso, translator; *Canti Popolari dei Classici Poeti Sardi*, Sassari, 1854.
Plutarch; *Lives*, ed. John and William Langhorne, 3d ed., Vol. IV, London, 1819.
Poesie Italiane Inedite; see Trucchi.
Poeti del Primo Secolo della Lingua Italiana, 2 vols., Firenze, 1816.
Poliziano (*i. e.*, Angelo Ambrogini); *Le Stanze, l'Orfeo, e le Rime*, ed. Giosué Carducci, Vol. I, Firenze, 1863.
Poliziano, *Le Stanze, l'Orfeo, e le Rime*, Carducci's text, with notes by A. Donati, Roma-Milano (Soc. Editrice Dante Alighieri), 1910.
Poliziano; *Prose Volgari Inedite e Poesie Latine e Greche*, ed. Isidoro del Lungo, Firenze, 1867.
Pontano, Giovanni; *Carmina*, ed. Benedetto Soldati, 2 vols., Firenze, 1902.
Pontano, Giovanni; *Opera Omnia soluta oratione composita*, Pars II, Florentiae, per haeredes Philippi Juntae, 1520.
Post, C. R.; *Mediaeval Spanish Allegory*, Cambridge (Harvard Univ. Press), 1915.
Post, C. R.; *The Sources of Juan de Mena*, Romanic Review, III, 223-279, New York (Columbia Univ. Press), 1912.
Prato, Giovanni da; *Il Paradiso degli Alberti*, ed. Alessandor Wesselofsky, Vol. II, Bologna, 1867.

Priorat, Jean; *Li Abrejance de l'Ordre de Chevalerie*, ed. U. Robert (Société des Anciens Textes Français), Paris, 1897.

Pucci, Antonio; *La Poesia Popolare*, ed. Ferruccio Ferri, Bologna, 1909.

Pulci, Bernardo and Luca; *Poesie*, in Lorenzo de' Medici's Poesie, II, 95–135, Londra, 1801.

Pulci, Luigi; *Morgante Maggiore*, 3 vols., Milano, 1806.

Raynaud, Gaston; *Rondeaux et autres Poésies du XVᵉ Siècle* (Société des Anciens Textes Français), Paris, 1889.

Règne de Fortune, Le; in Anatole de Montaiglon's Recueil de Poésies Françoises des XVᵉ et XVIᵉ Siècles, X, 75–84, Paris, 1875.

Reinach, S.; *Répertoire de la Statuaire Grecque et Romaine*, Vol. II, Paris, 1897.

Reisch, Gregorius; see *Margarita Philosophica*.

Renart le Nouvel; see *Roman du Renart*, IV, 125–461.

René, roi d'Anjou; *Œuvres Complètes*, ed. Le Comte de Quatre-barbes, Vol. III, Angers, 1846.

Ripa, Cesare; *Iconologia*, Roma, 1603.

Ritson, Joseph; *Ancient English Metrical Romances*, Vol. III, Edinburgh, 1885.

Robertus de Avesbury; *Historia de Mirabilibus Gestis Eduardi* III, ed. Thomas Hearne, Oxonii, 1720.

Roman de Fauvel, Le, ed. A. Pey, in Jahrbuch für Romanische und Englische Literatur, VII, 316–343, 437–446, Leipzig, 1866.

Roman de Fauvel, Le, par Gervais du Bus; ed. Arthur Längfors (Société des Anciens Textes Français), Paris, 1914–19. (References are to this edition.)

Roman de la Rose, Le, par Guillaume de Lorris et Jehan de Meung; ed. D. M. Méon, 4 vols., Paris, 1814.

Roman du Renart, Le, ed. D. M. Méon, 4 vols., Paris, 1826.

Romanz de la Poire, Li; see Thibaut.

Roscher, W. H.; *Ausführliches Lexikon der Griechischen und Römanischen Mythologie*, Vol. I (ii), Leipzig, 1886–90.

Rossetti, D. G.; *The King's Tragedy*, in Collected Works, ed. W. M. Rossetti, I, 148–175, London, 1888.

Rossi, V.; see Calmo.

Rothschild, James de, baron, *Catalogue des Livres composant la Bibliothèque de*, [ed. Émile Picot], Vol. I, Paris, 1884.

Rutebeuf; *Œuvres Complètes*, ed. Achille Jubinal, new ed., 3 vols., Paris, 1874–75.

Sacchetti, Franco; *Delle Novelle*, Vol. III, Milano (Soc. Tipogr.), 1805.

Saluzzo, Thomas, Marquis of; *Il Cavaliere Errante*, summarized in Gorra's Studi di Critica Letteraria, pp. 1–110, Bologna, 1892.

Sannazaro, Jacopo; *Opere Volgari*, ed. Gio. Antonio Volpi and Gaetano Volpi, Padova, 1723.

Sauer, J.; *Symbolik des Kirchengebäudes und seiner Ausstattung in der Auffassung des Mittelalters*, pp. 272 ff., Freiburg i. Br., 1902.

Saviozzo and others; *Alcune Poesie Inedite*, ed. Giuseppe Ferraro, Bologna, 1879.

Scarlattini, Octavio; *Homo Symbolicus*, published at Augustae Vindelicorum and Delingae, 2 vols. (in one), 1695.

Schmeller, J. A., editor; *Carmina Burana, einer Handschrift des XIII Jahrhunderts*, 3d ed., Breslau, 1894.

Schönbach, Anton E.; *Studien zur Geschichte der altdeutschen Predigt* (Kaiserl. Akad. der Wissenschaften, Sitzungsberichte, Philos.-Hist. Classe, Vol. CXLII, No. vii), Wien, 1900.

Schoonhoven, Floris van; *Emblemata*, Goudae, 1618.

Sedgewick, G. G.; *Dramatic Irony, Studies in its History*, etc. Dissertation, Harvard University, May 26, 1913, unpublished.

Sercambi, Giovanni; *Novelle*, ed. Alessandro d'Ancona, Bologna, 1871.

Sercambi, Giovanni; *Novelle Inedite*, ed. Rodolfo Renier, Torino, 1889.

Settimello, Arrigo da (*i. e.*, Henricus Septimellensis); *Arrighetto, ovvero Trattato contro all' Avversità della Fortuna:* Latin text, with Italian translation by D. M. Manni, Firenze, 1730; Italian text, Prato, 1841.

Sibbald, James; *Chronicle of Scottish Poetry from the Thirteenth Century to the Union of the Crowns*, 4 vols., Edin. and London, 1802.

Sieper, Ernst; *Les Échecs Amoureux, eine altfranzösische Nachahmung des Rosenromans und ihre englische Uebertragung*, Weimar, 1898.

Simund de Freine; *Œuvres*, ed. J. E. Matzke (Société des Anciens Textes Français), Paris, 1909.

Skeat, W. W., editor; *Chaucerian and other Pieces;* see Chaucerian.

Smith, G. Gregory; *Specimens of Middle Scots*, Edin. and London, 1902.

Solorzano Pereira, Juan de; *Emblemata*, Matriti, 1653.

Staveren, Augustino van, editor; *Auctores Mythographi Latini*, Lugdunum Batavorum and Amstelaed, 1742.

Stewart, John, of Baldynneis; *Poems*, ed. Thomas Crockett (Scottish Text Society), Vol. II, Edin. and London, 1913.

Suchier, H.; *Reimpredigt*, Halle, 1879.

Sylvius, Aeneas; *De Viris Illustribus*, Stuttgardiae, 1842.

Sylvius, Aeneas; *Opera Omnia*, Basileae, 1571.

Sylvius, Aeneas; *Storia di Due Amanti* (Bibl. Rara, Vol. XXXVIII), Milano, G. Daelli, 1864.

Sypherd, W. O.; *Studies in Chaucer's Hous of Fame* (Chaucer Society), London, 1907.

Taillevent, Michault; *Le Régime de Fortune*, in Alain Chartier's Œuvres, pp. 710–717, Paris, 1617.

Tasso, Torquato; *Opere*, Vol. XXVI, Pisa, 1830.

Tatlock, J. S. P.; *Astrology and Magic in Chaucer's Franklin's Tale*, Kittredge Anniversary Papers, pp. 339–350, Boston and London, 1913.

Tatlock, J. S. P.; *The Scene of the Franklin's Tale Visited* (Chaucer Society), London, 1914.

Taylor, H. O.; *The Classical Heritage of the Middle Ages*, 3d ed., New York, 1911.

Thibaut, Messire; *Li Romanz de la Poire*, ed. F. Stehlich, Halle, 1881.

Trissino, Giangiorgio (*i. e.*, Giovanni Georgio); *L'Italia Liberata da' Goti*, ed. A. Antonini, 3 parts, [Paris], 1729.

Trissino, G. G.; *Tutte le Opere*, 2 vols. (in one), Verona, 1729.

Trucchi, Francesco, editor; *Poesie Italiane Inedite di Dugento Autori*, 4 vols., Prato, 1846–47.

Uberti, Fazio degli; *Liriche*, ed. Rodolfo Renier (Raccolta di Opere Inedite o Rare), Firenze, 1883.

Vernon, W. W.; *Readings on the Inferno of Dante*, 2d ed., Vol. I, London, 1906.

Villard de Honnecourt; *Album, Reproduction . . . du Manuscrit Français 19093 de la Bibliothèque Nationale*, Paris, 1906.

Villon, François; *Œuvres*, ed. Paul Lacroix, Paris, 1877.

Villon, François; *Œuvres*, ed. J. H. R. Prompsault, Paris, 1835.

Vincentius Bellovacensis; *Speculum Historiale*, Venice, 1494.

Voigt, Ernst; *Florilegium Gottingense*, in Romanische Forschungen, III, 281–314, Erlangen, 1886–87.

Volpi, G.; *Rime di Trecentisti Minori*, Firenze, 1907.

Wace, Robert; *Le Roman de Brut*, ed. Le Roux de Lincy, 2 vols., Rouen, 1836–38.

Wace, Robert; *Le Roman de Rou*, ed. H. Andresen, 2 vols., Heilbronn, 1877–79.

Wackernagel, K. H. W.; *Das Glücksrad und die Kugel des Glücks*, in his Kleinere Schriften, I, 241–257, Leipzig, 1872.

Waddell, L. Austine; *The Buddhism of Tibet, or Lamaism*, London, 1895.

Wallace, Schir William; see Henry the Minstrel.

Watriquet de Couvin; *Dits*, ed. Auguste Scheler, Bruxelles, 1868.

Weinhold, K.; *Glücksrad und Lebensrad* (Philos. und Histor. Abhandlungen der Akademie der Wissenschaften zu Berlin), Berlin, 1892.

Werner, Jak.; *Beiträge zur Kunde der Lateinischen Literatur des Mittelalters*, 2d ed., Aarau, 1905.

Wissowa, Georg, and Kroll, Wilhelm, editors; *Pauly's Real-Encyclopädie der Classischen Altertumswissenschaft*, Neue Bearbeitung, Vols. XII, XIII, Stuttgart, 1910: "Fatum," XII, col. 2047; "Fortuna," XIII, col. 12.

Wolff, S. L.; *The Greek Romances in Elizabethan Prose Fiction*, New York (Columbia Univ. Press), 1912.

Wright, Thomas; *The Anglo-Latin Satirical Poets and Epigrammatists of the Twelfth Century* (Rolls Series), 2 vols., London, 1872.

INDEX

INDEX

figure, 31 f.; tragedy, 71 f.; astrology, 77 f.; Love, 92; the wheel, 160, 163, 169.
Other works, 54, 64, 98; tradition of the wheel, 153 f.
Chaucer's Dream, or *The Isle of Ladies*, 118, 119; cf. 130.
Chauntepleure, 54.
chess, 81 f. See *Échecs Amoureux*.
Chevalier Errant. See Thomas of Saluzzo.
Chrestien de Troyes, 50, 65, 68; problem of Fortune, 27; the wheel, 158. See *Perceval le Gallois*.
Christ, the wheel of, 58, 175.
Christian figure, 18 ff., 22, 24, 27 ff., 30 ff., 34, 35, 39 f., 48, 69, 77; as guide, 106; the wheel, 19, 147 f., cf. 58, 175.
Christianity, coming of, 3 f., 14 ff., 33 f.
Christine de Pisan, 42, 48, 51, 52, 56, 60, 61, 64, 65, 67, 68, 70, 71, 84, 91, 94, 96, 101, 102, 104, 105, 114, 117, 118, 119; the palace of Fortune, 144.
Church, the Christian, 15 ff., 26, 29; subject to injuries from Fortune, 58, 144. *See* Christianity, Fathers.
Cicero, 150.
Cino da Pistoia, 92, 103, 119.
cities, Fortune of the, 113 f.
classical allusions and figures, 3 ff., 10 ff., 22, 87, 120 ff.; islands, 130; the wheel, 149 ff., 152.
Claudian, 83, 97, 127; dwelling-place of Venus, 123 f., 136.
Colonna, Francesco, *Dream of Poliphilus*, 116.
combat, Fortune of, 89, 107 ff.
Complaynt of Scotlande, 42 f., 54; combat, 107 f., 109.

compromise, the attitude of, 17 ff., 34, 35.
Condé, Baudouin de, 39, 52, 60, 70, 172; the wheel and the prison, 161 f.
Condé, Jean de, 59, 70, 75, 110, 119, 156; Christian figure, 29; the mountain, 135 f.
Consolation of Philosophy. See Boethius.
Contention between Liberality and Prodigality, 136.
Conti, Giusto de', 77.
cornucopia, as symbol, 116, 120 f.
court, the, 59 f., 143 ff.; princes subject to Fortune, 112.
Court of Fortune, 92 f., 128, 143 ff., and plate 12.
Court of Love, 123 f., 128, 145.
Cousin, Jean, 43, 44, 45, 48, 49, 51, 53, 56, 60, 65, 76, 78, 79, 82, 83, 85, 92, 98, 100, 106, 114, 115, 116, 147, 148 f., 158, 168, 171.
Cranstoun, James, 40, 49, 54, 59, 69, 71.
Croesus, 64.
cults of Fortune. *See* functions, Fortuna Barbata, Fortuna Bona, etc.
Cumont, Franz, quoted, 15.
Cursor Mundi, the wheel, 162.

Dante, Christian figure, 18 ff., 22, 24, 27, 28, 29, 31; tragedy, 68, 69, 114.
Inferno, 54, 64, 99, 100, 111; Christian figure, 18 ff., 27, 28, 29, 31; tragedy, 114.
Purgatorio, 69, 146.
Paradiso, 50, 76, 85, 102, 175.
Other works, 68, 101, 109, 117, 130.
Death, 45, 89, 116, 117 ff.; Atropos, 89; city of Fortune and valley of